VOICES FROM BEYOND

Winner of the Walker Cowen Memorial Prize
for an outstanding work of scholarship
in eighteenth-century studies

Voices from Beyond

PHYSIOLOGY, SENTIENCE, AND
THE UNCANNY IN EIGHTEENTH-CENTURY
FRENCH LITERATURE

Scott M. Sanders

UNIVERSITY OF VIRGINIA PRESS
CHARLOTTESVILLE AND LONDON

University of Virginia Press
© 2022 by the Rector and Visitors of the University of Virginia
All rights reserved
Printed in the United States of America on acid-free paper

First published 2022

1 3 5 7 9 8 6 4 2

Library of Congress Cataloging-in-Publication Data
Names: Sanders, Scott M., author.
Title: Voices from beyond : physiology, sentience, and the uncanny in eighteenth-century French literature / Scott M. Sanders.
Description: Charlottesville : University of Virginia Press, 2022. | Series: Winner of the Walker Cohen memorial prize | Includes bibliographical references and index.
Identifiers: LCCN 2021052459 (print) | LCCN 2021052460 (ebook) | ISBN 9780813947327 (hardcover) | ISBN 9780813947334 (paperback) | ISBN 9780813947341 (ebook)
Subjects: LCSH: French literature—18th century—History and criticism. | Voice in literature.
Classification: LCC PQ265 .S264 (print) | LCC PQ265 (ebook) | DDC 840.9/353—dcundefined
LC record available at https://lccn.loc.gov/2021052459
LC ebook record available at https://lccn.loc.gov/2021052460

Cover art: From Jacques Cazotte, *Le Diable amoureux* (Beinecke Rare Book and Manuscript Library, Yale University Library); ltdedigos/Shutterstock.com

CONTENTS

	Acknowledgments	vii
	Introduction	1
1	The Physiology of Accent: Rousseau's Gendered Timbres	15
2	Fever Pitch: Songs of Temperance	52
3	Vitalist Voices in Diderot's Early Works	86
4	Sound and Sensibility: Music in *Le Neveu de Rameau*	109
5	The Haunted Listener: Voices of Possession in *Le Diable amoureux*	139
	Epilogue: Talking Heads	171
	Notes	183
	Index	225

ACKNOWLEDGMENTS

This book represents my approach to the voice as it is represented and constructed in eighteenth-century French literature. I am deeply indebted to many people, whose guidance and support inspired me and made it possible for me to write this book.

At an early stage of my project, my mentors gave me determined and demanding guidance for which I am forever grateful. The late Anne Deneys-Tunney was both a friend as well as a committed mentor whose deep knowledge of the Enlightenment and performance was instrumental in both developing my interest in and exploration of the voice. Suzanne Cusick gave me invaluable advice, and her feedback often considered the far-reaching implications of my ideas and enabled me to think beyond the narrow limitations of my initial thoughts. Finally, Benoît Bolduc provided the insights necessary to clarify the early stages of my project.

It is only fitting that I worked through my conception of the voice through conversations with colleagues. In the later stages of my project, I received generous advice and guidance from colleagues in my department. I am particularly indebted to Faith Beasley, who has consistently provided her invaluable support and feedback on the middle and late stages of my project. I likewise want to thank Lawrence Kritzman, whose mentorship and friendship I greatly appreciate. Finally, my thanks to Keith Walker, who was always available to discuss ideas and offered insightful comments.

This project would not have been possible without the generous support of the Leslie Center for the Humanities, which, under the stewardship of Graziella Parati, hosted Daniel Brewer and Tili Boon Cuillé. Their feedback, during the middle stage of my project, changed the direction of my scholarship, and their guidance came at a critical moment in my research. While the flaws of my book are mine alone, they enabled me to broaden the scope of my project.

I also wish to recognize the contribution of the Boston French History Group, to whose members I presented an early version of chapter 3. The feedback that I received from Robert Darnton, the respondent to my chapter; Jeffrey Ravel, the group organizer; as well as those in attendance was greatly appreciated and invaluable to me as I revised the chapter.

I could not have accessed and included the illustrations for this book without the support of research libraries. I wish to acknowledge the contributions of several rare book collections; namely, Rauner Special Collections Library at Dartmouth College, Beinecke Rare Book and Manuscript Library at Yale University, the Starred Books Collection from John Hay Library at Brown University, and the Bibliothèque Nationale de France. I am particularly thankful that the Morgan Library allowed me to read Denis Diderot's *Le Neveu de Rameau* in manuscript form.

Many of my colleagues deserve thanks for talking to me about my ideas and reading my work. These especially include Maeve Adams, Charlotte Bacon, Nancy Canepa, Andrew Clark, Annelle Curulla, Ryan Dohoney, Yasser Elhariry, Lynn Higgins, Lucas Hollister, John Kopper, David LaGuardia, Theodore Levin, Kathleen Lubey, Rena J. Mosteirin, Karen Santos da Silva, Analola Santana, Robert St. Clair, Andrea Tarnowski, and Kathleen Wine. Finally, special thanks to Victoria Malawey for sharing with me her illustration on the voice. I cannot thank Angie Hogan enough for her tireless work in shepherding my project through revisions.

I owe gratitude to my family, especially my mother and late father, Virgil and Judy Sanders, for their constant encouragement. I am also thankful to my sister, Julie Monberg, whose exuberance and interest encouraged me throughout this process. I also give thanks to my son, Rafael, who motivated me to complete my project.

Finally, there are no words sufficient to thank Mariana Pastore. Without her, I would not have been able to complete this work.

The book is dedicated to my dad, who spent a lifetime reading books. He is deeply missed.

PARTS OF chapter 4 were originally published as "Sound and Sensibility in Diderot's 'Le Neveu de Rameau,'" *Music and Letters* 94, no. 2 (2013): 237–62. They are reprinted with permission from Oxford University Press.

Parts of chapter 5 were originally published as "On Chanting, Wailing, and Spell-Casting: Haunting Voices in Jacques Cazotte's *Le Diable Amoureux,*" *The Eighteenth Century* 57, no. 4 (2016): 469–90. They are reprinted with permission from University of Pennsylvania Press. Copyright (c) 2016 University of Pennsylvania Press.

VOICES FROM BEYOND

Introduction

♪

In an article on song from the *Encyclopédie*, Louis de Cahusac notes that vocal physiology modifies the melodic beauty of bestial calls: "The inflections of animal voices are a true song ... and they are more or less melodious, according to the relative charm that nature has given to their organ."[1] This passage weighs in on a long-standing question: how does vocal physiology influence a host of qualities that define human and nonhuman voices? In the late seventeenth and early eighteenth centuries, French anatomists investigated vocal physiology and made major contributions to the field. In the late seventeenth century, Claude Perrault theorized that the voice arose from the collision of air in the throat. In the early 1700s, Denis Dodart completely reimagined vocal physiology by elevating the role of the glottis, which he argued was necessary for producing vocal sounds. Finally, by 1741, Antoine Ferrein had discovered vocal cords. The anatomists' approaches, however, often separated the physical causes of vocal sound from the intellectual faculty of speech. For instance, Perrault explained that "speech depends less on organs than on imagination."[2] They nevertheless speculated on how anatomy could modify the qualities of vocal sound. Antoine Ferrein even played like a musical instrument the vocal cords of dissected animals and noted how each one imitated specific animal calls.[3] A decade after Ferrein's discovery, François David Hérissant published a comparative anatomy of animal voices that both answered old questions and posed new ones about the influence of vocal physiology on animal and human voices.[4]

As scientists came to understand the mechanisms of the voice, its spiritual or supernatural power declined. Through an anatomical and acoustical understanding of the voice, scientists slowly secularized the organ, whose power lost its oracular force and gained a subjective, human, even animal identity. In this book, I examine traces of this material voice—which includes both the organs of vocal physiology and the sounds of vocal utterances—that appear in philosophical and literary works. Like Leigh Eric Schmidt, I show that the voice has played an underestimated but vital role in Western modernity, but whereas Schmidt finds in "narratives about modernity and the senses" a voice that lingers within the "cragged, contradictory presences of religion,"[5] I examine a voice whose biological and psychological forces are reincorporated into an unsettled version of the voice that ambiguously gestures toward spiritual and supernatural powers.

In particular, *Voices from Beyond* reconsiders how the embodied material voice is present in literary and philosophical representations of the human voice. I begin by showing how these representations responded to and commented upon developments in the French vocal sciences. In so doing, this work reconsiders contemporary critiques of the Enlightenment and its philosophical approach to the voice. As David Appelbaum argues, John Locke ushered in a "cultural laryngectomy" wherein the voice lost any acoustic features (such as coughs and babbles) that resist assimilation into a linguistic, phonemic system of meaning.[6] If we examine fictional depictions, however, we find a voice that still possesses a physiology and a sound. These depictions embed questions about the abstract nature of the human voice within thick descriptions of the voice's material existence.

In the process of describing, analyzing, and even attempting to record a physiological voice into print, writers created paradigms of the voice that explored sentience and sociability through an intricate web of moral, biological (and even supernatural) forces. *Voices from Beyond: Physiology, Sentience, and the Uncanny in Eighteenth-Century French Literature* interrogates the philosophical and literary works of well-known and lesser-known French writers—including Jean-Jacques Rousseau, Denis Diderot, François Baculard d'Arnaud, and Jacques Cazotte—and explores how their texts theorize, represent, and construct three interrelated vocal types: the sentimental, the vitalist, and the uncanny.

These vocal types are connected insofar as the conception of sentimental and vitalist voices—anchored to a physiological understanding of vocal organs—paradoxically led to the development of a disembodied, uncanny voice. The uncanny voice parodies and blends the rhetorical qualities that give sentimental and vitalist voices an embodied presence. Through its simulation of physiological voices, the uncanny voice alternates expressions of pathos with moments of raw vitalist energy that the reader perceives as both appealing and revolting.

To grasp this transition from embodied to disembodied voices, it is necessary to begin with the origin of these interrelated voices: they emerge from a scientific understanding of the voice that strips it of oracular power and replaces that force with biological and psychological energies. Whereas the sentimental and vitalist voices construct versions of human identity from biological and psychological energies, the uncanny constructs a parody of sentimental and vitalist voices in an attempt to unsettle the notion of a purely biological and psychological force behind the voice and leave open the possibility of a supernatural or spiritual force.

VOICES FROM BEYOND contributes to two disciplines: French literary scholarship and voice studies. In French studies, this book builds on the scholarship of Downing Thomas and Tili Boon Cuillé.[7] My work is indebted to Thomas's critique of Derrida's *De la grammatologie*—specifically the notion that music is not a supplement to but central to Rousseau's theory of language.[8] In addition to the linguistic function of music that Thomas analyzes, Cuillé examines the narrative function of musical tableaux, which she defines as a "musical performance staged for a beholder inscribed in the text."[9] I show how these texts invite the reader—a version of Cuillé's inscribed beholder—to imagine, experiment with, and feel the sensations that vocal performance engenders.

In this regard, this book contributes to the field of voice studies. As Martha Feldman explains in her theorization of the interstitial voice, scholars since the 1960s have developed approaches to the voice across a variety of disciplines and perspectives:[10] there are voices theorized from psychoanalytic, deconstructionist, cinematic, and feminist perspectives.[11] The richness of this field is in part due to the elusiveness of the voice as an object of study. This book follows the lead of recent studies of the voice that address its *grain*, or materiality.[12] In particular, recent scholarship has examined the voice as a material object in relation to vocal physiology, sound, cultures of listening, and listening technologies.[13] This book examines how eighteenth-century texts function as a recording technology for the voice in such a way that invites the reader to imagine and reconstruct the voice's materiality.

In this book, I also draw on Nina Eidsheim's argument that vocal sounds are the result of a series of movements and embodied actions; the voice is not a static object that we can reduce to a figure of sound.[14] The works I analyze deploy the textual means at their disposal to investigate and represent the voice as a physiological object and a thing in action. These textual representations come close to what Eidsheim defines as "the perspective of voice as action" because they invite the reader to understand the voice through its movement and action.[15]

Finally, I explore how the textual representation of the voice allows the reader to reconstruct, perform, and imagine a voice of performance, of movement, of bodily actions, and of sound. These textual representations, of course, are not all the same. These differences matter: the conventions of the genre in which a voice is heard or depicted influence the way the audience interprets that voice. Fictional representations of the voice differ from representations in medical texts, and the ones theorized in philosophical essays exist in stark contrast to the performed voices that listeners hear in operas. A series of letters in the *Mercure de France* illustrates how a reader can imagine the voice in part through the genre that represents it. In 1730, a sound event occurred north of Paris and was reported in the *Mercure de France*. In the months following the report, readers sent lengthy explanations to the editor. This event is a useful starting point for this cultural and intellectual history of the voice because it shows how readers rely on ontological and epistemological premises to interpret textual representations of the voice. From the reader's interpretations, we can reconstitute two critical methods of interpretation: how genre directs a reader toward a set of preconceived notions about the nature of the text, and how the text deploys various strategies to invite the reader either to imagine or perform the voice.

ON THE night of January 29, 1730, two middle-aged laborers and brothers, Charles and François Descoulleurs, returned home to Ansacq, a hamlet north of Paris, after a long journey from Senlis. Around two in the morning, they were approaching Ansacq's park when they heard inexplicable sounds in the air. In a sworn deposition almost four months later, Charles reported that from about twenty feet away a terrible voice had interrupted his conversation with François. In quick succession, he heard a similar voice from a gorge on the other side of town, which spread over the field. Finally, what sounded like a chorus of singers of all ages and genders sang "howling gibberish" that filled the valley.[16] On the opposite side of town, perched on a ridge overlooking Ansacq's valley, Louis Duchemin, a glove-maker, and his companion, Patrice Toüilly, a master mason, heard identical sounds emerging from Ansacq's park.

In all, more than twenty witnesses heard the sound event, and they described it with strikingly similar details. It was "un bruit confus, mais éclatant, de voix comme humaines, mêlées de differens instrumens" (a confused, but strident noise, of human-like voices, mixed in with different instruments).[17] A few witnesses peppered their descriptions with intriguing accents. For instance, at the end of the sound event, François Descoulleurs heard peals of laughter, which he imitated and described as the *a, a, a* sound of toothless old men and the *ho, ho, hi, hi* sounds of young men, women, and children.[18] Ansacq's former gate guard Claude Descoulleurs even identified the instrumental accompaniment as "*les sons des Violons, des Basses, Hautbois, Trompettes, Flutes, Tambours & de tous les Instrumens*" (italics in original) (*the sounds of violins, of basses, oboes, trumpets, flutes, tambourines and other instruments*).[19] Across these multiple versions of the same event, the witnesses reported a similar sonic experience: the noise started abruptly around two in the morning. They heard a loud ensemble of singers and instrumentalists. The voices came from multiple directions around Ansacq, and seemed to originate from the air and the ground. Those in the center of town heard the voices migrate from one end of town to the other.

By Sunday, January 30, Ansacq's parish priest, the curé Treüillot de Ptoncour, was au courant of the curious event and decided to initiate an informal inquiry. Of a slightly Pyrrhonean disposition, Ptoncour was initially skeptical. In fact, he started his inquiry mostly in jest, explaining that as a rule, he did not believe in "tous les contes nocturnes qui se débitent si souvent dans l'apparition des Esprits, des Sabbats & de tant d'autres bagatelles de cette espece" (nocturnal tales which so often begin with the appearance of ghosts, witches' Sabbaths, and so many other little trifles of that variety).[20] He pursued his investigation half-heartedly, hoping to convince his parishioners that nothing had happened.

A few months passed without further incident. Then, on the night of May 9 into the morning of May 10, several parishioners again heard a strange nocturnal chorus. After the second event, Ptoncour decided to start an official inquiry, for which he deposed more than twenty witnesses. From May 17 until June 2, he recorded his parishioners' sworn and signed depositions.

Later that same year, sometime between summer and early fall, Ptoncour and his parishioners tried to re-create the sound event. As he explained, "J'ai voulu moi-même faire l'expérience pendant une belle nuit & un tem[p]s calme."[21] (I tried myself to experiment with the natural and ordinary causes of noise during a beautiful night in calm weather.) Ptoncour positioned fifteen villagers at the top of ridges on either side of Ansacq's valley. As the curé recounted in exacting detail, Ansacq's topography resembled a fork (*patte-d'oie*) with three northern gorges that joined together to form a central valley. This unique topography might have produced bizarre echoes and sound shadows. Despite Ptoncour's exhaustive efforts, the principal witnesses concurred that their experiment only approximated the terrifying *sabbat* of the previous winter.[22]

In late fall, Ansacq's parishioners experienced the inexplicable sounds one final time. On October 31, 1730, the eve of All Saints' Day, a number of villagers heard a horrendous sound originating from Ansacq's park. This third sound event was so alarming that it dispersed a herd of sheep. What's more, the shepherd's wife, sleeping next to her husband, "en fut si épouvantée qu'elle en est tombée malade" (was so frightened [by the event] that she fell ill).[23] After three peculiarly similar events, the skeptical Ptoncour was perplexed. Even though his fellow parishioners had called on him to witness the subsequent events, he had never heard the strange phenomenon. He finally decided to collate his findings with a dual purpose in mind: to entertain the Princess of Conty, to whom he addressed his report, and to allow her to relay his story to scholars at court. Ptoncour's tale was subsequently published in the December 1730 edition of the *Mercure de France*, in which he described the Ansacq event as an *akousmate*.[24]

While Brian Kane has offered a compelling study of the Ansacq event, his study is intended to historicize the concept of acousmatic sound in relation to the concerns and preoccupations of sound studies. I want to draw attention instead to the rhetorical strategies deployed to represent and to reconstruct the haunting sounds. These strategies reveal the genre in which a text represents the voice, which in turn provides the reader with a framework in which to interpret the vocal object: a voice of medical science or a voice of fantasy.

Months after Ptoncour's initial report, a handful of readers offered their interpretation of Ansacq's sound event. A few commentators questioned the veracity of Ptoncour's inquest, claiming either that the sense of hearing was particularly susceptible to confusion or that Ptoncour's story was clearly a mere fabrication because it used the literary devices of a fairy tale.[25] Those who took Ptoncour's account seriously considered human, natural, and spiritual causes. One commentator proposed that a ventriloquist could have hidden behind a partition and thrown his voice.[26] A more spiritually inclined reader insisted that demons could interact with air particles to produce sound.[27] Two respondents suggested that Ansacq's nocturnal voices originated from meteorological and terrestrial phenomena.[28] By adapting contemporaneous theories of vocal anatomy, these last respondents formulated a scientific theory for the Ansacq sound events: terrestrial miasmas and celestial particles had collided in such a way as to reproduce the acoustical properties of the human voice.

THE READERS of the Ansacq article offered wildly divergent explanations in part because they made assumptions about the textual genre of Ptoncour's description. Depending on the reader, the Ansacq article followed the rhetorical logic of a fairy tale, a police inquest, a thaumatological investigation, or a scientific report. Based on this initial assumption, the reader then formulated a set of plausible explanations. In the process, the various readers created different types of voices. In the letters of those who believed that Ansacq was a hoax, we find the fictional howls of an inventive writer along with the haunting performance of a ventriloquist. For others, the voices were either a natural phenomenon that followed the laws of acoustics or a supernatural event that proved the spiritual essence of air. In other words, readers performed a genre analysis of Ptoncour's description, and through this process, they produced different disciplinary versions of the voice.

The Ansacq event reveals the extent to which a textual genre can define the essential attributes of a voice. When writing about an anatomical voice in a medical report, a doctor reduces its function to the mechanical, biological, and acoustical attributes that make the voice possible. To produce a literary voice, a writer imitates the sound, dynamic, timbre, and register through a series of literary conventions, such as adjectival descriptions, onomatopoeia, simile, and reported speech. Each genre comes with a set of textual strategies for representing the voice, and these strategies in turn influence how a reader interprets the voice's attributes.

Ansacq's acousmatic voices also come with a compelling twist. Ptoncour realized that his parishioners could not completely explain or understand the sound event without imitating the voices they had heard. His written description, moreover, could not re-create the acoustical sensations that his parishioners had experienced. Given the shortcomings of oral and written accounts, Ptoncour devised a process through which to test and reexperience the sound event. His article described how his parishioners attempted to reenact the voices. Their vocal experiment gestured to the materiality of the voice. Its sounds, accents, and timbre have a material cause that includes both the speaker's organ and the space where she speaks. Ptoncour even speculated on the effects of the local topography and weather on the voice's echo and movement.[29]

The Ansacq article thus relies on two ways of theorizing the voice: through literary simulation and vocal performance. This text creates two versions of the voice, one textual and one material, one simulated through rhetorical strategies and one imitated through performance techniques. Ptoncour's inquest is notable because it demonstrates reading and performance practices that are well adapted to the archive this book investigates. Indeed, I have analyzed novels that include parts of musical scores. In novels from Samuel Richardson's *Clarissa* to Jacques Cazotte's *Le Diable amoureux*, readers encounter descriptions of voices set alongside musical scores. These scores, which we can call musical paratexts, are similar in function to Ptoncour's vocal experiment: they supplement descriptions of the singing voice with a performance medium. As a lyric baritone who trained under the Heldentenor James King at Indiana University, I became keenly interested in how vocal performance could transform the reading experience. I even learned, practiced, and performed inserted scores from the novels analyzed in this book so that I could appreciate how literary description differs from vocal performance. This unique perspective has proven invaluable in my research on the voice. By performing these musical scenes, I was able to distinguish between two media through which literary texts theorize the voice: first a simulated medium, created by drawing on multiple disciplinary discourses, and then a performed medium, which the reader reenacts. The archive in this study invites readers to theorize the voice through literary simulation and performance because scientific reason alone offers a partial understanding of the voice.

THIS BOOK follows the development and theorization of two physiologically embodied voices (sentimental and vitalist) that paradoxically led to the creation of a disembodied vocal type: the uncanny. Each chapter investigates one of these three distinct vocal types, and explores their attributes through their materiality, their textual representation and their function as an organ of human identity. This book, then, disentangles three versions of the voice through their representations in eighteenth-century French fiction [and philosophy].

The first two chapters examine how the voice regulates the impulses of physical desire. Through the concept of moral hygiene, writers such as Rousseau and Baculard d'Arnaud demonstrate how the voice can be trained through physical and moral exercises, which enable a person to reverse the deleterious effects of desire and cultivate the moral sentiments of marital love, sociability and familial harmony.

Chapter 1, "The Physiology of Accent: Rousseau's Gendered Timbres," examines how Jean-Jacques Rousseau took issue with biomechanical conceptions of the voice, including the comparative anatomies published in the Académie royale des sciences. In so doing, Rousseau created a sentimental voice that retained a connection with vocal physiology but also became a tool for cultivating moral sentiment. Across a wide variety of genres—including articles in Diderot's *Encyclopédie* and Rousseau's *Dictionnaire de musique*, essays such as the *Essai sur l'origine de langue*, and the sentimental novel *Julie*—Rousseau deploys different methodologies and discourses through which to theorize and represent the voice. As part of a moral and social understanding of the voice, Rousseau's theories primarily identify vocal inflections, and melody in particular, as a medium through which to express and exchange emotion. Whereas previous scholars of Rousseau have identified the relationship that he traces between music and language, this chapter argues that Rousseau reserved a role for the physical attributes of vocal organs.[30] First, in terms of melody, Rousseau's work identifies flexibility as a crucial characteristic that enables certain individuals and people to perform emotionally vibrant melodies. Next, Rousseau's work identifies timbres as an acoustic mark of gender: women's voices should be soft and men's resonant. Disputing the Derridean critique of the voice in Rousseau's writings, this chapter argues that Rousseau was keenly aware of vocal physiology and theorized its impact on the voice.[31]

In chapter 2, "Fever Pitch: Songs of Temperance," I analyze period editions of sentimental novels in which musical scores accompany lyrical scenes. Beginning with Samuel Richardson's *Clarissa* (1748–49), which served as an important literary model for French writers, I trace the sentimental voice's migration from England in the 1750s to France of the 1760s to 1770s. Contextualizing Clarissa's musical scene in relation to contemporaneous medical notions about music making, I demonstrate how Clarissa's song serves as a form of moral therapy, represented in the novel and also performed by her readers. Crossing back to France, I show how the popular best-selling writer François Baculard d'Arnaud blended Richardson's version of musical therapy with Rousseau's approach to moral therapy. For Baculard d'Arnaud's version, music therapy served to domesticate male desire and to transform it into a form of marital love.

Chapters 3 and 4 examine an even deeper connection to the voice and human physiology insofar as the vitalist voice allows the body to express through sound a limited form of sentience. Vitalism here refers to a strain of thought that imagined that matter had a living life force, or *vis viva*. Vitalist thought rejects a binary opposition between the inert mechanical body and the spiritual mind. Instead, the vitalist body is composed of smaller structures that possess their own drives, sympathies, and energies.

Chapter 3, "Vitalist Voices in Diderot's Early Works," discusses the emergence of voice connected and reactive to human physiology, particularly the fibrous tissue and reproductive organs of the human body. Starting in 1745, Diderot adapted the voice of English moral and natural philosophy. Diderot first articulated the musical qualities of human *fibres* through his translations of works by Robert James and Anthony Ashley Cooper, the third Earl of Shaftesbury. He finally examines the acoustics of the vibrating string from the perspective of physics. By investigating the acoustics of vibrating strings from the perspective of morality, medicine, and physics, Diderot proposes a multidisciplinary approach to the voice.

In 1748, Diderot continued his implicit theorization of vitalist voices with the publication of *Les Bijoux indiscrets*, which represents the voice as reactive to the desire and aversion of reproductive organs. From the vibrations of fibrous tissues to the volitions of bodily organs, this early version of the vitalist voice allows the body to express through sound a limited form of sentience.

Chapter 4, "Sound and Sensibility: Music in *Le Neveu de Rameau*," analyzes Diderot's posthumously published philosophical dialogue, which explores the unique physiological temperament of its antihero, Rameau's nephew. Here, I explore both the performed and represented voice of the nephew, and specifically examine how the diaphragm, an organ essential to singing and one that Diderot theorized in relation to human temperament, is related to Diderot's conception of sensibility. In the dialogue, the nephew performs his defective diaphragm, and in the process, creates a musical representation of a very reactive voice, an organ from which issues both the beauty and monstrosity of bodily desire. His musical performance reenacts the chaotic experience of the nephew's embodied sentience.

In the first four chapters, I explore voices whose function it is to uncover aspects of human experience. They are voices of discovery whose sound reveals a singer's temperament, sexuality, and moral disposition. Whereas the vitalist and sentimental voices are defined in part through their materiality, the uncanny voice, discussed in chapter 5, unsettles the relationship between vocal physiology and the sound of the voice. Instead of revealing to the listener a singer's physical and emotional disposition, the uncanny voice projects a simulated form whose presence traps the listener between a state of revulsion and desire. Although the term *uncanny* in modern theories of subjectivity can refer to a variety of experiences, here I follow Diane Long Hoeveler's argument that uncanny voices developed "alongside" the sentimental and "in tandem with the growing science of psychology"—and, I would add, influenced by the forces of vitalism.[32] Similar to the vitalist voice, the uncanny voice is organized around the forces of desire and revulsion. These forces, however, no longer reveal how vocal physiology relates to the moral and physiological composition of the speaker. Instead, they are unleashed on the listener, who becomes consumed by feelings of desire, revulsion, and uncertainty.[33]

In chapter 5, "The Haunted Listener: Voices of Possession in *Le Diable amoureux*," I examine Jacques Cazotte's critique of vitalist and sentimental voices. Cazotte depicted these voices as deceptive objects that awaken in the listener aversion and desire. In *Diable*, the protagonist listens to a character whose voice both repulses and seduces him. First, the demon Béelzébuth frightens Alvare with an orotund yawl. Later in the novel, Béelzébuth changes shape to become an alluring transgendered Italian servant named Biondetto/Biondetta. Across these two parodies of vitalist and sentimental voices—the creaturely, demonic voice of Béelzébuth and the dulcet tones of the transgendered Biondetta—Cazotte reimagined the voice as an illusory object of desire.

The epilogue brings the uncanny voice of literature into dialogue with the mechanical voice of vocal sciences. With Abbé Mical's mechanical voices—the *Têtes parlantes*, displayed in 1784—vocal physiology reemerged as an avenue of philosophical inquiry. Natural philosophers, still keen to unlock the secrets of the voice, wanted to use Mical's mechanical voices to understand the hidden mechanisms of vocal physiology and its role in speech. Mical's *Têtes parlantes* failed to capture the audience's attention, however, in part because its robotic sound did not evoke the uncanniness its listeners desired. The public sought the thrill of uncanny sounds that could inspire monstrous desire, such as the voices of Biondetta in Cazotte's *Diable* and later of Zambinella in Balzac's *Sarrasine*. Here the use of fictional representation changes imagination's role from providing insight about the singer, to awakening in the listener the contradictory feelings of desire and revulsion. Whereas Rousseau and Diderot created fictional versions of sentimental and vitalist voices so that readers could imagine how vocal physiology influenced and was influenced by aspects of human experience (sexuality, gender, temperament), those writers who created the uncanny voice ask the reader to imagine the voice as a fabrication that awakens in the listener a monstrous form of desire. Their fabrication is made possible through a blending of the sentimental and vitalist forms. Whereas the sentimental voice constructs a legible gender identity, and the vitalist one makes audible the unspoken desire of the human body, the uncanny voice simulates gender identity while also awakening in the listener a bodily desire that he finds revolting.

1

The Physiology of Accent
Rousseau's Gendered Timbres

♪

In a letter dated February 16, 1766, David Hume recounted a curious story concerning Jean-Jacques Rousseau. During Rousseau's visit to London, David Garrick, a famous English actor who was known also in France, offered Rousseau his box seats for that evening. As Hume explained, the king and queen, whose loge faced Garrick's, were informed of Rousseau's visit and expected him to attend. "When the hour came," however, Rousseau told Hume "that he had changed his resolution, and would not go: for—what shall I do with Sultan? That is the name of his dog."[1] Rousseau could not bear to leave Sultan alone because he worried that during his absence, his dog would bolt out of the townhouse in search of him. After much cajoling, Hume finally convinced Rousseau to lock his dog in his room, noting: "as we went downstairs, the dog howled and made a noise; his master turned back, and said he had not resolution to leave him in that condition."[2] Rousseau finally relented and attended Garrick's performance. In the pathos this scene evokes, I wish to highlight the fact that Rousseau reacted to the voice of his dog, its howl a call for fellow feeling, a cry for empathy from his master. Sultan's howl came from an animal body with a vocal organ.

Across the rich field of Rousseau studies, many scholars have defined versions of Jean-Jacques Rousseau's voices: Derrida deconstructs the Rousseauan voice of metaphysical presence; Michael O'Dea contextualizes the voice within affective forms of communication; Downing Thomas relates the voice to a prelapsarian loss; and Cynthia Verba focuses on the importance of accent.[3] Among the voices that return in Rousseau's corpus we find *la voix de l'amitié, la voix secrète de la conscience, la voix intérieure, la voix publique, la voix de la raison, la voix de la vertu,* and finally *la voix de la nature.* These voices often appear as imaginary, silent, or even Husserlian voices of the interior self.

To be sure, Rousseau referred to metaphorical voices. For instance, in a letter dated 1769 to Monsieur Moultou, Rousseau asked, "Voulez-vous étouffer l'instinct moral? La voix interne s'élève dans votre cœur et foudroye les petits arguments à la mode, et vous crie qu'il n'est pas vrai que l'honnête homme et le scélérat, le vice et la vertu ne soient rien."[4] (Do you want to stifle moral instinct? The inner voice rises in your heart, thunders minor fashionable arguments, and yells at you that it is not true that the honest man and the scoundrel, vice and virtue are nothing.) This metaphorical voice retains physiological features, from its "moral instinct," which must be suffocated, to its screams at moral depravity. Because the voice is merely a literary trope, however, its physical manifestation does not influence its sound.

In addition to the metaphorical voice, Rousseau also referred to an actual vocal organ, whose material conditions influenced the quality of vocal performance. In a letter to Monsieur Laliaud dated November 28, 1768, Rousseau wrote about his "voix cassée et déjà tremblotante" (broken and already quivering voice):[5] "Si j'avais une pauvre petite épinette pour soutenir un peu ma voix foiblissante, je chanterois du matin jusqu'au soir."[6] (If I had a poor little spinet to sustain my weak voice, I would sing from morning to evening.) By characterizing his voice as weak, Rousseau provides the reader with an idea of the material condition of his brittle vocal organ.

As I mentioned in the introduction, the physiological voice appears across a network of writers whose texts construct the materiality of the voice through two main strategies: description and speculative experimentation. In science, vocal physiologists dissected, blew through, and examined the anatomical structure of vocal organs. In literary and philosophical texts, I define speculative experimentation as a combination of imaginative re-creation and performance practice whereby the reader either imagines how vocal physiology modifies a voice's sound or experiences changes in vocal physiology through performance. It is in the spirit of speculative experimentation that I interpret Rousseau's vocal organs as well as participate in the speculative experimentation that his texts propose.

In terms of description, writers construct slightly different versions of the voices' materiality through conventions of genre. For Rousseau's textually constructed vocal organs, he relies on philosophical and literary descriptions. Whereas the vocal organs that his texts represent may privilege the sound and emotional affect of the voice, his description of the *organe musical* remains rooted in an understanding and adaptation of vocal physiology.

In this chapter, I trace the story of Rousseau's vocal organs, what he refers to in his novel *Julie, ou La Nouvelle Héloïse* as *l'organe musical* (the musical organ), across a range of texts, from the 1749 *Encyclopédie* articles through the 1781 *Essai sur l'origine des langues*. Between these works, I examine the *Lettre sur la musique françoise* (1753), *Lettre à d'Alembert sur les spectacles* (1757), *Julie, ou La Nouvelle Héloïse* (1761), *Émile, ou De l'éducation* (1762), and the *Dictionnaire de musique* (written between 1753 and 1764, published 1768).[7] However, I organize the story of Rousseau's vocal organs—plural, not singular—thematically instead of chronologically. First, I contrast Rousseau's approach to an *organe musical* with that of French anatomists. Second, I discuss how Rousseau imagines vocal physiology through social and linguistic difference. Finally, I investigate how timbre—a notion outside the traditional dichotomy of melody versus harmony—returns in Rousseau's writings. This notion is a crucial but overlooked aspect of Rousseau's intersectional theory of the voice, which envisions vocal physiology as influenced and marked by cultural and gender differences.

By drawing attention to Rousseau's references to the physical organs of the voice, I will show how Rousseau's writings make room for physiology in his theory of the voice. This Rousseauan voice is in direct opposition to the Derridean voice described in *Marges . . . de la philosophie* (1972). According to Derrida: "Rousseau rejects any pertinence of the physiological point of view in the explanation of language. The physiology of the phonic organs is not an intrinsic part of the discipline of linguistics."[8] It is true that certain passages within Rousseau's oeuvre explicitly reject anatomical explanations that account for differences across vocal performance and linguistic capacity. Yet this rejection of anatomical science does not translate into a complete rejection of physiological influences. Specifically, vocal physiology, described and theorized across a range of Rousseau's texts, has qualities that are intrinsically associated with different languages and affective registers.

Moreover, without a properly tuned and sufficiently sensitive organ, people in Rousseau's philosophical and fictional universes are physically incapable of vocalizing specific linguistic and melodic tones. By attending to the physiological voice present in Rousseau's musical, philosophical, and literary writings, we encounter a theory of the vocal organ that reclaims vocal physiology from a purely mechanical and anatomical conception of the voice. Indeed, Rousseau's texts specifically target the anatomical voice that we find in the writings of Denis Dodart, Antoine Ferrein, and François David Hérissant.

Rousseau defines the influence of vocal physiology on what I call his "sentimental voices" in relation to external factors—such as social, cultural, and environmental forces. Here I add the notion of vocal practices to Lynn Festa's definition of sentimentality as "a rhetorical practice that monitors and seeks to master the sympathetic movement of emotion between individuals and groups of people."[9] These vocal practices modify a person's physiology so that he or she can produce specific timbres, dynamics, and melodic flexibilities that either help or hinder the exchange of emotion.

The sentimental voice is similar to but distinct from the aesthetic objects normally defined as sentimental. Scholars have noted that sentimental novels (and operas) use similar rhetorical (and musical) devices to represent emotion, such as the natural language of tears, sobs, and sighs.[10] In novels and operas, the rhetorical and musical representation of emotion often coincides with the depiction of human or animal suffering. The representation of misfortune is deeply entwined with moral sentiment and human sensibility.[11] It first elicits from the reader or audience a sympathetic response in which the observation of suffering translates via human sensibility the physical sensations of suffering. This sympathetic response in turn helps the reader/spectator identify with the suffering subject.[12] As a result of this experience, the reader/spectator increases his or her sense of social solidarity with those less fortunate.[13]

This sentimental form of social solidarity creates a hierarchical boundary between the suffering subject and the observer.[14] By constructing a class, gender, or racial-based distinction between the suffering victim and the observer, sentimental novels and operas often depict sympathetic identification in a way that perpetuates social inequality. Although the spectators/readers empathize with the suffering of young women, children, the working poor, and the enslaved, they are not expected to question the underlying injustice of social inequality. Instead, they experience redemption through the paternalistic desire to help those who suffer.

Although we usually associate sentimentality with its narrative version, the typical sentimentality of novels and operas does not align exactly with the sentimental voices that Rousseau represents in his novel and theorizes in his essays. It is true that Rousseau defines the musical and vocal features that are best suited for communicating and sharing emotional experiences, similar to the rhetorical and musical features that represent sentimental expression. What's more, suffering has a place in Rousseau's work: from *Essai de l'origine de l'inégalité parmi les hommes* to his novel *Julie*, readers hear the cries, tears, and sighs of suffering victims. In his broader discussion of sentimental voices, however, human (and animal) suffering is not the only emotional means through which he represents and theorizes sentimentality. The expression of love becomes a defining characteristic of sentimentality—a characteristic that separates sentimental voices, which promote social bonds, from the voices that erode social solidarity.[15] The sentimental voices in Rousseau's work thus map out a slightly different social and cultural relationship in which certain people have access to the full depth of emotional experiences, and others do not. Environmental and cultural factors modify vocal physiology in ways that either promote or hinder the development of sentimental voices.[16]

Throughout this chapter, I examine sentimental voices across literary and philosophical genres. In the process of theorizing Rousseau's vocal physiologies, I analyze representations of the voice in *Julie* alongside those in his philosophical essays. By doing this analytical work, I do not wish to flatten distinctions across these genres. Each textual construction of the material voice serves a slightly different purpose. Rousseau's speculative anthropology constructs a version of vocal physiology that is anchored in a long view of human development. Meanwhile, the fictional descriptions of a character's vocal physiology are intimately associated with the characters' emotional experiences. While it may be possible to reconstitute versions of Rousseau's embodied voices from his *Confessions* or from his musical *intermèdes* such as *Le Devin du village* and *Pygmalion*, in this chapter I interpret the theoretical and fictional voices in Rousseau's work in relation to my own embodied practice as a singer.

As the Ansacq anecdote served to illustrate in the introduction, the works that I have chosen for this book invite the reader to experience the voice through experimentation, either as an imaginative re-creation or a vocal performance. This is why I consider Rousseau's texts as an invitation for the reader to imagine and experience the vibrations, sonorities, and timbre of his sentimental voices.

IN ORDER to situate how Rousseau's texts explicitly and implicitly gesture toward vocal physiology, it is important to consider contemporaneous anatomical approaches to the voice. In eighteenth-century Paris, there were three major approaches to vocal anatomy. In a series of science articles from the early 1700s, Denis Dodart proposed a version of vocal anatomy that emphasized the role of the glottal opening in producing sound. By midcentury, Antoine Ferrein offered an alternative theory, that of vocal cords. While chapter 3 dedicates more space to the development and critique of Dodart's and Ferrein's vocal anatomies, for this chapter, I draw attention to the comparative anatomy of François Hérissant, who theorized differences across animal physiologies. For Hérissant, animal voices were either an *organe simple* or *composé*.

After being elevated to the rank of anatomist of the Académie royale des sciences in 1748, Hérissant published a treatise on the voices of quadrupeds and birds. This treatise, which appeared in 1753 under the title *Recherches sur les organes de la voix des quadrupèdes et celles des oiseaux*, proposed a compromise between Dodart's and Ferrein's approaches. While Hérissant retained Dodart's emphasis on the glottis, he borrowed Ferrein's definition of the human voice as "un instrument à cordes & à vent en même temps" (a wind and string instrument at the same time).[17]

Hérissant then formulated a comparative anatomy of the animal voice. Across his taxonomy of voices, he identified two major types, the voice of quadrupeds and that of birds. Four-legged creatures, cats, sheep, bulls, deer, and camels possessed a glottal voice that oscillated under air pressure. Hérissant called this humanlike voice the "*organe simple*" (simple organ).[18] Horses, mules, donkeys, and pigs had slightly different voices, called "*organe composé*" (compound organ), which included tissues that resembled either tambourines or bagpipe-like pneumatic sacs.[19]

After detailing the different voices of quadrupeds, Hérissant turned to birds' vocal organs. He noted that although birds' song seemed to indicate that their vocal anatomy resembled that of humans, they possessed a strikingly different set of organs.[20] Expanding on Claude Perrault's seventeenth-century research, Hérissant identified two important differences across avian and quadrupedal voices: in birds, he discovered a secondary larynx, lined with multiple membranes and absent in quadrupeds. Subsequently, he theorized that with exhalation, these fibrous membranes vibrated to produce sound in a fashion similar to an oboe's reed.

Hérissant researched the material, organic composition of vocal organs and explained how its structure influenced the sound of animal voices. He modified this approach slightly when he acknowledged the limitations of comparative anatomy, specifically with regard to the acoustic features of the voice. On the one hand, human and avian voices could both produce songs through different anatomical features. On the other, human and feline voices shared the same organs while producing different sounds. In other words, similar design could produce differing sounds, whereas dissimilar anatomies could approximate the same type of song.

Reaching for an explanation, Hérissant framed his discovery in the same light as had his predecessors Dodart and Ferrein. Although this logical inconsistency was a mystery to him, he imagined it as part of God's design with which "l'Auteur de la Nature" (Nature's Author) had created human, bovine, equestrian, and avian voices.[21] He thus left off any speculation on the metaphysical differences that allow humans to speak and birds to sing.

In contrast to the comparative anatomy of the Académie royale des sciences, Rousseau distanced his musical-linguistic theories from the material, organic explanations of the French science academy. For instance, in the *Essai sur l'origine des langues* (conceived around 1755, posthumously published in 1781), he explains: "La parole distingue l'homme entre les animaux: le langage distingue les nations entr'elles."[22] (Speech distinguishes humans from animals: language distinguishes nations from each other.) In other words, our biological organization has a limited influence on our capacity to communicate: "Donnez à l'homme une organisation tout aussi grossiere qu'il vous plaira; sans doute il acquerra moins d'idées; mais ... ils parviendront à se communiquer enfin tout autant d'idées qu'ils en auront."[23] (Bestow humans with as crude a [biological] organization as one would like; without a doubt, they will acquire fewer ideas; but ... they will succeed at communicating after all as many ideas as they will have.)

According to the *Essai*, cooperative animals such as beavers, ants, and bees might communicate through gestures.[24] Dogs and cats, moreover, can express fellow feeling through their barks and meows.[25] Animals, however, lack the abstract notion of speech, which Rousseau calls a "langue de convention" (a conventional language).[26] *Convention* here refers to an agreement that two or more people make. In this regard, vocal anatomy does not contribute to the distance between animal and human forms of communication. According to the *Essai*, "cette seule distinction paroît mener loin: on l'explique, dit-on, par la différence des organes. Je serois curieux de voir cette explication" (this distinction alone seems to lead far: it is explained, by some, through difference in organs. I would be curious to see this explanation).[27]

By miming the comparative anatomy of Ferrein and later Hérissant, the *Essai* rejects a material, biological explanation of vocal differences. Instead, certain human capacities—including the abilities to imitate nature, to hear and empathize with the suffering of others, and to reflect on one's feeling of existence in relation to another person—lead to the invention of language. Since many scholars have already analyzed the nuances of this story, I propose to reflect on a specific portion of it.[28] Within Rousseau's work on music, certain passages both refute and accept the role of Rousseau's *organe musical* in the creation of musical language.

In these passages as well, the *Essai* rejects the mechanical systems of the science academy, including Ferrein's vocal cords and Hérissant's *organe simple* and *composé*. The *Essai* depicts a version of vocal physiology that resembles Étienne Bonnot de Condillac's speculation regarding vocal organs.

Condillac theorized the perfect form of prosody across three categories: "la qualité des sons" (the quality of sounds), "les intervalles par où ils se succédent [sic]" (the succession of intervals), and "le mouvement" (movement).²⁹ The quality of sounds refers to a mixture of sounds—including consonant attacks, vowel sounds, and possibly even timbred qualities, which Condillac defined as "doux" (soft), "moins doux" (less soft), and "durs" (hard).³⁰ In terms of pitch, Condillac referred to vocal accents, which rose and fell. Finally, movement covered the metric alterations between long and short syllables. With these final attributes of declamation—intervals and rhythm—we have the basic contour of melody. In this regard, Condillac's approach to language greatly influenced Rousseau's conception.³¹

In addition to the melodic features of language, Condillac also speculated on the physiological changes that made possible the invention of language. In a fictionalized account, Condillac explains how natural language arose from the combination of visual gestures and passionate cries. Among the causes for language's slow development, Condillac names the inflexibility of "l'organe de la parole" (speech organ):³² "L'organe de la parole étoit si inflexible qu'il ne pouvoit facilement articuler que peu de sons fort simples."³³ (The speech organ was so inflexible that it could easily articulate only a few very simple sounds.) The Edenic couple in Condillac's fictional tale have a child whose "langue fort flexible, se replia d'une manière extraordinaire, & prononça un mot tout nouveau" (very flexible tongue, folded over on itself in an extraordinary fashion, and pronounced a brand-new word).³⁴ These Edenic parents, surprised to hear a new word, try to imitate the sound. Due to the inflexibility of their articulating organs, they cannot reproduce it: "Faute d'exercice l'organe de la voix perdit bientôt dans l'enfant toute sa flexibilité."³⁵ (For lack of exercise the vocal organ soon lost in the child all its flexibility.) Within Condillac's speculative history of language, the relative flexibility of vocal organs—which Condillac explicitly connected to the tongue but could also include the mouth, lips, glottis, and larynx—limited the degree to which early humans could enrich their lexicon. The attributes of good prosody (inflection, rhythm, and the sonic qualities of softness and harshness) revealed not only a language's development but also a people's vocal flexibility.

Almost ten years later, Charles Pinot Duclos, a writer, historian, and *Encyclopédie* contributor, penned an additional chapter of Condillac's story. In the *Encyclopédie* article "Déclamation des anciens" (published in 1754 and again in *Mémoire sur l'art de partager l'action théâtrale,* published the same year), Duclos describes styles of vocal expression that evolve within a human's lifespan (childhood to adulthood) and across human ages (antiquity to the early modern age). Within his taxonomy of vocal expressions, Duclos includes four categories: "un son simple, tel que le cri des enfans" (a simple sound, like a baby's cry), "son articulé, tel qu'il est dans la parole" (articulated sound, like it is in speech), "le chant, qui ajoute à la parole la modulation et la variété des tons" (song, which adds to speech modulation and variety of pitches), and, finally, "la déclamation," which "peut s'unir à l'une et à l'autre, ou en être retranchée" (declamation, [which] combines and is cut off from [the sounds of song and speech]).[36]

Starting with the cry, Duclos explains that the voice is "produite par l'air chassé des poumons, et qui sort du larynx par la fente de la glotte" (produced by air escaping the lungs, and leaving the larynx through a glottal opening).[37] Describing the effect of resonance, Duclos also speculates that "les vibrations des fibres qui tapissent l'intérieur de la bouche, et le canal du nez" (vibrations from fibers which line the interior of the mouth and nose) increase the volume of simple vocal sounds.[38] Because Duclos was a proponent of a more material, biological definition of the voice, his approach also differs from Rousseau's focus on the musical accents inherent in each language.

Indeed, Rousseau defined the voice in opposition to Duclos's theory of declamation. In *Dictionnaire de musique*, Rousseau first quotes Duclos verbatim, starting with Duclos's taxonomy of vocal expression. Rousseau then takes issue with Duclos's distinction between singing and speech, which was influenced by Dodart's treatises on the voice. Paraphrasing Dodart, Duclos surmises that the configuration of vocal organs (larynx, glottis, throat, mouth, and tongue) changes from singing to speech because a "man whose speaking voice [*voix de parole*] is ugly, has a pleasant singing voice [*chant*]."[39] Moreover, we can only recognize a familiar voice: "if we haven't heard someone sing, whatever knowledge we have of his speaking voice [*voix de parole*], we will not be able to recognize his singing voice [*voix de chant*]."[40]

Duclos explains differences between the speaking and singing voices through an analysis of laryngeal movement: "La différence entre les deux voix vient donc de celle qu'il y a entre le larynx assis et en repos sur ses attaches dans la parole, et ce même larynx suspendu sur ses attaches, en action et mu par un balancement de haut en bas et de bas en haut."⁴¹ (The difference between the two voices comes therefore from that between the larynx seated and at rest on its ligaments in speech, and this same larynx suspended on its ligaments, in action and moving by an up and down swinging motion.) To be sure, the singing and speaking voices do differ in significant ways that relate to many factors, including how the diaphragm supports the voice, which part of the body the speaker/singer projects the voice, and what pitch the speaker/singer vocalizes. Duclos, however, focuses on a specific anatomical difference that accounts for the many qualities that change from speech to song.

For Rousseau, laryngeal movement fails to account for the differences between singing and speaking voices. Rousseau proposes three objections to Dodart, and by extension to Duclos's theory as well. First, a singer's larynx undulates only when the voice intones a vibrato. In those who sing with a straight tone, the larynx remains immobile. Rousseau then compares the singer's vibrato to instrumental sounds that do not include vibrato: "Secondement, les Sons des Instrumens ne different en aucune sorte de ceux de la *Voix* chantante ... & n'ont rien par eux-mêmes de cette ondulation."⁴² (Secondly, instrumental sounds do not differ in any way from those of the singing voice ... and have nothing in themselves of this undulation.) Finally, Rousseau refines his definition of vibrato as an aspect of pitch: "Cette ondulation se forme dans le Ton & non dans le Tymbre."⁴³ (This undulation takes shape in the pitch, and not in the timbre.) The violin vibrato serves as proof: a violinist's finger does not rock or sway (*balancement*); instead, it moves forward and backward, producing two different pitches. Pitch, Rousseau reminds us, does not come from this undulation. Rather, vibrato is the quick movement between two pitches. Across many articles in the *Dictionnaire de musique*, Rousseau explains the rapid movement between pitches (which occurs in vibrato as well as in other forms of vocal ornamentation, such as *trillo, port de voix, tremblement,* and *chevrotter*) as a fluttering of the throat (*battement de gosier*).⁴⁴

To distinguish singing from speaking, Rousseau advances two interrelated claims. On one hand, the singing voice (la *Voix* de Chant) intones pitches, which are sustained and *appréciable*, meaning that they are perceived and measured by the senses. The sense of hearing can measure a pitch in relation to a harmonic series of intervals, such as its unison, octave, or fifth. To be sure, Rousseau emphasizes only the melodic unison, while ignoring the harmonic ratios of the fifth. On the other hand, the speaking voice (la *Voix* parlante) does not sustain a single pitch. Its intonation, moreover, does not fluctuate to a degree that allows our sense of hearing to measure its harmonic ratios. The speaking voice, or rather the monotone speaking voices of certain languages, exists outside the musical parameters of melody with their sustained pitches, which in succession relate to each other according to a musical scale.

By identifying melodic features as the defining differences between speaking and singing voices, Rousseau develops a longer discussion on the quasi-melodic features of certain languages. This distinction is a rhetorically strategic move that does not fully account for the broad range of differences between the speaking and singing voices. Concluding his passage on the difference between speaking and singing voices, Rousseau explains how a language's accent influences whether a person hears the speaking voice as qualitatively different from the singing voice. For Rousseau, accent has a particular meaning associated with a language's inherent melodic qualities: "Il y a des Langues plus ou moins harmonieuses, dont les Accens sont plus ou moins Musicaux, on remarque aussi, dans ces Langues, que les *Voix* de parole & de Chant se rapprochent ou s'éloignent dans la même proportion."[45] (There are more or less harmonious Languages, whose *accents* are more or less Musical, one also notices, in these Languages, that the speaking and singing *Voices* approach or move away in the same proportion.) Rousseau also specifies the languages in which the speaking and singing voices approach each other or remain distant. French speakers, whose language Rousseau considers to be monotone, sounds very different in song and in speech. However, Rousseau speculates that speakers of ancient Greek during the Hellenic period had a speaking voice similar to their singing one because ancient Greek was a melodic, or songlike, language. In other words, when the language spoken requires of the speaker to vocalize a musical language, similar to a song, a listener cannot differentiate between the singing and speaking voices.

By inserting the notion of accent, Rousseau eliminates the material, biological impact of the voice while also explaining the existence of two voices, whose acoustic differences one can reduce to the product of linguistic inflection. As Verba argues: "Rousseau presents the concept of 'accent' as a central part of his theory of the origins of language and melody. Essentially, he views 'accent' as a kind of natural inflection of the voice that was characteristic of man's first language."[46] Unlike Verba, however, I situate Rousseau's voice at the point of convergence between language and vocal physiology.

According to the *Dictionnaire de musique*, the term *accent* covers a range of concepts, chief among them the melodic features of language: "Toute modification de la voix parlante, dans la durée, ou dans le ton des syllabes . . . ce qui montre un rapport très-exact entre les deux usages des *Accens* & les deux parties de la Mélodie, savoir le Rhythme & l'Intonation."[47] (Any modification of the speaking voice, in the duration, or in the pitch of syllables & words . . . which shows a very exact relation between the two uses of *accents* and the two parts of the melody, namely rhythm & intonation.) On the one hand, *accent* includes the metric scheme, the short and long pauses of syllables, and the rhythmic speed of a language. On the other, it refers to the relative inflection or intonation of the speaking voice, from the most melodic line of speech, with wide intervallic jumps, to the most monotone inflection, with relatively small fluctuations in pitch.

In addition to these two musical elements, Rousseau distinguishes types of accents. The oratorical or pathetic accent conveys to the listener a speaker's passion through changes in inflection and speed: "L'*Accent* universel de la Nature . . . arrache à tout homme des cris inarticulés (tandis que) l'*Accent* de la langue . . . engendre la Mélodie particulière à une Nation."[48] (The universal *Accent* of nature . . . rips from humans inarticulate cries [while] the language's *Accent* . . . shapes the particular Melody of a Nation.) For instance, when angered, "L'Allemand . . . hausse également & fortement la voix dans la colère (pour qu') il crie toujours sur le même ton (tandis que) l'Italien (influencé par) mille mouvemens divers agitent rapidement & successivement dans le même cas, modifie sa voix de mille manières."[49] (The German . . . raises his voice loudly and to the same degree [so that] he yells on the same pitch and tone [*ton*] [whereas] the Italian [influenced by] a thousand various motions rapidly and successively, modifies his voice in a thousand ways.) Across the various versions of accent, three in particular shift attention away from vocal physiology and toward vocal sounds:

the individual inflection of a performer, the more general intonation of a particular language, and finally, the universal expressions of human sentience. These three accents reveal the centrality of melodic inflection to Rousseau's conception of emotionally inflected forms of communication.

This melodic conception captures an important but incomplete version of Rousseau's vocal theory. To be sure, the articles discussed so far reflect a consistent version of Rousseau's approach to the voice, in which he criticizes anatomists who explain the difference between singing and speech as a product of vocal physiology. By expanding the frame of reference to include other articles, however, we can begin to appreciate Rousseau's experimentation with an alternate approach to vocal physiology. For instance, in his *Lettre sur la musique françoise*, a pamphlet published in 1753 as part of the Querelle des Bouffons, Rousseau refers to particular voices. In analyzing the vocal demands of French and Italian song, Rousseau claims that singing in each language demands a distinct set of vocal attributes. First, French song differs from Italian because only remarkable singers such as Marie Fel and Pierre de Jélyotte may attempt to perform French music, whereas all voice types are well suited for Italian music.[50] He then characterizes French technique as requiring the following attributes: a wide register with swelling sounds, an open mouth, pneumatic force, and an ability to belt "toute votre voix" (all your voice) to the point of screaming.[51]

Italian song, however, requires a much lighter touch, a more flexible organ, and less forceful breath. These vocal attributes, in turn, produce an Italian sound, softer and more pleasant than the French style. As Rousseau explains, a richer, less forced vocal timbre allows Italian singers to fill vast concert halls with a soft, pleasant, and sweet resonance. In a word, Rousseau characterizes Italian vocal technique as the acoustic opposite of French technique: an Italian voice performs melodies that sound soft, effortless, "flexibles & coulans" (flexible and fluid).[52] "Pour ces momens rares & passagers où il faut surprendre & déchirer" (For those rare, passing moments where it is necessary to surprise and make one feel deeply), an Italian voice judiciously reveals its brilliance.[53]

Across Rousseau's essays, fiction, and philosophical texts, which examine different forms of vocal expression, two constellations of acoustic attributes emerge to express different affective registers. At one end of the spectrum, we hear the softness, resonance, and flexibility of impassioned vocalizations. At the other end, we hear forceful, harsh, staccato articulations, conveying a very different aspect of human experience: physical needs, social antipathy, or rational thought. Instead of focusing on how sound influences meaning, I propose to locate the physiological attributes that make these constellations of sounds possible.

A new story on musical expression emerges when vocal physiology is integrated into Rousseau's conception of music. Indeed, after Rousseau's first engagement with the Querelle des Bouffons, he began writing a version of what would later become his *Essai sur l'origine des langues*. After drafting a pamphlet titled "Du principe de la mélodie ou reponse aux erreurs sur la musique," Rousseau later borrowed from this text to create two musical essays: *Essai sur l'origine des langues* and *Examens des deux principes avancés par M. Rameau dans sa brochure intitulée Erreurs sur la musique dans l'Encyclopédie*.[54] The term *organe*—along with references to its relative flexibility or softness—appears in a digression on the *Origine de la mélodie*. Referring to the impact of vocal physiology, the digressive fragment states: "Outre cela les organes étoient plus ou moins déliés et flexibles selon la températance des climats et voilà déjà l'origine de l'accent national même avant la *formation* du langage."[55] (Besides, the organs were more or less delicate and flexible according to the temperature of the climates, and this already constitutes the origin of national accent even before the formation of language.)

Well after the *Lettre sur la musique françoise* and the fragment on the origin of melody, Rousseau continued to imagine vocal flexibility on two levels: as a matter of physiological dexterity and as a singer's capacity to stir feelings in the listener. A digression in the *Origine de la mélodie* paints another important yet incomplete version of Rousseau's voices. Throughout Rousseau's corpus, only certain vocal organs possess the sought-after quality of flexibility. In the *Origine de la mélodie*, the Rousseau of the 1750s attributed vocal flexibility and delicacy to nature, and specifically to climatic differences. In the early 1760s, Rousseau continued to mention the voice as an organ. For instance, the titular character in *Julie, ou La Nouvelle Héloïse* has "un organe ... sensible" (a sensitive organ), which enables her to perform Italian music. Her Swiss upbringing among mountains, lakes, and streams and away from the corrupting influence of city life has presumably helped develop her flexible organ. In contrast, "la dureté de l'organe musical" (the rigidity of the musical organ) in France becomes synonymous with voices that sound "rudes et sans douceur" (harsh and without sweetness).[56]

Likewise, in *Émile*, Rousseau's treatise on education from the early 1760s, the narrator situates the relative flexibility of vocal organs in relation to a child's developmental stages. For young children, "leur organe encore engourdi ne se prête que peu à peu aux imitations des sons qu'on leur dicte."[57] (their still-numbed organ lends itself little by little to the imitations of the sounds that are dictated to them.) In creating a composite version of Rousseau's vocal organs across his works, I discovered that a variety of internal and external factors influence vocal physiology: physical sensations (climate, physical needs); social interactions (emotions); and linguistic habits. Rousseau examines physiological modifications as a product of social, linguistic, and natural pressures.

Among the writings that clearly articulate social, linguistic, and natural influences on the voice, the *Essai* provides the most systematic explanation of the voice's interaction with climate, language, and society. Within Rousseau's anthropological theory of language, its melodic profile influences and even modifies a speaker's *organe musical*. To be sure, the habitual exercise of speaking a specific language can transform vocal physiology. A language's melodic qualities exist in direct proportion to "la délicatesse de l'organe" (the finesse of the organ).[58] Habitual vocal exercise leaves a physiological imprint on the voice. Indeed, Rousseau notes, "Cette habitude dépend des sortes de voix usitées dans le langage, auxquelles l'organe se forme insensiblement."[59] (This habit depends on the sorts of voices used in the language to which the organ imperceptibly shapes itself.) This formulation explains in part the distinction that the *Dictionnaire de musique* makes between French and Italian singers, insofar as the French language, which sounds monotone and harsh, not only modifies a singer's vocal organs but also demands a certain type of *organe*. According to this formulation, the *Essai* slightly reverses the order of vocal transformation from the one articulated in Étienne Bonnot de Condillac's *Essai sur les connaissances humaines* (1749). Language acquisition essentially changes the relative flexibility and finesse of the vocal organs, which include the mouth, glottis, tongue, lips, and ear. The ear is included among the vocal organs because a speaker can only modify the other organs if she hears her own vocal sounds.

By reversing the order of influence (that is, language's transformative power over vocal organs rather than vice versa), the *Essai* also claims that the transliteration of language not only modifies the inflective, melodic qualities of language but also shapes the very mouths that speak written languages. Rousseau lays the blame for this transformation in part on writing, which "décompose ... la voix parlante à un certain nombre de parties, soit vocales, soit articulées" (deconstruct[s] ... the speaking voice into a certain number of elementary parts, either vocal, or articulated).[60] As Rousseau states, "on écrit les voix, non pas les sons" (we write voices, not sounds).[61] Writing thus attempts to capture the *accent* of a language: an attempt that ultimately habituates the reader to a specific melodic profile and renders the reader's vocal organs more or less flexible.

During the speculative portion of the *Essai*, Rousseau again modifies Condillac's original premise that the flexibility of vocal organs influences the complexity of human expressivity. Whereas Condillac evaluates linguistic sophistication in terms of lexical variety and syntactical complexity, Rousseau evaluates language in terms of its capacity to express emotions, an attribute associated with the melodic flexibility of the voice. Melody is one of the major extralinguistic features that define Rousseau's sentimental voices.

Within his speculative history of language development, Rousseau proposes that two original languages constituted the protolanguage from which modern ones emerged. One language evolved among southern cultures; these dialects expressed passion through a melodic form of prosody. The other evolved among northern cultures, whose people expressed physical need through harsh, guttural articulations. Among the sonic qualities characterizing these two languages, southern languages were "vives, sonores, accentués" (lively, resonant, accentuated), whereas those of the North were "sourdes, rudes, articulées, criardes, monotones" (mute, harsh, articulated, crying, monotone).[62]

From these attributes flow the melodic and rhythmic features of the *organe musical*. Where the accentuated nature of southern language refers to its melodic line, the monotone characterizes the droning quality of northern idioms. What's more, the lively movement of southern language evokes a rhythmic dynamism, whereas the articulated northern dialect brings to mind a harsh staccato movement in the prosodic line of the language. As I have noted, a language's melodic features impact the relative flexibility of people's vocal organs. Language thus leaves a lasting physiological impression on a culture's collective voice.

In addition to language's influence, Rousseau considers how temperature and climate modify vocal physiology. As he develops this idea in subsequent works, his climatic theory comes to resemble that of Condillac, who envisions language formation across a mixture of environmental and cultural factors.[63] Among the climatic influences, the *Essai* describes causality between temperature and physical development. For instance, the coldness of the North left a physical impression on its inhabitants' constitution: "On voit déjà que les hommes, plus robustes, doivent avoir des organes moins délicats, leurs voix doivent être plus âpres & plus fortes."[64] (We already see that humans, stronger, must have less delicate organs, their voices must be harsher and louder.) This observation attributes biological qualities to climatic influences, which in turn impact the voice's melodic flexibility. When discussing this early stage of linguistic development, Rousseau modifies Condillac's notion that the first humans lacked vocal dexterity and situates the malleability of vocal organs within a climatic model.

For northerners, Rousseau adds two complementary notions: physical needs and coarse passions, which also influence a person's vocal physiology. Living in the North, where subsistence was tenuous, required cooperation. This in turn necessitated linguistic clarity, a quality that Rousseau associates with the inhospitable environment of the North, and that northerners expressed through "articulations fortes & sensibles" (loud and distinct articulations).[65] As northerners endured months of frigid temperatures, they eked out a tenuous existence, in competition or cooperation with other humans. During their limited social interactions, they often expressed negative emotions such as anger and threats.[66] In turn, northern inhabitants translated these feelings into a specific set of sonic features; for example, "La colère arrache des cris ménaçans, que la langue et le palais articulent."[67] (Anger rips out menacing screams that the tongue and the palate articulate.) Their repeated expressions of anger modified vocal physiology and rendered the *organe musical* more apt at articulating harsh sounds. As their language became fixed, their glottal dexterity deteriorated and left northerners with a limited melodic range—and by extension, I would speculate, with less open vocal organs, whose strength and harshness aptly expressed their coarseness through lingual and palatal articulations.

To imagine the configuration of the northerner's *organe musical*, I apply Nina Sun Eidsheim's "sound-based notion of singing" in which a singer relies on a "sonic ideal . . . to change her voice to match this ideal."[68] Whereas Eidsheim evokes the "sound-based notion of singing" to deconstruct Western vocal traditions that naturalize certain ideal sounds, I imaginatively and performatively experiment with her approach to change my voice to match a sonic ideal of northern voices. Indeed, the texts that I analyze invite readers to imagine and experiment with the voice. In so doing, they guide the reader toward a conception of the voice as a combination of sound and embodied action that influences a person's moral and physical being.

By borrowing Eidsheim's "sound-based notion of singing," I am not proposing that my experiments reveal an objective truth about Rousseau's theory of the voice. Instead, I believe that Rousseau's theorization of the voice is based on a speculative methodology that relies on the subjective knowledge of the writer as well as on the process of speculative experimentation. For my analysis of Rousseau, I rely on vocal performance to approximate the sounds of Rousseau's voices. This experimentation in turn provides me with embodied, physiological knowledge of the voices that construct cultural identities and gendered subjectivities. For this chapter as well as those that follow, I perform vocal experiments to understand how the voice through its materiality is an embodied action that constructs versions of identity, subjectivity, and sentience.

For the northern voice, I experiment with a harsh, nasal, guttural and melodically rigid sound that configures vocal organs around a narrowing aperture. The mouth—rather than the nasal cavities and the throat—produce a harsh, shallow, nasal tone color.[69] This closed aperture characterizes the voices of northerners: "Ces hommes grossiers . . . accoutumerent insensiblement toutes les oreilles à la rudesse de leur organe; leur voix dure & dénuée d'accent étoit bruyante sans être sonore."[70] (These vulgar men . . . accustomed all their ears without knowing to the coarseness of their organ: their harsh voice, lacking any accent, was noisy without being resonant.) As these clans dispersed and subjugated other nations, their imported language took precedence over the climatic and emotional factors that shaped vocal physiology: "Ce chant bruyant, joint à l'inflexibilité de l'organe, obligea ces nouveaux venus & les peuples subjugués qui les imiterent, de ralentir tous les sons pour les faire entendre. L'articulation pénible & les sons renforcés concoururent également à chasser de la mélodie tout sentiment de mesure & de rhythme."[71] (This noisy song joined to the inflexibility of the organ forced these newcomers and the subjugated peoples who imitated them to slow down all the sounds to make them heard. The painful articulation and the reinforced sounds also helped to drive out of the melody any sense of musical timing and rhythm.) As evidence of his theory, Rousseau cites the Emperor Julius, who "comparoit le parler des Galois aux croassement des grenouilles. Toutes leurs articulations étaient aussi âpres que leurs voix étaient nazardes et sourdes" (compared Gaul's speech to croaking frogs. All their articulations were as rough as their voices were nasal and dull).[72] Retracing this circuitous chain of cause and effect, we arrive where the *Dictionnaire de musique* picks up the story of the voice: at the point where language, with its accent, articulation, and timbre, trains vocal organs to become more or less flexible, pleasant (*doux*), and resonant (*sonore*).

The *organe musical* retains the memory of northerners' languages in the form of harsh consonants and hoarse vowels whose acoustic energy pools in the mouth. By focusing on vocal physiology, I propose a new direction for discussing Rousseau's music theory. Whereas scholarship across Rousseau studies has often emphasized the relationship between language and music, I propose that Rousseau's approach to timbre opens up a field of inquiry into the materiality of vocal organs. In his comparison of northern and southern languages, Rousseau implicitly describes two vocal physiologies. One physiology produces closed, guttural, nasal articulations of loud consonants whose percussive force and coarse vowels imperfectly resonate in a closed mouth. This vocal type would resemble what Dodart describes as a nasal voice, which refers to resonance in the mouth, in which the soft palate closes off nasal cavities.[73] In other words, the northerners articulate language through closed vocal organs and project the sound near the front and back of the mouth. In contrast, southern languages cultivate open, flexible, and delicate vocal organs with a dexterous glottis that quickly shifts between melodic intervals. The tongue lightly articulates consonants, while the open larynx and mouth resonate with rich tones. This vocal physiology—privileging the back and bottom of the throat—is conducive to three types of sound: melodic dexterity, soft consonant articulations, and rich, sonorous timbre.

Southerners' melodic dexterity flows from a distinctive set of natural, social, and moral pressures. Rousseau strategically ignores the possibility that warmth could influence vocal physiology. Unlike the unbearable cold, which hardens the physical constitution of northerners, warm, bountiful climates allow most physical needs to be easily met. Only thirst, stimulated by heat, sporadically propels southern clans to cooperate and build wells. Language arrives when these pastoral people meet habitually around the wells. During these chance encounters, love sparks a language of melodic passion.

As part of the southerner narrative, Rousseau describes how passion produces a relatively open and flexible vocal physiology: "La voix de la tendresse est plus douce, c'est la glote [sic] qui la modifie, & cette voix devient un son."[74] (The voice of tenderness is more pleasant, its glottis modifies it, and this voice becomes a sound.) The glottis returns again in a discussion of "une langue accentuée et chantante" (a songlike and accentuated language), where the habitual exercise of instinct trains the glottis to move delicately in a middle spectrum of vocal inflection: "L'organe prit un milieu & tomba naturellement sur des intervalles plus petits que les consonnances, & plus simples que les comma."[75] (The organ took a middle ground, and naturally fell on intervals smaller than consonant ones, & simpler than commas.)[76]

Within this middle ground between large consonant intervals and minute quarter tones, southerners' vocal organs can intone tiny intervals, which in turn express "des genres des plus pathétiques" (some of the most moving genres).[77] By referring to these minor variations as genres, Rousseau evokes the musical definition of the term *genre*: the intervallic division of the tetrachord, or a scale of four notes. Among the genres Rousseau defines, the chromatic, which involves melodic movement by half-step, expresses "la douleur & l'affliction" (pain and affliction).[78] In other words, the glottal flexibility of southern people permits them to express subtle pitch variations, which their inhabitants then associate with specific emotional meanings.

In addition to this speculative history of melodic dexterity, Rousseau applies a similar set of attributes to characterize the positive and negative qualities of opera singers. In an article on the operatic voice, Rousseau delineates the qualities of a lyric voice: "Mais par ce mot *voix*, j'entends moins la force du timbre, que l'étendue, la justesse, & la flexibilité."[79] (But by this word *voice*, I mean less the strength of timbre, than the range, preciseness, & flexibility.) Rousseau also explains that harsh and noisy voices cannot render the emotional movement of a song. The singer's task involves a melodic interpretation, judged by his capacity to "saisir & rendre avec intelligence la partie musicale de ses rolles [sic]" (seize and render with intelligence the musical part of his roles).[80] By diminishing the importance of timbre, Rousseau elevates the importance of melodic dexterity.

Across descriptions of these theoretical voices, certain features help to distinguish one voice type from another, from the melodic quality of southern language to the monotone accent of northerners. To bring clarity to my discussion of these extramelodic features, I borrow from Victoria Malawey's "comprehensive model" for voice analysis (see fig. 1).[81] Malawey breaks down the voice into six categories: "loudness, grain, timbre, turbulence, resonance and clarity."[82] She goes on to refine each category: turbulence refers to "softness, breathiness, huskiness, grit"; resonance refers to "ring, nasality, warmth, color, relation of sound to formant frequencies"; and clarity refers to "focus, degree of nonharmonic noise."[83] Between these categories, Malawey also identifies areas of overlap such as "registration," meaning "glottal fry, modal registers [of] chest, middle/mixed and head, falsetto, [and] whistle."[84]

In adapting Malawey's diagram to interpret Rousseauan voices, I acknowledge a fundamental difference between the objects that Malawey and I analyze. Whereas Malawey's diagram describes the auto-tuned voice as a linguistic-spatial map, I am analyzing literary description of voices that are either imagined or remembered by Rousseau. Malawey's diagram, however, is a useful tool to imagine how literary description can map out and record the sonic attributes of a voice. Among the attributes I borrow from Malawey, I map the sounds of resonance, clarity, turbulence, and agility onto Rousseau's descriptions of voices. This is not to say that Malawey's diagram offers a translation of or an equivalent model of Rousseauan voices. The two models do share commonalities. Under the category of resonance, I would place Rousseau's

FIG. 1. Victoria Malawey's "comprehensive model" for voice analysis. *A Blaze of Light in Every Word: Analyzing the Popular Singing Voice* (Oxford: Oxford University Press, 2020), 7.

binary notions of *éclat* (ring) and *sourd*. Turbulence approximately covers Rousseau's oppositional qualities of harshness (*rude, âcre, aigre*) and softness (*doux*). Finally, Malawey's notion of agility comes closest to Rousseau's description of voices that are *coulant* or that have *flexibilité*. From these broader categories, Rousseau constructs the archetypal voices of the northerners and southerners as well as the cultural voices of French and Italian performers. By adapting Malawey's diagram to the analysis of Rousseau's voices, I identify the importance of vocal quality in his construction of various voices.

As Deirdre Loughridge notes, Rousseau characterized timbral qualities along two opposing axes: dull/bright (*sourd/éclatant*) and harsh/soft (*aigu/doux*).[85] According to Loughridge, *éclat* refers to a "brilliant or bright tone,"[86] to which I add Rousseau's description of the violin's timbre as blending softness with *éclat*. I would define *éclat* as ring, a quality that so intensifies the resonance of an instrument that its vibrancy cuts through ambient noise and gives the instrument's sound an intense, shimmering quality.

Furthermore, the term *doux*—which Loughridge defines as "not only a simple decrease of sound but also a manner of playing more gently and sweetly"[87]—can also refer to a legato attack. Indeed, Rousseau's musical definition of *doux* has multiple meanings, including "une manière de jouer *più soave*, plus douce, plus liée" (a gentler, more connected way of playing).[88] In other words, *doux* blends the vocal quality of softness with the pitch/prosody attribute of legato. In this regard, softness inhabits a space between vocal quality and melodic flexibility.

Across an array of musical writings, Rousseau refines his ideas about vocal organs in relation to vocal register. For his description of natural singing, he begins with the vocal features of southerners' language: "aisé, doux, gracieux, facile" (natural, pleasant, graceful, easy).[89] He then adds a description of supple vocal inflection, which sounds "ni forcé ni baroque ... ni trop haut ni trop bas, ni trop vîte ni trop lentement" (neither forced nor bizarre ... neither too high, nor too low, neither too fast, nor too slow).[90] In this middle region, Rousseau identifies the ideal human voice: the tenor, whose register "convient le mieux à la voix d'homme" (best suits the man's voice).[91] Rousseau admires the tenor register so much that he dubs it the "*Voix humaine* par excellence" (*Human Voice* par excellence).[92]

As Lynn Festa notes, French sentimentality often begins with a universal conception of humanity.[93] If Rousseau's sentimental voices do possess a universal quality, it would inhabit a paradoxical space with the relativistic notions of Rousseau's aesthetic theories. He often defined the voice in relation to historical, cultural, and gender differences. According to Matthew Gelbart, the universality within Rousseau's music aesthetics is a process rather than a quality: it resides in Rousseau's "belief in an inescapable, linear degeneration of styles."[94] The construction of the "*voix humaine* par excellence," however, suggests that Rousseau did not believe so straightforwardly in a narrative of linear degeneration and pinpoints an audible record of the universal voice. Rousseau's definitions of the tenor voice come from an impulse to transcribe the male voice as a symbolic organ that retains traces of a prelapsarian human race.[95]

Indeed, among all of the male voice types, the tenor possesses the most attributes in common with the speculative voices of southern clans: this Italian voice type is "plus flexible, aussi sonore, & beaucoup moins dure" (more flexible, as resonant as, and a lot less harsh) than the bass voice type.[96] Rousseau again returns to that open and dexterous glottal voice that possesses a pleasing resonance (defined by softness) and lack of turbulence (defined as the absence of harshness). The tenor voice also possesses an important feature that distinguishes it from other vocal types: a middle range. In privileging the tenor voice as an embodiment of humanity's voice, Rousseau eliminates the extreme registers of bass and soprano.

This is not to say that the female voice is absent from Rousseau's work. Michael O'Dea, for instance, has noted a contradiction inherent in Rousseau's approach to female singers. In 1749, Rousseau praised the beauty of women's voices in his *Encyclopédie* article "Musique." He then reconsidered their beauty as dangerous in his 1757 *Lettre à d'Alembert*.[97] This essay argues against creating a theater in the Republic of Geneva. Among other reasons, Rousseau asserts that actresses pose a twofold threat to a republic. First, as public role models, they undermine a virtue necessary to maintain republican values: women's modesty. Women onstage are outside the domestic sphere and thus are dangerous role models for the public. Second, with their seductive allure presented on stage as an artificial object of desire, actresses distract men from their duty. O'Dea locates actresses' seductive and distracting power in their voices, a power that men "cannot resist."[98] For O'Dea, Rousseau's *Lettre à d'Alembert* represents the female voice within an "affective theory," in which the female voice possesses "remarkable and irresistible powers":[99] "The passionate voice came to be exclusively associated with women, and women were completely excluded from society's workings in Rousseau's account of them."[100]

Although I agree with O'Dea that the female voice in Rousseau's work is a powerful instrument that arouses male desire, after 1757 Rousseau neither abandoned nor fully condemned the beauty of the female voice. In his *Dictionnaire de musique*, written in 1764 and published in 1768, Rousseau praises the timbre of women's voices: "Mais de toutes les *Voix* aiguës, il faut convenir, malgré la prévention des Italiens pour les Castrati, qu'il n'y a point d'espèce comparable à celle des femmes, ni de l'étendue ni pour la beauté du Tymbre."[101] (But of all the high-pitched voices, it is necessary to agree, in spite of the Italians' preference for the Castrati, that there is no voice type comparable to that of women, of its range or the beauty of its timbre.) The high-pitched voices of men, however, are quite disagreeable: for Rousseau the falsetto, used by the French *Haute-contre*, is "le plus désagréable de tous les Tymbres de la *Voix* humaine" (the most unpleasant timbre of all human voices).[102]

Rousseau modifies his critique of high-pitched male voices when he discusses the castrati. According to Rousseau, their voice has brilliance only near the top of their range, but they sing "sans chaleur & sans passions" (without warmth & without feelings).[103] As Martha Feldman notes, Rousseau's critique of the castrati was part of a larger discourse on the coldness of castrati, which associated them humorally through Galenic medicine to women.[104] Their coldness also served as a metaphor for the virtuosic precision of their performance style.[105] Rousseau was not merely targeting the sound of castrati. His larger critique was directed at the unnatural sacrifice that fathers imposed on their sons in pursuit of fortune.[106]

Across Rousseau's discussion of timbre, he is constructing sentimental timbres that promote a traditional patrilineal organization of familial and social relationships. The castrati's lack of warmth and feeling becomes a figure of sound that marks the castrati as outside of the natural order of familial and social hierarchies. For my discussion of the uncanny in chapter 5, I will return to the literary depiction of the castrato's voice. Within Rousseau's work, I wish to highlight the role of timbre in the construction of gender identities.

By accepting the natural beauty of the female voice, Rousseau sought a middle ground, arguing that women from large cities should be permitted to perform "les ris modestes, l'air dédaigneux, & les propos plaisans dont ils sont l'éternel objet" (modest laughter, with a disdainful air, and with the pleasing remarks of which they are the eternal object).[107] By giving women's voices a restricted public repertoire, Rousseau banished the castrato's voice from public space and left in its place the voice of "humanity" and "modesty": "Faisons entendre, s'il se peut, la voix de la pudeur & de l'humanité qui crie contre cet infâme usage."[108] (Let us hear, if possible, the voice of modesty and of humanity who cry out against this vile practice.) By mentioning the voice of modesty after a condemnation of castrati, Rousseau gestured toward a vocal type of human modesty whose timbre emerges from the natural beauty of female voices.

To be sure, in *Lettre à d'Alembert*, Rousseau condemned the presence of female performers, in part because of the political and social context (the theater was in a Republican city that had not reached the moral depravity of Paris). In this regard, Rousseau implied a system of moral and aesthetic values analogous to the governmental institutions proposed in *Du contrat social*, in which an ideal form of governance does not exist. Instead, each nation must adapt a form of governance suited to its specific set of historical contingencies.[109] Yet female voices, with their seductive allure, had a place in Rousseau's social theory, specifically in *Émile* and *Julie, ou La Nouvelle Héloïse*. Paradoxically, in these works the female voice guides a male protagonist away from passion and toward moral forms of desire.

Several important distinctions must be noted. Rousseau's *Lettre*, for instance, theorizes the social utility of an actress's voice, which is an embodied organ whose speech circulates within a public venue. Unsurprisingly, this female voice, whose presence male spectators experience as a physical sensation, is the one that Rousseau most roundly condemns. On the other hand, southerners' voices are speculative creations that Rousseau imagines as part of his discussion of language's origin. As a theorization of the sentimental voice, the *Essai* develops a version that is both universal and differentiated across cultures. In this theoretical work, Rousseau follows a Gallic trend, noted by Lynn Festa, of imagining a universal example of sentimentality.[110] In contrast to these theoretical and embodied voices, the voices in *Julie* are fictional, intended to arouse the reader's imagination. With *Julie*, Rousseau begins to represent unique voices that are associated with the particular emotional and moral dispositions of characters.

While I develop the idea of the voice as a moral guide more fully in chapter 2, here, to round out my discussion of the voice as a flexible, sensitive organ, I focus on the ambiguous notion of timbre in Rousseau's work. As a quality incorporating both physical and moral attributes, timbre can draw the listener in one of two directions: toward pure physical sensation, or toward a moral feeling of communitarian love. Thus, in the final section of this chapter, I examine Rousseau's theorization of the voice in relation to its timbre, a broad term under which I include the singer's grain, resonance, and turbulence.

TIMBRE IS a slippery and interesting concept, and its definition relates to a third quality of sound. In Rousseau's definition of the voice, as we have seen, he relates vibrato to pitch instead of timbre. In contrast, in his article on sound, Rousseau defines timbre as an attribute that involves neither pitch variation nor dynamic force. Instead, it is a sound eminently connected to the material qualities of an instrument. Comparing the soft and pleasant tone of the flute to the harsh and shrill tone of the oboe, Rousseau admits that theorists have yet to find the source of timbre, which he imagines exists in a third cause associated with the *corps sonore*, the vibrating corpuscles whence sound originates.[111] Emily Dolan highlights Rousseau's role in conceiving of timbre in terms of tone qualities, explaining that Rousseau's "brief article" on timbre "is notable as the first explicitly musical definition of the concept of timbre, in isolation from particular performances."[112] Furthermore, Dolan notes that Rousseau ends his article on timbre with a reference to Diderot's *Principes généraux acoustiques*, which "explores the production of pitch, but does not tackle issues of tone quality."[113]

However, if we consider for a moment how Diderot formulates his mathematical notion of sound through an understanding of the materials used to produce pitch, it may become clear why Rousseau directs readers toward Diderot's work: Rousseau theorizes timbre in terms of the material configuration and construction of musical instruments. As a reflection of instrumental design and material composition, Rousseau first attributes specific timbres to individual instruments. Borrowing tactile, gustatory, and visual analogies, Rousseau categorizes instruments according to a series of oppositions: an instrument is either pleasant (*doux*) or harsh (*aigre*), muffled (*sourd*) or ringing (*éclatant*). For instance, flutes and lutes are pleasant (*doux*) with little ring (*éclat*), whereas those "sons éclatans sont sujets à l'aigreur, comme ceux de la Vielle ou du Hautbois" (ringing sounds are subject to sharpness, like those of the viola and oboe).[114] The harpsichord has the worst timbre, "à la fois sourds & aigres" (both muffled and harsh), while the violin possesses a "beau *Tymbre*" (beautiful *Timbre*) "qui réunit la douceur à l'éclat" (that brings together softness and ring).[115]

Absent from this description of timbre is an assessment of individual instruments whose material attributes distinguish them from their families. For the voice, Rousseau at least acknowledges the existence of unique vocal sounds, without elevating timbre to the level of melody. In his article on the voice, Rousseau explains, "Chaque Individu a sa *Voix* particulière qui se distingue de toute autre *Voix* par quelques différence propre, comme un visage se distingue d'un autre."[116] (Each individual has its particular voice that distinguishes itself from another voice by some difference of its own, as one face differs from another.) Without specifying the acoustic qualities that render each voice unique, Rousseau implicitly defines uniqueness as originating in part from timbre. In his article on the voice, however, Rousseau reduces vocal uniqueness to a physical trait, like beauty.

Indeed, in Dictionnaire de musique, the Acteur, which includes the operatic singer, needs "un bel organe pour la parole" (a beautiful organ for speech) that is "tout aussi beau pour le Chant" (just as beautiful for song).[117] In Émile, the narrator offers a slightly different version of the voice in his description of women's education. In a passage deriding the futility of personal grooming, which, according to the narrator, does not enhance a women's natural attractiveness, Émile's narrator envisions puberty as a moment when "la voix s'étend, s'affermit, et prend du timbre" (the voice stretches out, strengthens, and gains some timbre).[118] Female maturity occurs when a woman marries her physical traits, including the maturity of her voice, to a capacity to imitate "un accent flatteur" (a caressing accent).[119] Timbre, unlike accent, comes from the natural and purely physical trait of beauty, which accompanies female puberty.

As a result, the beautiful and unique timbre of a female voice may refer to its physical and sensual allure, an attribute that is far from the moral accents of Rousseau's mythical originary languages. By discussing this less explored realm, I argue that as a purely physical aspect of the voice, timbre may have the most in common with Rousseau's version of harmony. For instance, the Essai attempts to separate "impressions purement sensuelles" (purely sensual perceptions) from "les impressions intellectuelles & morales que nous recevons par la voie des sens" (intellectual and moral impressions, which we receive by the way of the senses).[120] Within his taxonomy of moral and sensual impressions, Rousseau classifies color and harmony as pure physical sensations whose sensual pleasure derives from the physics of art, namely painting and music. An artist generates moral sensations through the imitative arts of drawing and song.

Accordingly, the narrator of Émile encourages young women to learn how to sing and dance. This encouragement follows his description of puberty, when women's voices gain timbre. As the narrator of Émile states, "les bras se dévelopent [*sic*], la démarche s'assure" (the arms mature, and the gait becomes confident).[121] In other words, the narrator associates physical beauty with the cultivation of the art of imitation, and specifically the arts of song and gesture. Moreover, to this cultural education, the narrator associates a marital benefit in which a wife cultivates "talens agréables pour plaire au mari qu'elle aura" (agreeable talents to please the husband that she will have).[122] Herein lies the moral utility of a beautiful timbre. By combining natural, sensual beauty with the art of imitation, women can deploy their voices to please men, thus fulfilling (in part) their moral duty within marriage.

Imitation alone, however, does not produce moral sensations. The article on taste (*goût*) defines fashionable singing as the following practice: "donner artificiellement à la voix du Chanteur le tymbre, bon ou mauvais, de quelque Acteur ou Actrice à la mode" (to give artificially to the singer's voice the timbre, good or bad, of a fashionable actor or actress).[123] Among the imitated sounds, this article includes the tone coloring, "nazilloner . . . canarder" (nasalizing . . . squawking).[124] In addition to these nasal-sounding styles, the article mentions the techniques "chevroter . . . glapir" (quavering . . . shrieking), which refer to the blended features of loudness, turbulence, and vocal attack.[125] Across these forms of imitation, the *goût* article re-creates the harsh, inflexible features of the northerners' vocal organs. While the nasalized sounds of *nazilloner* and *canarder* combined with the loudness of *glapir* are consistent with the originary northern organ, *chevrottement*, as a melodic feature, seems to depart from it. This term, however, does not refer to a trill (an alternation of pitches). Instead, it refers to a staccato repetition of the same note in which a glottal stop and forceful air pressure create a trembling quality.[126]

By defining *le goût du chant* as a form of imitation that seeks to reproduce the timbre and voice of a popular singer, Rousseau distances this form of imitation from the form that conveys moral sensations. Through the direct imitation of a unique voice, the singer artificially re-creates a purely physical and mechanical sound: "Les sons annoncent le mouvement, la voix annonce un être sensible."[127] (Sounds announce movement, the voice announces a feeling being.) This distinction between sound and the voice returns in the *Essai* when Rousseau re-creates a scene with his cat. While Rousseau imitates feline meows, his cat responds with a mixture of attention, worry, and agitation.[128] For

David Kusinic, this passage is a critique of emotional deception: "The nonhuman imitation of human sound can create, using Rousseau's language, 'moral impressions'—that machines, necessarily insincere, can sing."[129] But to convey moral sensations to another living creature, a person cannot merely approximate the timbre of a voice—neither a cat's voice nor that of a famous singer. This imitation of timbre approximates the physical sensations of nonhuman sounds. Without the same vocal organs, there is an uncanniness to this imitation. It is easy to sense this uncanniness through sight and sound. The nonhuman listener does not see a cat when it hears an approximation of a cat's voice. The articulation of a meow from a feline voice is also part of the moral impression of timbre.

Likewise, southerners' vocal organs, which develop material and anatomical qualities, produce sounds (timbre and melodies) that convey moral sensation. As noted earlier, southerners' voices possess a flexibility that enables them to perform tiny inflections called accent. In addition to their melodic flexibility, southerners' voices also have *douceur*, meaning softness or pleasantness, accompanied by an internal resonance, *sonore*.

Besides southerners' voices, Rousseau attributes these qualities to Italian singers, whose voices, according to Rousseau, are softer than their French counterparts. In the *Lettre sur la musique française* (1753), Rousseau describes the force of Italian singing as associated with the tone color of these singers. To account for Italian singers' ability to fill performance venues, Rousseau explains that they possess "le timbre le plus fort & plus harmonieux" (the fuller and more harmonious timbre), which enables the singer to be heard in "les théâtres immenses de l'Italie" (the immense theaters of Italy).[130] He also describes the melodic feature of flexibility blended with the Italian tone color of softness (*douceur*) and ring (*éclat*).

To translate the qualities of *douceur*, *sonore*, and *éclat* for modern ears, I apply Malawey's taxonomy of vocal sounds to the qualities of *douceur* and *sonore*. I define *douceur* first as the vocal qualities of loudness and turbulence, and second as a legato form of vocal attack. As for *sonore* and *éclat*, I situate them under Malawey's category of resonance.

Given that Rousseau accords timbre little importance, why does he mention it in the *Lettre sur la musique françoise* and recycle the qualities of softness and resonance for his description of southerners' voices?

I propose that we distinguish different types of Rousseauan timbre: the unique *grains* of individual voices and a cultural *grain* shared by people who speak with a similar cultural voice. The qualities of softness and resonance are most often associated with the cultural *grain* of southerners' voices but can also appear as part of the individual *grain* of fictional characters. Certain people—such as those belonging to southern cultures, Italian singers, and even certain Rousseauan characters, like Julie—possess a vocal organ with a very specific timbre that conveys moral impressions. In terms of vocal technique, softness and resonance appear to be related. As qualities of the voice, they may have less social and communicative usefulness than the flexibility of the glottis. These timbred qualities, however, may accompany a flexible glottis as a secondary vocal feature because looser and more open vocal organs would make possible the somewhat surprising convergence of softness, fullness, resonance, and ring. Indeed, a singer whose open vocal organs project sound into the *mask*, or the nasal cavities, can produce a fuller, more resonant sound, capable of filling an entire concert hall.

The opposite of this rich, resonant voice is a shallow, nasal-sounding voice. In reconstructing the northerners' voice type, I have relied on my experience as a singer. For the northerners' voice, I imagine tighter vocal organs that push up the larynx and collapse the soft palate. This vocal configuration would produce an excessive breathiness with less resonance and more nasality. By drawing on my performance practice, I speculate that Rousseau describes two types of vocal configurations: the southerners' voice has the softness and resonance of an open and flexible voice, whereas the northerners' voice has the harsh nasality of a closed and rigid organ.

Among the southern people, softness (*douceur*) and resonance (*sonore*) characterize the expression of communitarian feeling. Rousseau mentions softness or pleasantness in connection with southern clans' "voix de la tendresse" (voice of tenderness).[131] This voice, furthermore, is articulated through a modification of the glottis. Within a prelapsarian context, softness and resonance exist in a gender-neutral milieu, wherein southerners intone language with an open and flexible organ that produces resonant and pleasant sounds. After this prelapsarian moment, however, the voices most similar to southerners' voices possess only a portion of the originary vocal qualities. Furthermore, the voice branches off into masculine and feminine voice types. The *doux* tone color becomes a feature of female voice types, and resonance characterizes male voice types.

Among the female characters in *Émile* and *Julie, ou La Nouvelle Héloïse*, voices are often described in terms of softness. For instance, in *Émile*, Sophie discovers that the dry and harsh timbre of the harpsichord brings out the softness of her voice.[132] Likewise, in *Julie*, an adaptation of the Eloise and Abelard love story, the character Saint-Preux falls head over heels for Julie d'Étange. In the first of six volumes, Saint-Preux refers to the softness or pleasantness of Julie's voice: "Je t'apperçois & et mon sein palpite; le doux son de ta voix y porte une agitation nouvelle."[133] (I see you, and my chest beats; the sweet sound of your voice introduces into it a new stirring.) The timbre of *douceur* as the tone color par excellence of tenderness first reveals itself as a sensation; it rhythmically seizes Saint-Preux's vital organs and manifests itself as heart palpitations. Similar to the *voix de la tendresse* from Rousseau's essay on language, *douceur* as a timbre of the voice exists between physical sensations and moral impressions. As Saint-Preux's desire transforms from a physical sensation into the moral emotion of love, and then, painfully, after Julie marries and becomes Julie de Warens, into loving friendship. Throughout the course of the novel, Saint-Preux responds to the *douceur* of Julie's voice differently. It first arouses desire and then slowly transforms from a physical to a moral sensation.

In this chapter, I have emphasized that Rousseau represents the voice in terms of gender and theorizes the voice in terms of cultural heritage. These intersectional qualities—gender and cultural heritage—develop at different historical moments. The cultural *grain* of southern voices does not have such starkly delineated vocal features. While the clans clearly organize labor around gender-specific roles—men tend to their flocks, and women fetch water—Rousseau's speculative descriptions of these originary voices blend softness with resonance. Gender distinction arises once humanity has left the prelapsarian moment described in the *Essai*. For instance, vocal *douceur* becomes a feature of female voice types that is implicated in the story of domestication. Julie and then Sophie, whose sweet voices arouse the desire of male admirers, first pique their lovers' interest and then guide them toward a moral existence.

Gender, as an attribute of fictional voices, imprints differences on vocal organs.

As such, his characters take on specific gender qualities that accompany clearly defined feminine and masculine spaces. *Douceur*, as a quieter quality, fills the domestic space, while resonance fills public forums. *Émile*'s narrator, for instance, represents Sophie in a domestic scene. Her pleasant singing voice accompanies the strident tone color of the harpsichord. The female voice functions as a softening element within the domestic sphere. Outside the home, male voices are expected to fill up space and reach distant listeners. The narrator's male ward, Émile, possesses a resonant organ similar to those possessed by male children educated in "la rusticité champêtre" (pastoral rusticity).[134] Unlike city children, whose voices are only "[un] confus bégaiement" (a confused stuttering), or villagers, who speak with colloquial accents and expressions, children raised in rustic settings develop a robust vocal organ and "une voix plus sonore" (a more resonant voice).[135] Moreover, when Émile grows older and learns to sing, his voice becomes "juste, égale, flexible, sonore" (in tune, even, flexible, resonant).[136] Surprisingly, Émile's voice possesses almost all of the qualities of southerners' voices—their resonance, their accuracy of pitch, and their melodic flexibility. Émile, however, does not possess the sweetness through which Sophie expresses tenderness, because sweetness (*douceur*) accompanies an affective register associated with feminine spaces, whereas resonance covers the public domain of persuasion.

This notion of resonance returns when Rousseau describes the voice within the public sphere: such a voice can fill public forums and be heard. Indeed, in a section on the postlapsarian voices that followed the northern and southern languages in the *Essai sur l'origine des langues*, the narrator describes a voice similar to a southern one: Muhammad's "voix sonore & persuasive" (resonant and persuasive voice), the rich tone color of which "séduisoit les oreilles avant le cœur" (seduced one's ears before one's heart).[137] To be sure, Muhammad of the *Essai* marries his resonant voice to "l'accent de l'enthousiasme" (the accent of zealotry).[138] Whereas the resonance of southern voices gives shape to an accent of communitarian feeling, Muhammad's voice combined with an accent of zealotry turns his persuasively melodic voice into an intoxicating and purely physical sound. Within the broader universe of Rousseau's voices, resonance appears as part of a male voice type, deployed to persuade a gathered public.

By describing Muhammad's resonant voice as a seduction of the ears, Rousseau recycles an eighteenth-century French notion of Islam as a religion of intolerant zealotry. Within this context, Muhammad's tone color falls within the spectrum of physical sensation rather than moral impression. Surprisingly, within these public spaces evoked in the *Essai*, the voice of a zealot—however persuasive—is not a moral voice: it does not preach a message of tolerance, inclusion, and social cohesion.

Like the tender voice, the resonant, public speaking voice can elicit both physical and moral responses. Although the *Essai* does not specifically explain what differentiates the moral resonance of southern voices from the physical resonance of Muhammad's voice, I speculate that behind Rousseau's critique of Muhammad's work lurks the recycled trope attributing Islam to fanaticism. The cultivation of a resonant voice turns into a pure physical sensation when its expression does not come from a genuine expression of fellow feeling, of a near-egalitarian notion of collective belonging for which the southern languages are known. Indeed, Rousseau's version of Muhammad ends with the voice of fanaticism, whose sound provokes a horde of believers to kneel, to chant the prophet's name, and to pledge to die for his cause.[139]

Among the voices of passion and persuasion described in the *Essai*, one finds a series of tensions in which the acoustic features of resonance and sweetness, melodic flexibility and consonant turbulence are posited as both physical sensations and moral impressions. The affective register that these qualities express is not dependent merely on the sounds. The speaker must possess the proper organ to intone these persuasive and tender pitches. Although Rousseau appreciates the sound of several organs—flexible, resonant, sweet, and sensitive ones—only one voice possesses political power: the resonant one. In a letter to Julie, Saint-Preux speculates that politically oppressed people lack the organ to express their grievances: "Souvent les opprimés ne le sont que parce qu'ils manquent d'organe pour faire entendre leurs plaintes."[140] (Often the oppressed are only because they lack an organ to make their complaints heard.) Among the voices that can be heard in public, Rousseau includes those of the ancient Greeks and the one cultivated in *Émile*, because these voices are audible through their resonance. As a result, they project political power.

While physiology influences how the sentimental voice sounds, external factors, such as environmental and cultural forces, shape and modify the vocal physiology. It is these external factors that in turn construct different types of sentimental voices. Whereas sentimentality in narrative (novels and operas) distinguishes the suffering victim from the sympathetic observer, Rousseau's voices organize social relations and cultural interactions around two major spheres of human activity: the effective communication of emotion, especially sentiments that contribute to social solidarity, and the audible demarcation of gender roles around feminine and masculine spheres of influence. Although these sentimental voices do not reproduce the same social hierarchy that is present in sentimental narratives, they do configure social and cultural interactions around affective and gendered boundaries. Two vocal features construct these boundaries: glottal flexibility determines the affective capacity of a people's voice, and vocal timbre performs a person's gender role.

The physical attributes of the vocal organ, which certain passages from Rousseau's corpus appear to minimize, nonetheless influence the way a person vocalizes. While contradicting the scientific discourse of anatomists, Rousseau's œuvre on the voice represents the physical and material properties that make certain sounds possible as a product of social and environmental interaction. The construction of the vocal physiology does not determine whether humans and animals can speak. Social interaction and the physical environment, however, modify the vocal organs in ways that make them more or less conducive to certain styles of speech—resonant and sweet, harsh and guttural, melodic and monotone.

This chapter, then, has described what we might call a physiological version of the sentimental voice. Chapter 2 continues this discussion by exploring sentimental literature, and in particular the notion of resonance. Instead of investigating vocal configurations that produce resonance, as I have done in the present chapter, I analyze fictional settings that influence the vocal qualities of characters. In particular, I examine how fictional settings represent a voice's resonance and tenderness, and in so doing, transform the voice's function into an external object whose sound serves as a moral guide for the singer. We thus transition from a sentimental voice that controls and prescribes the vocal qualities necessary to exchange emotion across individuals to a sentimental voice that enables the singer to control the circulation of feeling within his body.

2

Fever Pitch

Songs of Temperance

♫

IN AN essay praising Samuel Richardson's novels, Denis Diderot highlights the audible character of the Englishman's epistolary voices. Addressing readers who are moved by Richardson's novels, Diderot explains how Richardson's writing makes passion speak as if the letters themselves had voices.[1] For Diderot, the voices of Richardson's characters ring with "bursts of passion," which in turn "strike" the reader's "ears."[2] Epistolary fiction thus becomes a conversation that transcends the narrative frame to include readers who "take a role" and "join in on the conversation."[3]

Diderot's reference to conversation was a refrain among eighteenth-century French and English critics of the epistolary genre. From Samuel Johnson to the Chevalier Jaucourt, these critics recommended that letter writers imitate the familiar and natural style of conversation. In England, Samuel Johnson defined "the stile of *letters*" as "free, easy, and natural; as near approaching to familiar conversation as possible."[4] Across the Channel, in Diderot's *Encyclopédie*, the sociable, as opposed to philosophical, epistolary style was "a sort of conversation between absent individuals; [this] *style* must resemble that of a discussion such as you would have with a person even if he were present."[5] In Diderot's praise of Richardson, he extends this notion of conversation between friends into an imaginary conversation with fictional characters.

Thus far I have argued that certain literary and philosophical texts construct the voice with attention to the influence of vocal physiology. In the previous chapter, I analyzed Rousseau's ideal vocal sounds that result from physiological modifications. These vocal sounds then become the acoustic marker of a person's gender and cultural identity. Through my analysis of the voice, I demonstrate that the voice is not merely a sound. It is an extension of an embodied collection of organs whose physical changes transform their sound.

For this chapter, I direct my analysis of the voice toward its presence in sentimental literature. I am specifically interested in sentimental scenes that invite the reader to re-create lyrical scenes either through their imagination or through performance. Here, I borrow from Nina Eidsheim's notion that singing is a "multisensory physical activity"[6] and posit that sentimental accents are a multisensory activity that interact with and modify a singer's emotional state and physiological state. Sentimental accents become a form of physiological control that seeks to transform not only the sound of the voice but also the emotions and sensations of the singer.

By attending to and analyzing the voices of characters, I uncover how a textual representation of the voice allows the reader to imagine a physiological, sonorous voice that approaches what Roland Barthes describes as the grain, particularly as it relates to "the materiality of the body."[7] The literary representation of the voice guides the reader to feel and imagine the materiality of a character's voice.

The voice that I theorize is multimodal in its form and multisensorial in its materiality.[8] It is multimodal insofar as I analyze voices represented in several forms: prose description, typographical experimentations, medical observations, illustrations, and musical scores. These multimodal representations of the voice then aid the reader in his imagination of, and experimentation with, a multisensorial voice. This multisensorial voice is partly tactile (that is, the breath, the movement and configuration of vocal organs, and the vibrations of sound), partly audible (that is, the sound of the voice as it departs from the body and returns in the form of resonance or echo), and partly visual (that is, the surroundings of the singer inform the reader's acoustical imagination). This multisensorial voice then interacts with the materiality of the body as well as the acoustic medium through which vocal sounds move and are reflected: air and the character's surroundings.

Here I depart slightly from my approach to vocal materiality. In chapter 1, I defined the voice as a set of physiological organs whose configuration impacts vocal sounds. In this chapter, I add to that definition the influence of a singer's material surroundings insofar as the voice's reflection (echo or resonance) retains an imprint of the singer's physical surroundings. This definition of the voice broadens the sphere of influence on vocal sounds from inside (mouth, glottis, larynx) to outside the singer's body (the location in which a singer performs).

When the singer hears his acoustical reflection, he reexperiences his voice as both sound and vibration. This acoustical reflection becomes a feedback loop through which the singer can modify his physiological and emotional disposition. This type of vocal performance—which I anachronistically describe as a form of vocal therapy—is rooted in the sonic reflection of sentimental accents that the singer hears and reexperiences through his body.

My study of vocal therapy begins with two canonical novels: Samuel Richardson's *Clarissa* and Jean-Jacques Rousseau's *Julie, ou La Nouvelle Héloïse*. My readings of these novels inform my analysis of a popular French writer, François-Marie-Thomas Baculard d'Arnaud, who penned a short story in which the protagonist, Lorezzo, performs eight romance songs. Baculard d'Arnaud's story is notable because it is representative of a novelistic trend that started in the 1760s and continued until the 1780s. During this period, certain novelists inserted musical scores into their fictional depictions of lyrical scenes. By foregrounding my analysis of Baculard d'Arnaud with a discussion of music in *Clarissa* and *Julie*, I show how Baculard d'Arnaud builds on Richardson's and Rousseau's depictions of the voice to notate, transcribe, and describe an embodied, physiological voice. Through Baculard d'Arnaud's experimentation, the novel invites the reader to hear, feel, and experience a voice as a living, breathing organ. Whereas sentimental novelists often represent emotional accents through typographical exuberance (in the form of ellipses) or onomatopoeic transcriptions, Baculard d'Arnaud experiments with musical form and prose description to invite the reader to modify their vocal physiology and feel how the voice interacts with the singer's body.

My analysis of the voice differs from more traditional approaches in literary studies because I examine the voice as a set of vocal organs whose sound interacts with the singer's material surroundings. From a more traditional literary perspective, there is a continuum of perspectives on the literary voice that shifts between an inaudible thought to an audible presence.[9] While Ian Watt imagines Clarissa's letters as the "flow of" Clarissa's "consciousness," made possible through the print medium,[10] Tom Keymer takes issue with the notion that Richardson's epistolary genre offers an unmediated and immediate representation of a character's consciousness. Instead, he shows that Clarissa's letters are premeditated, intended as carefully crafted pieces of writing that imitate speech.[11] Finally, critics who value the audible presence of the voice note their dramatic effect. For Mark Kinkead-Weekes, Richardson's style "attempts to catch living voices in a dramatic present."[12] Kinkead-Weekes's voices remain anchored to a private consciousness, which manifests as "a distinctive mental voice, speaking on paper to its correspondent, analysing, commenting, arguing."[13]

Among critics who have an interest in the voice's audible presence is Cynthia Wall, who analyzes the sounds of Harlowe Place. According to Wall, sonic descriptions give readers a sense of the implied rooms that exist in *Clarissa*'s fictional space.[14] In a contemporaneous analysis of *Clarissa*, Diderot noted such implied sounds. For Diderot, an attentive and sensitive reader of *Clarissa* "listens well ... [and] will hear a dissonant tone" that unveils "the secret feeling" of a character.[15] These voices not only reveal the characters' intentions or the flow of a mental voice; they also provide the reader with the implied sounds of characters' voices.

If we return for a moment to the writing of real letters, we catch a glimpse of Clarissa's conversational practice in Richardson's correspondence to friends.[16] Replying to the young Sophia Scudamore a few years before publishing *Clarissa*, Richardson sets the scene for an imaginary conversation in which he hears, sees, and even feels the presence of his "pen daughter": "While I read [your letter], I have you before me in person: I converse with you.... I see you, I sit with you, I talk with you, I read to you, I stop to hear your sentiments, in the summer-house: your smiling obligingness, your polite and easy expression, even your undue diffidence, are all in my eye and my ear as I read.—Who then shall decline the converse of the pen? The pen that makes distance, presence; and brings back to sweet remembrance all the delights of presence; which makes even presence but body, while absence becomes the soul."[17] For Richardson, epistolary conversation at its best allows the reader to have a virtual experience in which he becomes an active spectator of the letter's contents. Indeed, Richardson describes how he reconstructs Sophia's presence from memory in a way that confirms Cynthia Wall's interpretation. Seeing and hearing a virtual Sophia, he even situates their conversation "in the summerhouse." This is not an abstract conversation that occurs between the author's prose and the reader's mind; instead, Richardson explains that Sophia's epistolary voice awakens in his imagination a virtual discussion, a process that has the paradoxical effect of making Sophia's absence felt as presence. Richardson also states that this virtual presence is idealized because it comes with none of the "intrusions" of physical needs. Freed from the impediments of the body, an epistolary conversation allows the writers' souls to commune with each other.

This virtual presence, however, still awakens physical sensations in the reader. The reader first imagines a letter writer's voice, and this virtual sound in turn elicits feelings associated with the person that the reader experiences as physical sensations. If the reader has positive feelings toward the letter writer, his imaginary audition produces physical sensations associated with joy. Richardson's correspondence even hints that sentimental novels represent virtual voices whose imagined presence the reader hears. In letters written the year Richardson published *Clarissa* (1748–49), he recommends reading his novel through a virtual form of listening. He advises Dorothy Bradshaigh to "hear" the "Testimony" of Mr. Belford, to "hear what my Girl says," and to "hear how Mr. Lovelace expresses himself."[18] Writing to Edward Moore, Richardson likewise directs his friend to "hear Lovelace's *farther Remorses.*"[19] Richardson encourages his readers to imagine characters' voices and create their virtual presence, including their voices, gestures, and appearance.

Reading these letters alongside the 1746 letter to Sophia Scudamore, I propose to use a similar method to analyze the voice in sentimental literature. By studying the voice as a sound that inhabits a fictional space, I revise our understanding of its function in sentimental literature and consider the sonic presence of the voice during the reading of, and imaginative re-creation of, sentimental literature. According to Tadmor's local history of reading, women read novels, such as *Clarissa*, aloud to their families.[20] In this regard, the voice's sonic presence is crucial to understanding how characters rely on the voice to control their emotional state. Scholars often analyze sentimental voices as signs of suffering or involuntary vocalizations of affect.[21] These vocal signs thus represent a character's sincerity and depth of feeling. The sentimental voices in this chapter are quite different: the characters control and instrumentalize these voices. Through musical expression, the characters learn to exercise the vocal organ as a bodily and sonic regime of emotional control.

These virtual voices not only have an imagined presence but also invite the reader to re-create them through performance. For instance, as early as the seventeenth century, French and British novelists began to integrate musical scores into prose fiction.[22] Inserted scores, which I call musical paratext, appeared in a wide range of novelistic genres. In the early eighteenth century, French writers inserted musical scores into fairy tales and pastoral narratives. By the midcentury, British writers were including scores in sentimental and satirical works. From the 1760s until the end of the century, French writers incorporated scores into medieval-inspired historical novels, pastoral works, and—most notably—sentimental literature. These experimental works asked the readers to reenact lyrical scenes and listen to their own voices. The performed voices thus externalized the voices imagined by the reader.

In sentimental literature, the voice's audible presence is intimately connected to notions of sensibility and human physiology. As chapter 1 argued, external forces—environmental, social, and cultural—shape a person's vocal physiology, and so affect the person's ability to exchange emotion with other individuals. In sentimental literature, however, characters can control environmental factors, and in turn devise a form of physiological and emotional control that modifies their physical sensations as well as influences their emotional disposition. For instance, sentimental characters perform a sort of vocal therapy to modify their physical and emotional state. In locations where the voice reverberates or echoes, it becomes an external, reflected sound whose vibrations the character feels. Thanks to the acoustical properties of echo and reverb, characters can then impact their physical sensations through vocal performance.

We find a compelling example of this vocal control in a lyrical scene found in Richardson's *Clarissa*. This type of scene evidently made an impression among at least some of Richardson's readers: similar scenes later appeared (though with several telling differences) in the sentimental fiction of François Baculard d'Arnaud, a popular French writer and an admirer of Richardson.[23] Clarissa's scene as well as the one analyzed in Baculard d'Arnaud's novel represent a moment of heightened emotion when the narrative action slows down while the protagonist sings about his or her emotional turmoil. Singing then allows the protagonist to control his or her emotional response. In this way, both the protagonist and the reader learn a moral lesson through music.

Clarissa's moral lesson teaches her to compose her dysregulated emotions, in part through a contemplation of virtue and wisdom. After *Clarissa*, this musical form of morality migrated to French sentimental literature through Jean-Jacques Rousseau's version of sentimentality to Baculard d'Arnaud. Showing how Baculard d'Arnaud draws on Jean-Jacques Rousseau's approach to music and emotion, I trace Baculard d'Arnaud's blending of British and French versions of sentimentality. Baculard d'Arnaud's short story differs from *Clarissa* in two substantive ways: Baculard d'Arnaud situates moral education in nature itself, and he directs that education toward a male protagonist. His work is an informative counterpoint to *Clarissa* because his version of musical control involves the domestication and even valorization of masculine desire, a notion that is not only antithetical to Lovelace's rakish behavior but also in contrast to the many French depictions of men seducing women through song. Through Baculard d'Arnaud's adaptation, the sentimental voice becomes a therapeutic device for calming masculine desire.

To IMITATE conversations, Richardson's characters rely on a variety of strategies, including punctuation, typographical emphasis, repetition, short phrases, and dialogue form. These strategies allow his characters to write "to the Moment," which for some critics generates a false sense of unmediated representation.[24] Instead of recording the present moment, as a court stenographer would, the letter writers re-create a moment that has already passed and whose details the letter writer can judiciously select to her advantage. Although Richardson believed a letter could transport the reader into a virtual reality, his characters' letters do not represent the action as a transparent and unmediated event.

The virtual conversation created by a letter dramatizes the memory of a recent event through specific print and literary strategies. Richardson's characters, that is, write a reenactment that the reader, relying on the letter's form and style, imaginatively re-creates.

To imitate conversation in a way that avoids repetition, Clarissa stylistically differentiates the virtual voices of reenactment from the style of written prose. For instance, during a heated argument, Clarissa re-creates "an angry dialogue, a scolding-bout rather [that] . . . passed between" her and her sister.[25] In her sister's rant, Clarissa italicizes a few keywords; *witty, prudent, dutiful,* including the word *pi-ous,* which her sister "sneeringly pronounced."[26] She then increases the rhythm of their virtual dispute with "arch expression[s]" plucked from her sister's mouth.[27] Her sister's assault becomes a stammering tongue-wagging, verbalized as a series of rapid and repetitive phrases. Among Arabella's clever mannerisms, Clarissa includes a rhetorical question: "Let me ask you (affecting archness), Has, has, has, Lovelace, has your Rake, put it out at interest for you?"[28] To represent Arabella's virtual voice, Richardson, the printer and writer, relies on italicization, short phrasing, and repetition. To these stylistic elements, Clarissa adds exclamation points, question marks, commas, and em-dashes, which function as cues that distinguish the speech of Arabella's "rising voice" from Clarissa's description. Arabella's voice here audibly expresses the pent-up tension and anger that is mounting in her nerve fibers, vessels, and sinews.

Even when Clarissa speaks, she supplements her reported speech with observations that evoke the embodied, physiological voices of characters. During a conversation with Aunt Hervey, Uncle Antony, and Mr. Solmes, Clarissa attempts to defend Lovelace, to which her audience responds in utter shock. Visualizing their sheer surprise, Clarissa brackets together her interlocutors' expressions of disbelief and emphasizes the simultaneity of their speech with the expression "all in one breath" (see fig. 2).[29] The reader can almost hear the vocal organs at work. Their breath forcefully issuing from their lungs causes each torso to collapse simultaneously. To this unison choreography of breath, the reader can also imagine how their voices start in unison and descend into garbled, incoherent noise. This imaginative re-creation is only possible through typographical experimentation. In this scene, there

> —Yet he may have as bad :—Worfe, pardon me, he cannot have, in my poor opinion : For what muſt be the man, who *hates his own fleſh?*
> You know not, Madam;
> You know not, Niece;   } All in one breath.
> You know not, Clary;
> I may not, nor do I deſire to know his reaſons : It

FIG. 2. Samuel Richardson, *Clarissa, or, the History of a Young Lady*, vol. 2 (1748), 205. (Rauner Rare Book Collection, Rauner Special Collections Library, Dartmouth College)

is supple interaction between description, reported speech, and typographical experimentation, all of which combine to depict a dynamic conversation, filled with sounds and represented in print.[30]

In *Clarissa*, virtual voices that are perceptibly present or absent reveal an underlying power dynamic that motivates first the Harlowes and then Clarissa's captor, Lovelace, to silence the protagonist's virtual voice. During an argument with her sister, Clarissa "was going to speak with vehemence; but [Bella] put her handkerchief before my mouth, very rudely—You have done enough with your pen, mean listener, as you are!"[31] Using several means, her family attempts to isolate Clarissa from her friends and neighbors. Her family forbids her to attend church; her father terminates her contact with Anna; James, empowered by her father, severs Clarissa's correspondence with Mrs. Norton and Lovelace; and finally her parents dismiss Clarissa's chambermaid, who delivered Clarissa's clandestine correspondence to Anna and Lovelace. Even after Clarissa leaves Harlowe Place, Lovelace directly and violently attempts to silence the protagonist. Her cries for help are nearly lost in the din of London's urban soundscape until, in a moment of panic, she "rushed by" Lovelace, "and attempted once more to throw up the sash—Good people! Good people! cried she."[32] The same effort to silence her is made at the moment of her rape, when Lovelace has her drugged. This determination to control Clarissa's physical voice extends to her epistolary voice. When the Harlowes and Lovelace forbid the letter exchange and then intervene in Clarissa's correspondence, they are attempting to control her verbal and vocal expression. In a letter to Anna, Clarissa alludes to the danger that her voice poses: "If consent of heart, and assent of voice, be necessary to a marriage, I am sure I never can, nor ever will be married to Mr. Solmes."[33] To suppress Clarissa's dissent, her family and Lovelace take great pains to mute the articulation of her will.

As a silenced captive of Harlowe Place, Clarissa becomes acutely aware of the voices that surround her. As Cynthia Wall notes, "both at Harlowe Place and in London, Clarissa's perspective is that of imprisoned and, therefore, imperfect apprehension of spaces beyond her immediate boundaries, and, thus, she needs to interpret motives, events, and possibilities by deciphering the sounds coming out of those spaces—pacings, shoutings, door closings, silences."[34] It is precisely these sounds, which pass between walls and through doors, that Clarissa represents as virtual voices on the page, and whose meaning Clarissa interprets for her correspondent. Eavesdropping on a heated argument in her sister's adjoining parlor, Clarissa "heard a confused mixture of voices, some louder than others, drowning, as it seemed, the more compassionating accents. *Female* accents I could distinguish the drowned ones to be."[35] Here, Clarissa provides a sonic description that layers voices on top of each other, with the harsh tones of the Harlowe family washing over the compassionate "*female* accents" that condemn the Harlowes' "cruelty." Clarissa later overhears her brother, "as talking to somebody, in my sister's apartment just by, I stopped; and heard the barbarous designer say, speaking to my sister, This works charmingly, my dear sister! It does! It does! said she, in an exulting accent."[36] Confined, isolated, and silenced, Clarissa must piece together any shreds of evidence she can pick up from the acoustic sphere surrounding her.

Indeed, Clarissa's hypervigilant ear helps make Lovelace's abduction possible. In volume 3, which begins the second installment of *Clarissa*, the protagonist is convinced that her family will force her to marry Mr. Solmes. Lovelace, sensing an opportunity, enlists the Harlowes' gardener, Joseph Leman, to assist with Clarissa's abduction. Rehearsing their escape, Lovelace dictates to Leman his signal for action: "If you hear our voices parleying, keep at the door, till I cry Hem, hem, twice: But be watchful for this signal, for I must not hem very loud, lest she should take it for a signal."[37] Lovelace is aware that the sound of one's voice can betray meaning, and he chooses a cue that Clarissa will interpret only as the clearing of someone's throat. His awareness of sound extends to Leman's role: while discussing the plan for Leman to pretend to break down the garden door, Lovelace—ever the actor—recommends that Leman put less force against the door while also making more noise. Finally, he advises Leman to speak in "as terrible a voice, as you can cry out with."[38] This imitation of anger is intended to provoke a physical and emotional response in Clarissa. By dictating Leman's tone and sounds, Lovelace performs the roles of playwright, dramaturge, and director. He is not "writing to the moment" as much as he is *creating a moment*, which, as Kathleen Lubey argues, is intended to confuse her consciousness.[39] His staged abduction is adapted to Clarissa's situation as a prisoner in her home. While much is made of Clarissa's fear of a forced marriage, her apprehension would not have existed had she not been so isolated from her family. Her solitude heightens her awareness of her acoustic sphere and drives her to interpret the intentions behind overheard voices.

In Richardson's novel, the sounds of virtual voices have a presence that influences the protagonist's actions and reactions. Here, I refer to voices that are virtual to the letter recipient in the novel. As the previous scenes illustrate, Clarissa often interprets and responds to the sounds of scenes she cannot see. She even differentiates the compassionate accents of older female voices from the harshness of male ones. In her cloistered existence, the sounds she overhears connect her to her family's emotional state, and by extension offer indirect access to their deliberations on her fate. These virtual voices constitute what I call an acousmatic regime—where *acousmatic*, a concept developed in the introduction, refers to unseen sound. *Regime* has a dual meaning; I define it as both a system of control and the routine that gives cadence and rhythm to Clarissa's daily life.[40] In Harlowe Place, Clarissa's acousmatic regime is composed of a chorus of voices in which Clarissa can hear the rising accent of anger and the conspiratorial tone of whispered stratagems. My reading of virtual voices suggests that at the moment Clarissa reacts to Leman's angry cries, she is running from the terrorizing acousmatic regime that has kept her body and mind captive at Harlowe Place.

IN THE first two volumes of *Clarissa*, the Harlowes often deny the protagonist an opportunity to control her acoustic sphere. For Tita Chico,

Clarissa's closets are paradoxical spaces where the hope of liberation sporadically shines light into the darkness of her subjugation.[41] If we turn our attention away from the commercial and sexual purpose of her isolation and analyze the acoustical features of her room, we find an exceptional scene during which Clarissa drowns out the sounds outside her room with her own sonic regime, which is to say that Clarissa can see the origin of the sound. In *Clarissa*, the protagonist's sonic regime likewise involves a material alteration of her physical surrounding, and by altering her environment, she is able to regulate her sensibility.

Near the beginning of volume 2, Clarissa, accompanying herself on a harpsichord, sings alone in her room. In this scene, Clarissa directs attention toward herself, specifically focusing on her dysregulated emotions: "I have been forced to try to compose my angry passions at my Harpsichord; having first shut close my doors and windows, that I might not be heard below."[42] This scene is especially significant when we recall that the characters surrounding Clarissa wish to silence her. Completely alone and separated from her family, Clarissa, for one sublime moment, has complete control over her acoustical space.

To interpret this scene, I turn to an excerpt from Anna Howe's eulogy from the third edition of *Clarissa* that offers important context for Clarissa's musical performance. Detailing her departed friend's voice, Anna distinguishes different styles of vocalization, including speaking, reading, and singing. When Clarissa "re'd-out to her friends," her voice was melodious and graceful in part because it did not draw attention to itself with "buskin elevation" or "tragedy-pomp."[43] Instead, she guided her listeners with an "admirably placed" "accent," a "forcibly laid" "emphasis . . . as the subject required," and she even "gave grace and significance" to passages that had none.[44] In Anna's recollection, Clarissa's voice navigated with aplomb between her unique understanding of a text and the social customs regarding public reading as she unselfishly embellished a writer's work with the grace of her voice. In her attitude toward singing, Clarissa similarly embraced the idea that musical performance was for the sake of others. We learn through Anna that when she was "*very young*," she "was guilty of the fault of those who want to be courted to sing."[45] Clarissa then taught Anna—"by her own *example*"—that singing acquires moral value owing to its "*act of obliging.*"[46] According to Clarissa, the young Anna's desire to be courted reduced singing to a transactional form of self-interest. By expecting solicitous attention in return for singing, Anna transformed an act of kindness, service, and courtesy into a form of self-adoration.

The adult Anna does not, however, completely adopt Clarissa's belief that singing is a form of solicitous obligation. While her suitor, Mr. Hickman, engages in "submissive courtship," Anna distracts herself with music. "I am frequently forced," she writes, "to go to my harpsichord, to keep me awake, and to silence his humdrum."[47] In this passage, although Anna eschews the accolades that she once sought, she does not display a generous, courteous, or kind spirit. Instead, she relies on the harpsichord for its sheer volume, its ability to dominate a room's sonic sphere, and its capacity to enliven her spirits. Music here achieves a dual purpose: she is relieved of social obligations while retaining the appearance of civility.[48]

Clarissa's solo performance in volume 2 is not quite like the virtuous singing that she recommends to Anna or Anna's subversive harpsichord playing. Clarissa does not sing and play to oblige a listening audience but rather to soothe her irritated and dysregulated nerves. In this regard, her performance extends and modifies Anna's use of music. While both women achieve a form of social isolation through music, Clarissa relies on musical composition to harmonize her feelings.

Clarissa's song scene also differs from the previous sonic examples because Richardson accompanies it with a musical score. In other words, the narrative and the book itself stage through sound a period of intense emotional reflection. At the editorial level, the first, second, and third editions include a pop-out musical score. Folded between the pages, the score jumps out of the manuscript as if to dramatize an epistolary moment. The materiality of the codex imitates Anna Howe's discovery of an inserted song. As Clarissa explains, she has composed the musical piece, performed it for herself, and then inserted the score into a letter so that her friend could enjoy it. Among the four editions that Richardson directed, three contain the pop-out engraving of the musical score, and the fourth contains a smaller, woodblock version. To put this moment into context, this score is the only large visual figure to appear in the first edition. With more than 2,500 pages, the first and second duodecimo editions include illustrated initials and print ornaments such as arabesques, rosettes, and indices. There are other experimental practices, such as the simultaneous interjection that I mentioned earlier. In the third edition, Richardson also experimented with adding marginalia.[49] However, there are no illustrations. Only the fourth edition includes a portrait of Samuel Richardson. Within the paginated space of *Clarissa*, the engraved score literally stands out among reams of letters.

In terms of the editorial process, this scene is an example of Richardson's attention to paratextual elements. This paratextual insertion followed the practice of contemporaneous authors and editors who likewise supplemented prose descriptions of songs with inserted scores. For many of these novels, we do not know whether it was the author or the publisher who chose to incorporate the music. In the case of *Clarissa*, Richardson took great pains to find a poem and musical setting that suited his protagonist's situation.

For the poem, he borrowed Elizabeth Carter's "Ode to Wisdom" because he wanted Clarissa's moral lesson to come from a female author.[50] "But the Ode being shewn me as written by a lady," explains Richardson, "and the intention of my work being to do honor to the sex, to the best of my poor ability, I was so pleased with it."[51] Richardson then hired a very competent composer to craft a song equal to the artistic merits of Carter's poetry.[52] Finally, Richardson involved himself personally in the printing process. He chose the most expensive type of musical copy, an engraved score. He then inserted this song in his first London edition and three subsequent editions (see fig. 3). By paying particular attention to the materiality of Clarissa's score, Richardson demonstrated an interest in verisimilitude. He could have chosen cheaper methods for inserting the score, such as a woodblock copy that could be mounted on his printing press. Instead, he paid an artist to create an engraved musical score that resembled a written composition.[53] The score itself was then folded between the pages, which gave the reader an experience similar to that of Anna Howe, or possibly even Lovelace, who could have rifled through her letter in the woodhouse. As a result, the reader could discover Clarissa's song almost as though it were a sheet of music inserted into a letter.

With her departure in mind, Clarissa sits at the harpsichord and meditates on female independence. Clarissa's performance, as Leslie Ritchie notes, is a "subversive" form of "self-discipline" because her harpsichord playing—a skill paid for by her family—is not part of a family-sanctioned activity.[54] In other words, Clarissa is subverting the

FIG. 3. "Ode to Widsom," lyrics by Elizabeth Carter, music by anon., in Samuel Richardson, *Clarissa, or, the History of a Young Lady* (1748). (Rauner Rare Book Collection, Rauner Special Collections Library, Dartmouth College)

traditional moral value of music making, which rests on its capacity to promote social unity and familial harmony.

Clarissa's performance also transforms the purpose of her bedchamber: whereas once it enforced filial obedience, it now is the source of independence. In the first volume, Clarissa equates her confinement with a system of sequestration and surveillance: "I *am* to be watch'd, banish'd, and confin'd."[55] Before her performance, however, she seizes control of her isolation: "I have been forced to try to compose my angry passions at my Harpsichord; having first shut close my doors and windows, that I might not be heard below ... the distant hooting of the Bird of Minerva, as from often-visited Woodhouse, gave the subject in that charming Ode to Wisdom, which does honour to our Sex, as it was written by one of it."[56] Her sealed bedchamber affords her a modicum of privacy and muffles the sounds from the garden and the rest of Harlowe Place. In Clarissa's search for independence, her closed bedchamber symbolizes not only her divided family but also an active form of defiance.[57]

As she "was closing the shutters of the windows,"[58] hoping to create a quiet retreat in which to discover the inner turmoil of her soul, Clarissa hears the hooting owl—the symbol of Minerva, the chaste goddess of wisdom—presages Clarissa's song because Carter's poem begins with two stanzas about "the solitary bird of night" whom the poet "hear[s]" "with joy": "the solemn sounds, which midnight echoes waft around, and sighing gales repeat."[59] With Carter's poem as a silent, intertextual partner to Clarissa's performance, we perceive that sound is an important medium through which wisdom, thoughts, and emotions circulate. And by controlling the manner of her confinement, Clarissa replaces the acousmatic regime of virtual voices with her own sonic regime. As explained earlier, the sonic regime modifies Clarissa's physical surroundings, which in turn influence her sensibility.

To re-create this sonic regime, I propose a hybrid reading of Clarissa's performance that imaginatively re-creates her song in a way that resembles Richardson's virtual conversation with Sophia Scudamore. For Clarissa's musical performance, I imagine how the sound of her voice moves and resonates within the wooden interior of her bedchamber—an acoustically rich space whose materiality would modify Clarissa's voice. Given that Clarissa is constantly eavesdropping on her family, her voice, though contained within her room, might seep out through the door of her sister's adjoining parlor. We can assume that her room includes a few traditional items (curtains, rugs, wainscoting). With closed shutters and doors, these sonically reflective wooden surfaces would enhance the resonant capacity of her acoustic space. With little ambient noise, her voice would fill her bedchamber and reverberate after each verse. Of her performance, Clarissa only states: "I flatter myself, that I have not been quite unhappy in the performance."[60] Her understated evaluation may not only speak of her ability; Clarissa may also be referring to the sensation of performing in that space. She hears the plucking of a spinet mixing with her song. In addition, the reverb would reflect back to her the warmth and richness of her voice. The acoustic properties of this scene would allow Clarissa to feel the vibrations of her melody and hear the consonant endings of each verse. Clarissa achieves an important feat. Her musical scene serves as a sounding mirror through which she externalizes her emotions and hears them reflected back.[61]

My sonic re-creation follows the spirit of Richardson's imagined conversation with Sophia Scudamore in which he feels her presence, hears her voice, and even visualizes her sitting in the summerhouse.

The acoustics of Clarissa's bedchamber, in other words, circulate vocalized emotions against objects (walls, chairs) and around her body. Clarissa's bedchamber and its materiality interact with her voice as an object of feeling that moves around and through her. In this regard, Clarissa's enclosed bedchamber creates a space in which she can listen to the reverb of her voice, and by virtue of the room's resonance, Clarissa feels the vibrations of her emotionally charged lyrics. Finally, by drowning out external noises, she replaces the acousmatic regime of terrorizing voices with a sonic regime of her own making, a musical composition.

Her sonic regime not only controls her acoustical sphere, it also functions as a form of emotional and physiological control. By singing, she actively regulates her emotions through a mental and physiological exercise. Indeed, Clarissa's performance aligns well with contemporaneous medical approaches to music. As Noelle Chao notes, British readers became familiar with music's physiological and mental effects through the medical writings of Richard Browne and Richard Brocklesby.[62] Chao also argues that these works created a discourse of musical effects that subsequent writers exploited to make musical experience more accessible to readers.[63] Indeed, *Clarissa*, published before Charles Avison's essay on music and well before the gothic soundscapes of Ann Radcliffe, includes a musical scene that resonates with the medical effects of music as they are articulated and described by Browne and Brocklesby. For instance, in *Medicina Musica: A Mechanical Essay on Singing, Musick and Dancing* (1727 or 1729), Richard Browne describes the physiological and emotional benefits attributed specifically to singing. He also prefaces his essay with a direct appeal to women, because "this Treatise is principally for their Good, whose tender and delicate Constitutions render them most liable to the Disease I have enquired into."[64]

Although Richardson did not comment on Brocklesby or Browne's medical theories, he maintained a long relationship with the doctor George Cheyne (1671–1743). In his letters to Richardson, Cheyne offers remedies for Richardson's ailments. Advising against Richardson's "sweating Machine for the Head," Cheyne explains that the writer's "giddiness" comes from "Fumes arising" from the digestive tract, from thick blood, and a "Want of Perspiration."[65] As for Richardson's tinnitus,

Cheyne reassures him that it is a "common Symptom of nervous Hyp and of no possible Consequence."⁶⁶ Cheyne firmly advises against Richardson's "cold Bathing" and instead recommends treating nervous disorders with a combination of diet, vomiting, and exercise.⁶⁷ For the sedentary Richardson, Cheyne also prescribes an eighteenth-century exercise machine. "I wonder you get not," he remarks, "the Chamber-horse which is now so universally known and practiced in all the studious Professions in London."⁶⁸ The Chamber-horse, a large wooden and leather armchair, replete with metal springs, mimicked the bouncing motion of horseback riding.⁶⁹

Within his health regime, Cheyne examines both the causes of and the cures for passionate maladies. In diagnosing nervous disorders, he often blames a sedentary life. He recommends exercise accompanied by a diet light in animal protein and alcohol. In *An Essay of Health and Long Life* (1725), Cheyne explains how exercise and diet are crucial to health because they "prevent the *thickening* of fluids, . . . [and] keep the Fibres in due *Tension*."⁷⁰ Cheyne here blends two approaches to the body: the pneumatic theory of the body and the string theory of interconnected nervous fibers. By the 1740s, doctors had begun to adopt the fiber theory of the human body, which held that nervous fibers had a string-like vibratory response to external sensations.⁷¹

For Cheyne, human physiology intersects with affect. Through exercise and diet, a person can cure their nervous disorders. For exercise, he specifically recommends a mixture of aerobic activities ("*Walking, Dancing, Fencing, Tennis*"), strengthening ones ("*Digging,* Working at a *Pump, Ringing* a Dumb Bell"), and less strenuous activities such as "*Riding* a Horse-back, or in a Coach, playing at *Billiards, Bowls*."⁷² Through exercise, he explains how a person can "shak[e] the whole *Machine* . . . variously *twitching* the *Nervous Fibres*, to brace and contract them."⁷³ With the term *machine*, Cheyne is referring to a human body whose organs are connected to a network of nervous *fibres*. Through exercise, a person can maintain the proper tension across his mind and body.

Elaborating on a fiber theory of human physiology, Cheyne makes a metaphorical connection between the human body and musical instruments that strongly resembles the connections made by Diderot and Shaftesbury. Likewise, Cheyne imagines the body and soul as part of a larger musical instrument with external and internal "keys."⁷⁴

The external keys allow people and things to influence a person's mind through the body, while the internal keys allow the mind to influence the body.⁷⁵ Within the logic of this musical metaphor, the fiber's tension plays an important role: its ability to receive vibrations enables it to pass sensations back and forth between the body and mind. Cheyne's health regime thus plays, calibrates, vibrates, and shakes the various threads that hold the human organism together.

To this musical metaphor, Cheyne adds the notion of elasticity, which determines how sensations influence a person. Cheyne describes how a person's character is directly related to the tautness of the nervous fibers. For instance, "Those who have very *springy, lively,* and *elastick* Fibres, have the *quickest Sensations,* a *weaker Impulse* producing a stronger Sensation in them."⁷⁶ In contrast, "those of *rigid, stiff* and *unyielding* Fibres" are those who "excel most in the *Labours* of the *Understanding,* or the *Intellectual Faculties*" because they "retain their Impressions longest, and pursue them farthest."⁷⁷ Finally, "*Ideots, Peasants* and *Mechanicks*" who have "*un-elastick*" fibers, barely register "any *Passions.*"⁷⁸ Across these three character types, Cheyne reduces passionate disposition to the construction of the human body. The elastic fiber, then, is a key factor in the intensity of an individual's feeling. Here we see an affect theory akin to Shaftesbury's, which Diderot refined in the 1740s. While Cheyne relates fibrous tension to mental capacity, his musical metaphor also suggests a version of the vitalist voice: the voice translates into sound the lively vibrations of "*elastick* Fibres," the less resonant and subdued sound of "*rigid . . .* Fibres," and finally the atonic expression of "*in-elastick*" and passionless "Fibres."

Returning to Clarissa's chamber, we see parallels between her situation and Cheyne's medical theories. In Harlowe Place, she is confined to her room, her movements restricted and her person isolated from those who love her. What's more, her family, with their voices raised in anger and resentment, invade her space, turning what could be a sanctuary of contemplation into a space of anxiety and agitation. Her passions, coupled with her nearly constant confinement, have a deleterious effect on her health. Cheyne would not have been surprised: "Those," according to Cheyne, "who are tender and *valetudinary,* lead *sedentary* Lives, or induce *contemplative* Studies ought to avoid Excesses of the *Passions.*"⁷⁹ With little opportunity to exercise, Clarissa has few ways to relieve her agitation. Whereas Cheyne never associates music making with salubrious exercise, Richardson's musical scene dramatizes this connection.[80]

Indeed, Clarissa relies on music to "compose" her "angry passions."[81] She even alludes to the physiological and emotional effects of her singing when she describes how "her heart went with her fingers."[82] Through performance, she replaces her "selfish Resentment [and] violent passions"[83] with the "intellectual light"[84] of her ode. When Clarissa calms her tumultuous emotions, she literally means that musical sound allows her to regulate her passions through the sympathetic vibrations of melody and the soothing effect of diaphragmatic breathing. Singing produces pneumatic and elastic effects on Clarissa. The movement of fluids (blood, animal spirits, and digestion) allows her to purge her emotional turmoil, and the vibration of nervous fibers recalibrates her elastic body.

Her song, however, functions as more than a physical exercise because it provides Clarissa with a moment of self-reflection. In the song, her "thoughts" rise up in "flight" toward an "intellectual light."[85] The "all-perfect mind['s] . . . discerning eye" sees through "the mists of error" and "ev'ry fair disguise."[86] It pierces the erroneous shadows that plague humanity. Transporting her mind away from its temporal, physical existence, she hovers on a purely intellectual plane. Clarissa's ode prefigures a sentiment that the character Mr. Belford expresses: he refers to Clarissa as "all Mind."[87] For him, Clarissa is an "Angel" who should not "be plunged so low as into the vulgar office of Domestic Life."[88]

Through her musical performance of Carter's poem, Clarissa represents an untethered mind that briefly departs from the physical constraints of domestic life.[89] Her musical lesson reshapes the traditional purpose of music making. Scholars have compared Clarissa's musical ode to moral conduct books, which included musical lessons.[90] To be sure, her song imitates the devotional or prayer-like quality of a moral conduct book. However, she does not sing a pedantic tract on domestic or filial duties.[91] Instead, she directs her energy toward a life of the mind and praises self-directed intellect and wisdom. In other words, her song replaces the communitarian appeal of music making with a meditation on female independence.

Moreover, the complexity of her moral lesson extends beyond the traditional realm of female wisdom because Clarissa blends physical sensations with intellectual reflection. The lyrics, set to the melody, represent the interaction between physical sensation and cognition. While her borrowed words depict a grave and circumspect tone, her voice flies into melismatic passages (see fig. 3). Indeed, her "flight" at first leaps downward (mm. 9–10), which could be a musical depiction of her current struggle between her physical and intellectual existence. Across the three stanzas, her melismas emphasize two paths; her sustained melody on "flight," "road," and "show" evoke an appealing journey with Lovelace, while the musical runs on "light," "good" and "woe" redirect her attention toward the unappealing yet morally acceptable choice of remaining at Harlowe Place. Clarissa's reflected voice has a dual nature. On the one hand, it teaches a moral lesson intended to moderate her emotional turmoil. On the other, its melismatic passages retain a hint of passion. Her song allows her to experience two contradictory demands at once: the desire to which she cannot succumb and the filial duty to which she must remain subservient. By literally reflecting back her contradictory feelings, her performance harmonizes these feelings into a resonant sound. As a remedy for *raging* and *tumultuous* passions, Clarissa's song offers a path toward female independence, one that marries intellect with chastity.

CLARISSA'S VOICE differs from the sentimental voices from chapter 1 in two substantive ways: its relationship to the speaker, and its capacity to control the speaker's sonic sphere. In chapter 1, we encountered voices that Rousseau conceived within a social setting. Within the Rousseauan context, a speaker is normally intended to intone emotional accents that a listener will hear. In *Clarissa*, the protagonist directs the emotional energy of her voice inward. By channeling vocal energy toward herself, Clarissa also controls the environmental factors that impact a person's moral disposition. In chapter 1, I discussed how cultural and environmental factors modified the voice to create specific vocal identities, Clarissa's voice, however, takes over her sonic sphere. She does so in order to perform a sort of vocal therapy. While scholars often consider sentimental voices to be involuntary expressions of sincere emotion, Clarissa's musical scene represents a sentimental voice in control, a voice that brings harmony to the character's passions and physical sensations. This sentimental voice is not a passive recipient of environmental and cultural forces but rather the generator of forces, which influence her moral disposition.

In addition to *Clarissa*'s representation of vocal sentimentality, the musical scene invites the reader to perform the protagonist's musical version of moral sentiment. The musical score thus functions in parallel with prose description. On the one hand, readers imagine Clarissa's virtual recital, which produces sympathetic vibrations in the reader's fibrous tissue. On the other, the novel invites readers to sing "Ode to Wisdom" and, through its performance, to feel the vibrational and resonant forces of Clarissa's song. The novel thus asks the reader to interact with two media: a virtual voice represented in print and a performed voice that the reader reenacts. This musical scene serves a pedagogical purpose.[92] By moving between imaginary and embodied practice, readers can receive Clarissa's moral lesson as a haptic, auditory, and imaginary experience.

As I noted at the beginning of this chapter, my analysis of *Clarissa* is part of a comparative diptych between Richardson's *Clarissa* and the popular French writer Baculard d'Arnaud. This movement between an imagined and an embodied voice is crucial in Baculard d'Arnaud's adaptation of Clarissa's vocal therapy. Baculard d'Arnaud's sentimental voice retains a therapeutic function that helps moderate the protagonist's intense passions. The narrative itself makes clear that the protagonist must reimagine intense moments of passion and then use art as a form of emotional therapy. In this regard, Baculard d'Arnaud's protagonist teaches the reader how to approach the novel as both an imaginary and an embodied lesson.

Baculard d'Arnaud's music therapy differs from Clarissa's, however, because it is directed at masculine desire. Unlike Clarissa's scene, which involves the contemplation of female virtue and wisdom, the lyrical scenes in Baculard d'Arnaud's short story domesticate male desire through the contemplation of nature. Baculard d'Arnaud does rely on an art song, but he chooses the *romance*, a popular strophic genre with a bucolic character. In contrast to art songs, arias, and airs, which are often structured as binary, ternary, or through-composed works,[93] the *romance*'s strophic structure has a single melody, which the singer performs for each stanza. In England, ballads were a popular example of this folk-type genre. In France, the *romance* song genre became increasingly common after the 1750s. Baculard d'Arnaud capitalized on their popularity when he inserted *romance* songs into his short story "Anecdote sicilienne." In it, the protagonist relies on strophic songs, much as Clarissa does, to purge unhealthy and destabilizing emotions. Clarissa's sonic regime can be said to have migrated to France as a naturalized form of vocal therapy in which the protagonist listens to his voice accompanied by the sounds of a pastoral landscape.

As part of Richardson's sentimental project, Clarissa's sounding mirror deploys music as a moral exercise that in many respects imitates George Cheyne's medical theory, specifically the impact of passion on one's health. In the French context, music qua moral lesson was rare, but it became more popular around the midcentury.[94] Among literary examples of musical therapy, Baculard d'Arnaud's "Anecdote sicilienne" is noteworthy because the protagonist performs eight newly composed *romances*, whose musical scores the reader could find in the volume's appendix. Much like Clarissa, the protagonist of Baculard d'Arnaud's story, Lorezzo, performs music to himself and relies on music to purge intense passions.

Richardson's influence partly sheds light on the role of vocal performance in Baculard d'Arnaud's short story. To illustrate how "Anecdote sicilienne" deploys music, I must briefly take a detour through Rousseau's novel *Julie, ou La Nouvelle Héloïse* so that I can explain how Baculard d'Arnaud transforms the function of lyrical scenes from the Richardsonian example, which promotes female temperance, to a Rousseauan model that cures the excesses of masculine desire.

With *Julie*, Rousseau attempted to cure obsessive passion by turning it into friendship. For this cure, he relied on a moral therapy called *morale sensitive*, premised on the idea that external sensations modify a person's internal dispositions. As Anne Vila notes, Jean-Jacques Rousseau had deep and influential ties to promoters of the practice of moral hygiene, which originated in the mid-eighteenth-century Montpellier medical school.[95] In a passage describing his unfinished work *Le Matérialisme du sage*, for instance, the *philosophe* envisions the environment as an external regimen through which a person may modify and maintain his moral consciousness. As Vila shows, Rousseau incorporates the notion of *morale sensitive* into the narrative of *Julie, ou La Nouvelle Héloïse*.[96] The protagonist Saint-Preux, who is the former lover of Julie, needs to be cured of lovesickness, and he can only manage his dysregulated sensibility through a process that stimulates and naturalizes desire's physical sensations. By first awakening Saint-Preux's insalubrious desire, Julie allows him to feel its negative effects. She then reminds Saint-Preux of her maternal status: the sight of Julie as a mother and wife helps bring Saint-Preux's heart back into balance. Vila identifies this cure in visual and gustatory objects that arouse and modify a dysregulated sensible constitution.[97]

Song also played a role in this cure. To understand it, we must know something about how music therapy was regarded within the broader Montpellier school of thought. One of the Montpellier doctors, Joseph-Louis Roger, published a Latin treatise on the effects of music on the body, *Tentamen de vi soni et musices in corpus humanum* (1758). In it, Roger argues that music can become part of a person's "hygiène" or "exercice," especially for sedentary types such as women or literary men, because there is a "rapport exact entre le tremblement sonore et le tremblement vital" (exact correspondence between sonorous trembling and vitalist trembling).[98] By connecting music to the material fabric of a listener's soul, Roger proposes that music not only leads to a virtuous life but also furnishes "les parties d'un traitement moral" (parts of a moral treatment).[99] Roger finally contends that music's "empire sur l'âme est incontestable" (control over the soul is indisputable).[100]

Music's relationship to Rousseau's moral and social thought is complex, and a comprehensive discussion of it would exceed the scope of this chapter.[101] But because music does not play a major role in Vila's reading of *Julie*, I propose a brief analysis of music's moral influence in Rousseau's novel. In terms of the *romance* song and its effect on listeners, Rousseau departs slightly from the purely material conception of music as a sound object whose vibrations tremble the living force inside a listener's body. For Rousseau, music's influence over the soul is intimately connected to the social and linguistic context from which it emerges.

For instance, in *Julie*, music contributes to Saint-Preux's cure in the form of an audible souvenir, which first revives dormant passion and later purges emotional dysregulation. Saint-Preux offers a glimpse of music's therapeutic function during a postprandial session with Julie's family. Entertaining each other after dinner, Julie's family works alongside *les vendangeuses* (female grape harvesters), who sing "de vieilles romances dont les airs ne sont pas piquans; mais ils ont je ne sais quoi d'antique et de doux qui touche à la longue" (a few old *romances* for which the tunes are not dazzling, but they have a hint of Antiquity and a touch of sweetness that over time is deeply affecting).[102] Upon listening to the "simples, naïves, souvent tristes" (simple, naïve, often sad) lyrics, Julie blushes, and Saint-Preux sighs because the *romances* remind them of their past indiscretions.[103] Here, Saint-Preux takes the first step toward achieving moral balance. The *romance* becomes a mnemonic device that transports Saint-Preux into the somatic memory of lovesickness.

After seeing Julie blush, Saint-Preux suddenly experiences "un poids insupportable" (an insufferable weight) from his unsanctioned desire and feels it fall on his "cœur" (heart).[104] The *romance*, according to Saint-Preux, "me laisse une impression funeste qui ne s'efface qu'avec peine" (imprints on me a gloomy feeling that only fades away with difficulty).[105] Despite this heart-wrenching experience, he still finds in these evenings "une sorte de charme" (a sort of charm), which he cannot express in words, but to which he is "fort sensible" (extremely sensitive).[106] This moment allows different emotional states to flow through his body and mind. He progresses from gloom, to rest, then to harmony with a moment of brief tranquility, and finally to a feeling of peace. Saint-Preux then remarks that the evening's activities render these rather simple songs "plus intéressantes" (more interesting).[107]

In Rousseau's work, the *romance* has surprising moral effects in part because it is a mnemonic sign of social affection. In *Julie*, the grape harvesters' *romance* reminds the protagonists of their previous liaison.[108] Similar to Rousseau's theorization of song's relationship to memory, the song in this scene has a nostalgic impact on Saint-Preux. As Rousseau notes in *Dictionnaire de musique*: "La *Musique* alors n'agit point précisément comme *Musique*, mais comme signe mémoratif.... Tant il est vrai que ce n'est pas dans leurs actions physiques qu'il faut chercher les plus grands effets des Sons sur le cœur humain."[109] (*Music* does not act precisely as *Music*, but as a mnemonic sign.... It is true that it is not in their physical actions that one must seek the greatest effects of Sounds on the human heart.) At the end of this passage, Rousseau offers a key to uncovering music's mnemonic function—the human heart. Melodies awaken in the listener a specific type of affective memory. For Saint-Preux, the *romance* brings back the memory of his former love: its melody thus unlocks emotional memories.

In my analysis of the sentimental voice, songs of the *romance* genre awaken dormant desires in the listener's heart. A *romance* serves as a melodic memory of a singer's passion, feelings, and childhood affections. Rousseau's 1760s reflections on the *romance* are important to my story about the sentimental voice because they connect Richardson's strophic song in *Clarissa* to the *romance* songs that Baculard d'Arnaud inserts into his sentimental story "Anecdote sicilienne" (1775). With Baculard d'Arnaud, the sentimental singer returns as a hybrid figure that unites Rousseau's mnemonic sign and Richardson's (and to lesser extent Joseph-Louis Roger's) musical therapy. On the one hand, Rousseau depicts strophic songs as a receptacle of social and emotional memory. On the other, we have Clarissa's song, which I interpret as a Cheynian moral exercise that shakes and vibrates the human machine. In "Anecdote sicilienne," these two conceptions of moral singing come together during the musical performances of the protagonist, Lorezzo.

IN 1775, the popular sentimental writer and playwright Baculard d'Arnaud published the short story "Anecdote sicilienne" that refashioned Richardson's English sounding mirror into a French version in which songs contain moral lessons intended for a young man. Much like Clarissa's solo, the songs inserted into Baculard d'Arnaud's short story compose and temper the protagonist's intense emotions.[110]

Baculard d'Arnaud, while relatively unknown today, was a highly successful and widely read French novelist and playwright of the eighteenth century.[111] Acclaimed both in France and abroad, he was a friend of Voltaire and a guest of Frederick the Great. During his long career, he popularized a French version of the English gothic called the *roman noir*. The saccharine prose of these novels set the French reading public aflame, from the most humble chambermaid to the queen herself. Marie Antoinette even ordered Baculard d'Arnaud's major works bound by an accomplished artisan, a request repeated by the Comtesse de Provence and many other members of the aristocracy.[112]

Baculard d'Arnaud and Rousseau have a special kinship. Rousseau reportedly praised Baculard d'Arnaud for his capacity to write from the heart instead from his head and hands.[113] For his part, Baculard d'Arnaud incorporated Rousseau's call to bring humanity closer to nature in his depiction of pastoral figures. Among the short stories in Baculard d'Arnaud's collection *Épreuves du sentiment* (1770–72, 1775–78), there is a legacy of both Rousseau's and Richardson's visions of sentimental fiction. With the second edition of *Épreuves du sentiment* (1784), however, Baculard d'Arnaud distanced himself from English sentimentality and objected to those critics who described his work as a derivative expression of *anglomanie*, or Englishmania.[114]

Despite his disingenuous protests, Baculard d'Arnaud was a faithful reader of Richardson. In a short article on translation, Baculard d'Arnaud praised Richardson for his "extensive knowledge of the heart and nature."[115] Baculard d'Arnaud even analyzed the moral utility of *Clarissa* for his own fiction. In his preface to *Nouvelles historiques* (1774), he explained why Richardson did not reward Clarissa's virtuous life with a happy ending: "Richardson a voulu nous prouver combien la vertu étoit aimable, puisqu'il n'y a personne, après avoir lû son ouvrage, qui n'aimât mieux être Clarisse entraînée sous le poids de l'infortune, que Lovelace, fût-il au comble du bonheur."[116] (Richardson wished to prove to us how worthy of love virtue was, that there is no one, after reading his work, who did not prefer more to be Clarissa, dragged under by the weight of misfortune, than Lovelace, even for the utmost happiness.) Baculard d'Arnaud thus recognized that the sentimental novel can incarnate moral reflections in the characters that people its fictional universe. Because the readers identify with Clarissa, they empathize even more with her because she confronts a series of hardships. By accepting hardship as the price of virtue, she elevates its status. For "Anecdote sicilienne," Baculard d'Arnaud adapts Clarissa's moral lesson for a male protagonist. In Baculard d'Arnaud's pastoral tale, the protagonist Lorezzo confronts a series of hardships, and much like Clarissa's virtuous suffering, his response serves as a moral exemplar.

Baculard d'Arnaud's "Anecdote sicilienne" differs in many respects from Richardson's epistolary novel. The story is a third-person narrative that combines pastoral, sentimental, and gothic elements. The plot revolves around a harrowing love story between Lorezzo, the adopted son of the Sicilian farmer Serano, and the farmer's daughter, Nina. At the beginning of the story, Lorezzo has the misfortune to fall in love with his sister Nina. In a surprising turn of events, he discovers that he is not Nina's brother, but a foster brother of noble birth. This revelation replaces one obstacle (the taboo of incest) with another one (marriage between classes). The obstacles, which Lorezzo confronts with a mixture of despair and optimism, delay—but do not prevent—the lovers' eventual betrothal.

In the face of each obstacle, Lorezzo expresses and moderates his explosive passion through a series of musical lessons. In each scene, he performs within a pastoral setting. He carves his songs into trees, listens to his echo return from rugged escarpments, and serenades nature accompanied by the babbling of a brook. In this regard, his musical lessons, unlike Clarissa's domestic lesson, combine music with the moderating effects of nature. His lessons resonate with the French school of thought (discussed above) called the *morale sensitive*, which offered a "natural" path toward moral balance. The medical doctors who adhered to this school of thought prescribed hygienic regimens that brought stability to an individual's sensible constitution.[117] The goal of treatment was to rid the body of the insalubrious effects of civilization. As the Montpellier-trained doctor Roger stated: "L'influence de la musique devient chaque jour plus nécessaire dans ce siècle corrompu, où . . . l'amour [est] un vil libertinage, et la sensibilité un froid égoïsme; où les vapeurs, les maladies nerveuses, les consomptions, les manies, les suicides règnent comme une épidémie sociale."[118] (The influence of music becomes every day more necessary in this corrupted age, where . . . love [is] a vile libertinage, and sensibility a cold egotism; where . . . nervous diseases, consumption, mania, suicides reign like a social epidemic.) For Roger, music "isole [l'homme], le fait vivre avec lui-même, le ramène aux lois de la nature dont il s'écarte sans cesse" (isolates [a person], makes one live with oneself, and brings a person back to the laws of nature from which he constantly departs).[119]

Baculard d'Arnaud blends Roger's musical hygiene with Rousseau's musical memory because he frames the *romance* as an intrasubjective reflection: that is, the singer listens to the sound of his emotions. For instance, in "Anecdote sicilienne," Lorezzo performs three of his first four *romances* alone. In one scene, he even inscribes his song on the trunk of a tree. The fourth *romance* occurs at a particularly poignant moment following Lorezzo's declaration of his love to Nina. The latter, recognizing the social cost of their incestuous desire, vows never to see him again, although she loves him ardently. In this moment of despair, Lorezzo performs a song in a gothic setting, facing a dramatic waterfall that rushes over a cave whose floor is covered in moss and littered with fallen rocks: "Le jeune-homme, livré à sa sombre douleur, va chercher au bas du mont Eryx le vallon le plus isolé: il court s'enfoncer dans une espèce d'antre tapissé d'une mousse marécageuse, & prolongé sous la voûte d'un rocher qui sembloit menacé de s'écrouler."[120] (The young man, given to his dark grief, searches out the most isolated valley at the bottom of mount Eryx: he runs sinking himself into a kind of cavern, carpeted with a marshy moss that extends over a vaulted rock menacingly close to collapse.) The *romance* becomes a naturalized sounding board for Lorezzo's thoughts and passions.

As Lorezzo sings to himself, he hears a modified and enhanced voice that bounces off his gloomy surroundings. For this fourth *romance*, he stands in front of a cavern whose semi-enclosed space can create an echo. The cavern opens into a deep valley that amplifies Lorezzo's voice and creates a time lapse between his voice and his echo. The coldness of the cavern likely slows down the sound waves and slightly increases the time lapse. Finally, we can surmise that the surfaces—rock and moss—partially cancel out each other's effect on the resonance of his voice. Whereas rock reflects a relatively strident sound, moss dampens its sharpness.

Whereas Clarissa hears a warm and comforting reverb, Lorezzo's dark and dank cavern would create a strident echo, transforming his solo into an eerie-sounding duet. The narrator even includes soundmarks that overdetermine the sinister quality of Lorezzo's location. A "stream" with "slimy water" falls into a "vast precipice," producing a "horrible noise" and "bleak echoes." As if accompanying Lorezzo's sinister performance, "funereal birds" "make themselves heard."[121] The soundscape in Lorezzo's fourth *romance* hinges in part on the description of the cavern. The cascading water drowns out his doleful tune, and the cave, dangerously close to collapse, nearly entombs his forsaken love. Baculard d'Arnaud here deploys the sentimental voice as a form of music therapy in which the sound of sentiment, modified by the singer's natural surroundings, regulates and balances extreme passions.

The gothic gloominess that muffles Lorezzo's echo transforms the sound of his reflected voice and modifies the moral sensations embedded in his fourth *romance*. If Lorezzo is interested in externalizing his reflection, then the sinister timbre of his echo makes audible his suicidal ideation. In this regard, the fourth *romance* is not simply a moment during which Lorezzo reflects on losing Nina's love. He is also in dialogue with a palpable darkness inside himself. By hearing how sinister his reflected voice sounds, he listens to and confronts the dire consequences of suicide. This scene is representative of landscape's discursive function. By listening to reflected sound, Lorezzo gains deeper self-knowledge.

Lorezzo's sounding mirror does not purge his passion for Nina. Instead, each stanza allows him to hear different shades of feeling. By comparing his conflicted passions, he eventually brings his emotions into harmony. Lorezzo's *romances* dramatize and make audible a form of reception that arrives in waves. His reaction to the *romance* form closely resembles a reaction articulated in *Julie*. In the preface to *Julie*'s second edition, Rousseau's fictionalized persona, the character R., explains how the effect of the sentimental epistolary form on the reader is similar to the effect of the *romance* song on a listener. For R., *Julie* "est une longue romance, dont les couplets, pris à part, n'ont rien qui touche, mais dont la suite produit à la fin son effet. Voilà ce que j'éprouve en les lisant." (is a long Romance, whose stanzas in isolation are not touching, but whose sequence produces its effect at the end. That is what I feel when I read.)[122] Each letter ripped from its context would have little impact on the reader. It is only through the process of reading letters in sequence that the novel elicits a strong impression.

Lorezzo's *romances* invite such a gradual reception through their music, lyrics and vocal performance. Specifically, the *romance*'s strophic form allows Lorezzo to layer his emotional reactions one on top of the other. Since the melody repeats itself and generates associations across stanzas, Lorezzo transforms his melody into a *signe mémoratif* of his lovesickness, an illness that washes over him in waves of emotion. His melody rises and falls, traversing love and heartache, desperation and joy. For instance, Lorezzo's fourth *romance* has a distinctive melodic line in the third verse. Its half-step chromaticisms are suggestive of Lorezzo's plaintive accents (see fig. 4). This chromatic line provides the poet with an additional sonic tool. Traditionally, a writer deploys rhyme, assonance, and alliteration to generate surprising connections. The *romance*'s strophic form adds melodic associations, whereby different poetic lines set to the same melody are sonically related. The strophic form serves as an echo connecting various dimensions of Lorezzo's misfortune: his love for and loss of Nina, his contemplation

Fig. 4. Marc-Antoine Désaugiers, "Quatrième romance," *Épreuves du sentiment*. (Starred Books Collection, John Hay Library, Brown University)

of death, and so on (see ex. 1). With each repetition, Lorezzo adds another emotional layer to his plaintive remarks.

Furthermore, the melody allows Lorezzo to externalize and listen to the reflected melodic lines; it becomes the sonic substrate on which he combines layers of contradictory emotions (see ex. 1). While the material of the cave, the valley, and waterfall modify the emotional timbre of Lorezzo's echo, the strophic melody is a mnemonic sponge that retains many emotions. Melody, in essence, functions much like love in the novel. As the narrator states: "L'amour est une passion qui absorbe tous les sentiments qui lui sont étrangers" (Love is a passion that absorbs all feelings that are strangers to it).[123] Lorezzo's melody symbolizes a love that absorbs pain and regret, and in turn melds them with his desire. In this regard, Lorezzo's echo enables the protagonist to become emotionally mature. His musical therapy teaches him to accept and cope with a series of simultaneous and contradictory emotional experiences. By the same token, as his voice externalizes vibrations, he harnesses physical and emotional forces. The musical scenes become a sonic representation of Lorezzo's physical and mental state, and his voice guides him back into physical and moral alignment.

In fact, Lorezzo's eight songs are sung at pivotal moments during his emotional journey to moral maturity. In the first *romance*, Lorezzo reveals a budding passion for his sister. As the narrator prefaces his song, he notes: "sans y faire attention, il prenoit le langage passionné d'un amant" (without paying attention, [Lorezzo] borrowed the language of a passionate lover).[124] Every *romance* adds an emotional layer to his love, such as hope, disappointment, or happiness. Each performance also guides him closer to a moral awakening. Through this emotional progression, Lorezzo heals his lovesickness. By singing to himself, Lorezzo learns to moderate his incestuous passion and feel a pure marital love.

EXAMPLE 1. Marc-Antoine Desaugiers, "Quatrième romance," from "Anecdote sicilienne." mm. 7–8.

Through performance, he softens his desire with the beneficent effects of nature. This is why his violent passions are not purged but rather are blended with other natural emotions. Passion in itself does not constitute a moral failing because it comes from natural inclinations. Instead, Baculard d'Arnaud's sounding mirror harmonizes Lorezzo's passion with nature. As his reflected voice comes back from the walls of nature (forest, trees, and waterfalls), Lorezzo learns to moderate his passion by hearing how nature modifies and moderates his intense passion. With nature as his moral guide, he blends violent passion with more useful feelings of social obligation.

These solitary scenes even become a cornerstone of Lorezzo's governing philosophy. Paradoxically, to sustain his happy marriage, Lorezzo regularly leaves his family and retreats into a small cabin, which he calls his *cabinet d'étude*. Here, he paints the most touching scenes of his love story. His *cabinet* serves the same purpose as the sounding mirror, a moment of self-reflection aided, amplified, and brought to life through the senses. Lorezzo explains that his solitary retreat allows him to experience moral feelings through nature. Baculard d'Arnaud thus transforms Clarissa's sounding mirror in two substantive ways. First, he turns the sounding mirror into a therapeutic device for a sensitive male protagonist. As I noted near the beginning of this chapter, musical performance in *Clarissa* is mostly a feminine vocation. By turning musical performance into a form of moral therapy, Clarissa modifies its function for female readers: originally a form of domestic entertainment, it becomes a prayer for female independence. In Baculard d'Arnaud's work, in contrast, the male singer learns to moderate his passions through artistic reflection. The protagonist then naturalizes the sounding mirror. Lorezzo must commune with nature, blend his emotions with the reflected impressions of nature, and finally reintegrate that lesson into another medium.

ALTHOUGH THE life forces coursing through Lorezzo and Clarissa differ slightly in name and in features, behind the two authors' conceptions of music therapy lies a singing voice that shakes and vibrates the elastic, vibratory matrix of the human body. What is most compelling about the sounding mirror is the way the voice separates from the singer and returns to its body in the form of reverberation or echo. The voice's return plays a crucial role in the protagonists' moral therapy because it causes the singer's body to vibrate. To be sure, these therapies differ in their application; furthermore, the songs I have discussed have the capacity of musical performance to elicit moral reflection. But across these musical therapies, the writers have a shared sense that the singer's voice can modify a singer's emotional state and physiological disposition.

From chapter 1, I have expanded my definition of the voice in two distinct directions: the voice as represented in print and the voice as a multimodal object. First, I have examined how the voice—as a literary and musical representation—aids the reader in imagining and experimenting with the voice. Through this imaginative experimentation, readers can then appreciate the extent to which the voice is a multimodal object, which is to say an object that is embodied (the vocal organs), tactile, and acoustic. In this chapter, the multimodal voice extends beyond the singer's vocal organs because its sonic emissions interact with the singer's surroundings. Once the voice's echo returns to the singer, the echo becomes a disembodied, acoustical, and vibrational object that accumulates tactile and audible impressions from the singer's surroundings. Finally, the singer absorbs its echo as an acoustical and vibrational object that causes the singer's fibrous tissue to tremble and agitate. While the process of reabsorption (that is, the singer who listens to and feels his echo) is intended to temper the singer's emotional and physical state, the process itself transforms the voice into an object that transcends a physiological voice.

With the example of Lorezzo, his voice exists across a complex network of temporalities, meanings, and modalities. As a vocal expression of desire, the *romances* that Lorezzo sings are polysemous messages that convey multiple affective registers. As a material object of vibration and sound, the voice circulates and transforms into different objects. It first issues from the vibration of vocal organs into an acoustical emission that bounces off the singer's landscape. Finally, the echo comes back to be reincorporated into the singer's body as embodied vibration.

In this chapter, I am triangulating an implicit theory of the voice through texts that are not necessarily focused on the voice but whose form invites the reader to imagine and experiment with the voice, and whose cultural influence includes contemporaneous theories on the emotional and physiological effect of sound, music, and the voice. For the next chapter, I alter the direction of my theory of the voice and go deeper into the embodied, material aspect of vocal organs. As I depart from a more sentimentally inflected theory to a more biologically influenced approach, I examine how the voice amounts to more than the sum of its organs. The voice as conceived by Denis Diderot is intricately woven into the fibrous tissue that connects many parts of the human organism. From this chapter to the next, I transition from a sentimental voice to a vitalist one. This distinction, however, is not rigid: the vitalist and sentimental voices share commonalities that I do not wish to erase with the boundaries that arise from naming an object. Instead, I wish to highlight a new perspective on the voice that vitalism brings into focus. It is a voice whose biological and material mechanisms take a prominent role in its theorization.

3

Vitalist Voices in Diderot's Early Works

♪

IN MY investigation of the physiological traces of the voice in French literature, I started with the most familiar representation: sentimental voices. For these voices, external forces (cultural practices, language, sensations) modify the singer's vocal physiology in such a way that makes their voice more or less conducive to the exchange of and cultivation of socially beneficial emotions. In chapter 2, I showed how the singer can engage in a form of physiological and emotional control to temper dangerous feelings of passion. In this chapter, I focus on what I define as vitalist voices. While I continue to reveal the physiological traces of the voice in French literature, I do so from another perspective. Vitalist voices are the product of a direct link between the voice and human physiology. Unlike sentimental voices, which are the product of an altered or controlled physiology, vitalist voices translate through sound the hidden, silent (possibly even silenced) sensations, tensions, and temperaments of the human body.

This inquiry into vitalist voices centers around the early writings of Denis Diderot. In works published from 1745 to 1748, I uncover the implicit theorization of a vitalist voice. Although Diderot's early works do not directly discuss the voice, they implicitly theorize a version of the voice that is grounded in an understanding of human physiology. Instead of an anatomical understanding of the voice that focuses on the role of a collection of organs (larynx, pharynx, glottis, vocal cords, tongue, mouth, nose, lips), Diderot metaphorically and literally envisions the fibrous tissue of the body as instrumental strings whose tension and configuration influence the voice's sound. Diderot then implicitly extends this insight to consider how the body, specifically reproductive organs, influence the development, register, and timbre of the voice.

This chapter analyzes Diderot's early references to the voice by explaining the medical, acoustical, musical, and moral theories to which he responded. Three of Diderot's works implicitly theorize versions of the voice: his translation of Anthony Ashley Cooper, Third Earl of Shaftesbury's, essay on merit, entitled *Essai sur le mérite et la vertu* (1745); his 1748 libertine novel *Les Bijoux indiscrets*; and his 1748 mathematical treatise *Principes généraux d'acoustique*. Across these three works, we encounter three versions of an early vitalist voice. *Bijoux* is a fictional demonstration of a vitalist concept: the idea that organs have an independent sentience through which they experience and retain the impressions of aversion and desire. Diderot prefigured the notion of embodied sentience in his translation of Shaftesbury, for whom the body's fibrous tissue acts as a resonating chamber for the voice. Finally, Diderot's work in mathematics follows a different disciplinary path toward the vibrating, speaking body. Within the field of physics, Diderot describes a dynamic natural system in which multiple internal and external forces unlock the acoustical properties of the vibrating string. By reading these works together, I argue that Diderot's early vitalist voices, conceived through the literary figure of metaphor and the philosophical figure of analogy, go beyond abstraction to become intimately linked to the acoustical properties of matter itself.

THE VOICES in Diderot's early works differ from the mechanical voices advanced by the French science academy. Indeed, *Bijoux* is a parody of an anatomical discovery from the period. In 1741, Antoine Ferrein, the chair of medicine at the Collège de France, forever changed the history of vocal anatomy when he discovered vocal cords and realized that the voice was a wind and string instrument. By blowing through a dissected canine larynx, he demonstrated how "the violent collision of air and vocal cords cause[d] the latter to tremble, and that the more or less rapid vibrations [of these cords] produce[d] different pitches according to the laws governing string instruments."[1] As the summary from the Académie royale des sciences explains, Ferrein's experiment involved blowing through a dissected trachea while pulling on the "glottal ribbons."[2] Through Ferrein's discovery, the science academy also confirmed an important mechanistic notion about the voice: "the quality of matter influences the nature of sound."[3] In other words, the inert material of the human or animal voice differs in construction, which in turn modifies timbre.[4] These material differences successively produce specific sounds. By blowing through the larynx of a bull or a dog, one could hear the correspondent "bellowing of a bull" or "the yelp of a dog that is suffering."[5] Thus, dogs have a specific sound, attributable to their anatomy. In reconstructing the voice's material architecture, Ferrein even "play[ed]" it, like a musical instrument. Ferrein's anatomical discovery constituted another confirmation of the soulless *bête machine*, proven by the anatomist's mechanical imitation of the affective sounds of the creaturely voice.[6]

Surprisingly, Ferrein's major discovery was controversial. As Hans von Leden explains, Ferrein was the "founder of experimental voice physiology" who "correctly observed that [vocal pitches] vary with the [vocal cords'] speed of vibration."[7] His theory, however, sparked an immediate debate, pitting Joseph-Exupère Bertin, a supporter of Denis Dodart, against Ferrein's defender, Henri Joseph Bernard Montagnat.[8] Once the dust settled, a decade later, Dodart's version of the voice had prevailed. In fact, Denis Diderot, Charles Pinot Duclos, Jean-Jacques Rousseau, and Albrecht von Haller continued to defend Dodart's inaccurate and much older glottal theory over Ferrein's version.[9] In the *Encyclopédie* article on the physiological voice, a large portion of the text concerns Dodart's glottal voice, and Ferrein's alternative view is mentioned only at the end.[10] Likewise, Diderot's chapter on the voice in *Éléments de physiologie* retains the glottal structure of Dodart's voice.

In a parody of the 1740s voice wars, *Bijoux* guides the reader through the underlying philosophical issues regarding Ferrein's versions of the voice. In terms of Ferrein's voice, the narrative relies on parody to undermine the scientific import of his discovery. Depicting Ferrein as the fictional character Doctor Orcotome, the narrator describes how this revered figure of the Banza science community spends weeks perfecting a plausible anatomical explanation for talking genitalia. His theory hinges on structural similarities that he discovers between the trachea and the *delphus,* or womb.[11] Finally, in front of an esteemed assembly of experts, the doctor promises to demonstrate his discovery:

> Orcotome prenait un Bijou, y appliquait la bouche, soufflait à perte d'haleine, le quittait, le reprenait, en essayait un autre; car il en avait apporté de tout âge, de toute grandeur, de tout état, de toute couleur: mais il avait beau souffler; on n'entendait que des sons inarticulés, et fort différents de ceux qu'il promettait.[12]

> (*Orctomus* took up a Toy, put his mouth to it, blew into it till he was out of breath, quitted it, returned, tried another: for he had brought a variety of them with him, of all ages, sizes, conditions and colours: but in vain did he blow; nothing was heard but inarticulate sounds, vastly different from what he had promised.)[13] (italics in original)

In this satirical reenactment of Ferrein's experiment, the narrator pokes fun at the mechanical systems that the French science academy promotes to such an extreme that scientists assume the preposterous: inert matter can imitate the emotional and impassioned tones of sentient beings. By playing the organs of dissected cadavers, Orcotome extricates the voice from its living and embodied context, and so draws erroneous conclusions about its mechanical functions. This is a parodic critique of Ferrein's experiment in which the illustrious member of the French science academy excised the trachea from the body and used his breath to produce the voice's unique timbre.

The narrator represents Orcotome's experiment as spectacularly humorous in part to undermine the scientist's mechanical methodology but also to direct the reader toward a vitalist understanding of the body. The narrator relies on the imaginative power of literature to give a voice to female reproductive organs. Although this story can be read as an allegorical representation of the vitalist body, it also directs the reader toward a more scientifically grounded, more literal understanding of the vitalist body. This body is not a mute, unfeeling collection of organs. Instead, each organ has its own set of volitions, aversions, and memories. Following a vitalist approach to vocal organs, a scientist cannot reduce its sound to the movement of air over vocal cords. The sound of the voice rather comes into being through the complex interaction of a network of organs, glands, and tissues to whom the voice reacts, and for whom the voice expresses their silenced feelings.

To PUT Diderot's vitalist turn into context, I situate his early work during a transition period in French scientific inquiry. Although mechanical models of the body, called *iatromechanical*, still held sway among certain French scientists, a new approach to the body called vitalism was gaining ground. Adherents of these approaches differed in how they conceived of sentience and its relationship to the body. In iatromechanical approaches, the body was thought to be composed of inert matter whose movement was explained through the laws of physics. From the circulation of blood to the impulses of nervous fluid, scientists predicted these systems through an understanding of fluid dynamics. Sentience, however, was separate from the movement of bodily fluids, and it occurred only when a spiritual substance controlled and interacted with the mechanical body.

In vitalism, matter itself possessed the rudimentary properties of sentience. There were sentient molecules of matter, which, for some scientists, even retained memories and experienced aversion and desire.[14] Each practitioner of vitalism took a slightly different approach to biology, but they all believed that matter possessed a vital property, a *vis viva*, or life force. Although the Montpellier school of doctors, including François Boissier de Sauvages, Louis La Caze, and Théophile de Bordeu, are the scientists most often associated with vitalism, two intellectuals in Paris who had contact with Diderot—Pierre Louis Moreau de Maupertuis and Georges-Louis Leclerc, Comte de Buffon—also developed versions of vitalism. Buffon presented a version of the vitalist body in *Histoire naturelle* (written in 1746 and published in 1749) in which a living body was composed of an assemblage of little "organic living parts."[15] To destroy a living body, which he called an "organized body," it sufficed to separate these "organic living parts" from each other.[16] Central to Buffon's theories was the notion that reproduction was an essential activity of vitalist molecules. This generative or reproductive force was made manifest through the molecule's capacity to self-organize into more sophisticated organisms.

In addition to theorizing the generative capacity of matter, vitalists imagined how the parts of the body experienced and expressed their own form of sentience. Maupertuis speculated that each little part of the body preserved instincts of self-preservation and reproduction, and therefore that even the smallest part of the body possessed the instincts of aversion and desire.[17] This notion then filtered down into the various parts of the body, whose fibrous tissue and organs experienced various degrees of sentience.[18] By 1751, Théophile de Bordeu was claiming that the organs, glands, and vessels of the body had their own life and sensibility, which is to say a conscious feeling.[19] Organs, for Bordeu, moved much like a swarm of bees: individually they had control over certain parts of the body, and collectively they functioned in relation to each other.[20] A diseased organ thus impacted the life and sensibility of the neighboring organs. The vitalist body was a complex network of parts, including fibrous tissues, blood vessels, muscles, nerves, glands, and organs, which independently and collectively maintained the health and life of human and animal bodies.

In the 1740s, Diderot engaged with this emerging approach to the life sciences, but not wholeheartedly. From 1745 to 1749, Diderot was moving toward vitalist principles, a materialist conception of life, while he slowly and publicly shifted his stance away from deism, a divine approach to creation.[21] With his translation of Shaftesbury, Diderot began this journey toward a vitalist voice insofar as he described how the organization and composition of animal physiology influenced animal voices. As Ann Thomson notes, however, Diderot "was wary of attributing intelligence to the smallest molecules."[22] In *Pensées sur l'interprétation de la nature*, he warned against attributing to "organic molecules" "the most seductive type of materialism," which "attribute[s] to organic molecules, desire, aversion, feeling, and thought."[23] Although Diderot believed in a "muted sensibility" whereby "organic molecules" possess a "muted and obtuse sense of touch,"[24] he also proposed that our sense organs possess a form of "momentary consciousness" that perceives the organ's existence but not that of the "entire animal or human" body.[25]

Despite his circumspect approach to vitalism, Diderot did share with vitalist thinkers a desire to experiment with what Peter Reill calls a "language of nature."[26] For Reill, vitalist scientists, such as Buffon, developed a "language of nature" that first situated scientific discovery from an authorial perspective, and then created a set of rhetorical strategies to use as tools of scientific discovery. The language of nature served, first and foremost, to situate humanity at the center of discussions about nature. This language then rejected a divine explanation for nature's mechanical operation, and, instead, the scientist discovered nature through a series of "intuitive, experimental insights."[27] Among the rhetorical strategies developed, Reill notes a reliance on historical narrative and analogy, and a rejection of the purely arbitrary representation of nature through mathematics.[28]

In his early works, Diderot developed a slightly different language of nature that put into dialogue multiple forms of expression, reason, and logic. In his translation of Shaftesbury, we find mathematical logic placed alongside musical aesthetics, and even medical theory embedded within the acoustical properties of strings. In each work, we also find an authorial, editorial, or literary figure who directs the reader to translate meaning across multiple discourses, including music, mathematics, philosophy, and literature. Through the translation of meaning, the reader intuits and experiments with the properties of life. As a result, mathematics is not banned from the language of nature. Instead, it is one of many intermediary discourses intended to awaken in the reader his own ideas about the nature of life, the sensations of bodily organs, the sentience of living beings, and the articulation of sentience through the voice.

For my study of Diderot's implicit theorization of the vitalist voice, I begin with its smallest element—the fiber—whose tissue connects the body's organs and glands to the voice. As I discussed in chapter 2, the British doctor George Cheyne envisioned human temperament as the result of the relative strength or weakness of fibrous tension that binds the human body together. In Diderot's early translation work, he encountered variants of this theory in Shaftesbury's *An Inquiry on Virtue or Merit* and Robert James's *A Medicinal Dictionary*. Even though these works investigate the human condition through different disciplinary perspectives—medicine and moral philosophy—it is possible to see how a thinker like Diderot would discover points of contact between the metaphorical meaning that Shaftesbury imparts on strings and the literal meaning that James describes in his dictionary.

In my interpretation of Diderot's early works, I interpret certain elements such as the vibrating string as simultaneously holding literal and metaphorical meanings. It is the role of a reader to evaluate these simultaneously occurring meanings and understand how to translate them into language. Through this process, a literal reading informs a metaphorical interpretation of a word: a philosophical approach can lead to scientific discovery. The word *fiber* or *string*, in this context, does not have a fixed literal, metaphorical, philosophical, or scientific connotation. It is instead entangled with the nuance of each utterance, the sum of which produces a new dynamic, polyvalent word that accumulates layers of meaning as the text unfolds.

For my exposition of Diderot's *fibre* context, I reverse the order in which Diderot translated these British works. He completed his translation of James's dictionary in 1747 and his translation of Shaftesbury essay in 1745. Discussing his translation of James's dictionary first allows me to begin with a concrete, biological notion of the *fibre* and to end with a metaphorical notion of the vibrating instrumental string. This order reflects the organization that Diderot later imposed as the editor of the *Encyclopédie*. For instance, in the 1754 *Encyclopédie* article concerning strings (*corde*), Diderot first wrote about the fabrication and mechanical use of different *cordes*: in addition to catguts, he wrote about hemp ropes (*cordes de chanvre*) and other strings made from nerves, tendons, ligaments, and hair. At the end, he referred to the articles that followed, which explored more abstract scientific principles of strings, including their strength, flexibility, elasticity, and vibration. I take my cue from this encyclopedic study of objects in which an item, such as a string, has different yet interrelated meanings depending on the author's epistemological perspective.

The *fibre*, as an elastic and resonant tissue of the human body, is an ever-present element of mid-eighteenth-century medical discourse. According to Hisao Ishizuka, medical practitioners of the period, including Boerhaave, Robert James, and George Cheyne, conceived of the body by beginning with its smallest part, which was understood to be the fiber. As Ishizuka notes, "Eighteenth-century medical discourse from c. 1700 to c. 1740 is pervaded with fibre-related terms and descriptions such as 'membranes,' 'web,' 'stamina,' 'weaving,' 'vibrating,' 'folding,' 'tone' and 'tension,' rather than 'nerves' and the 'nervous system.'"[29] These threadlike filaments join together in parallel structures, which form larger membranes. In a cyclical pattern of development, these membranes then weave together to form vessels.

According to Diderot's translation of the *Dictionnaire universel de médecine*, this building block of life varies in elasticity, cohesion, durability, and strength based on environmental and innate factors. Among the environmental factors, the voice interacts with these filaments in surprising ways. For instance, a "loud cough," a "laugh," or a "loud cry" can disrupt the underlying matrix of *fibres* in such a way that their cohesion breaks and an embolism results.[30] Even "a sudden noise" can penetrate the fibrous walls of blood vessels and increase a person's blood circulation.[31]

To demonstrate how external forces can diminish a *fibre*'s strength, James mentions an experiment in which "une corde d'instrument de musique, au bout de laquelle on pend un poids, devient plus longue; elle s'allonge encore davantage, si on y en ajoute un nouveau, & casse à la fin: un instant avant la rupture, il y avoit encore cohésion; mais si peu qu'il ne falloit plus que le plus petit poids pour la romper" (a musical instrument string, at the end of which a weight hangs, becomes longer; it is lengthened even more, if one adds a new one, and breaks in the end: an instant before the break, there was still cohesion; but so little that it takes only the smallest weight to break it).[32] By describing this experiment with instrumental strings that come from fibrous entrails, James departs from mere simile: *fibres* are more than simply "like" instrumental strings. Indeed, instrumental strings share properties with the organic threadlike filaments that are woven through human and animal bodies.

In addition to translating James's material and medical notion of the *fibre*, Diderot encountered a similar analogy in Shaftesbury's *An Inquiry concerning virtue and merit* (1699), in which the English moral philosopher articulated an affect theory for social, sentient beings. Shaftesbury's moral philosophy rested in part on his interpretation of sentience through the sounds of creaturely voices. He noted how external signs of joy could communicate sympathetically to other animals: "It will be consider'd how many the Pleasures are, of *sharing Contentment and Delight with others*; of receiving it in Fellowship and Company; and gathering it, in a manner, from the pleas'd and happy States of those around us, from accounts and relations of such Happinesses, from the very Countenances, Gestures, Voices and Sounds, even of Creatures foreign to our Kind, whose Signs of Joy and Contentment we can anyway discern."³³ As Shaftesbury noted, animals have varying degrees of success in expressing and perceiving external signs of affect.³⁴ He attributed their social aptitude in part to the tuning of a creature's fibrous tissue.

To understand the external signs of natural affections, Shaftesbury described how the organization of the "Animal-Constitution" influences the expression of emotion:³⁵ "Upon the whole: It may be said properly to be the same with the Affections or Passions in an Animal-Constitution, as with the Cords or Strings of a Musical Instrument."³⁶ With this metaphor, Shaftesbury suggested a sonic blending of natural affections in which each passion represented a string individually tuned to the intervals of joy, fear, despair, and wonder: "It might be agreeable, one wou'd think, to inquire thus into the different *Tunings* of the Passions."³⁷ By relating animal constitutions to instrumental *tunings*, Shaftesbury implicitly referred to the different instrumental timbres that arose from early eighteenth-century tuning systems. Depending on the system of temperament—just, Pythagorean, mean-tone, well, or equal—the harmonic ratios performed in the same key transformed the relative consonance and dissonance of music intervals. These changes in turn modified the overall sound of a song. For instance, a trained musician who listens to J. S. Bach's *The Well-Tempered Clavier* in equal and well temperament should notice a marked difference between the two performances.³⁸

As in James's example of the *fibre*, Shaftesbury imagined a fibrous animal machine whose filaments resembled instrumental strings. This metaphor expressed an abstract notion of harmony through Shaftesbury's concrete experience with musical temperament. This music analogy makes sense when we reconstruct it with Shaftesbury's period ear. In referring to different tunings, Shaftesbury may have been drawing from knowledge acquired during his two-year tour of the Continent (1687–88), including Italy, where his son claimed Shaftesbury learned about "the polite arts."³⁹ During Shaftesbury's travels through Europe, he would have encountered different tuning systems. At the very least, his essay makes evident his appreciation for the ways tuning systems modified the consonant and dissonant intervals of music. Since local taste dictated tuning systems, Shaftesbury likely encountered many variations in temperament. While our modern ears may not appreciate the cultural connotations associated with various temperaments, to Shaftesbury's period ears, temperament may have communicated affective meaning.[40]

When Shaftesbury extended his instrumental metaphor to include a taxonomy of animal constitutions, he alluded to the different tunings of instruments. As he noted, "If these [cords], tho in ever so just proportion one to another, are strain'd beyond a certain degree, 'tis more than the Instrument will bear: The Lute or Lyre is abus'd, and its Effect lost."[41] These instrumental references implicitly nodded toward the equal temperament of lutes and the Pythagorean tuning of the ancient lyre. Based on this instrumental metaphor, Shaftesbury speculated that each species resembled a different instrumental design. Even within a species, the strings of emotion required precise, individualized tuning. In other words, behind the external signs of joy and passion, an internal, instrumental machinery varied across species and individuals. Among the many possible variations, Shaftesbury concluded that certain creatures could have broken, disorganized, and uncalibrated strings whose dissonant sound impeded the expression of social affect.

Shaftesbury finally recommended a process of recalibration to bring the animal constitution back into alignment with his community. A "*right* Balance," he claimed, would maintain the harmonic proportions of "tenderness, love, sociableness, compassion." With this notion of balance and calibration, he broadened his metaphor to include a consort of instruments that performed in harmony. By choosing the lute as a symbol of the "Animal-Constitution," Shaftesbury suggested also a tuning system that could perform in concert with other instruments. The equal temperament of the lute conveyed Shaftesbury's notion of harmonious affections, wherein an individual who listened to his fellow creatures accommodated and modified his own voice.

Within the context of Diderot's 1745 translation, musical temperament gestures toward both a metaphorical notion of harmony and a practical idea regarding the physical ratios of temperaments. Within French performance practice, equal and nonequal forms of temperament were used. As Rameau explained in 1726, mean-tone temperament offers the composer an expressive harmonic palette with which to depict various emotional accents. Rameau specifically noted that the major third normally "excites us to joy" but when "too large" "impresses upon us ideas even of fury."[42] Likewise, the minor third normally "transports us to sweetness and tenderness" but "saddens us when it is too small."[43] With mean-tone temperament, each key has a unique color because the intervallic relationships vary. As a metaphor for the animal voice, mean-tone temperament encompasses a range of individual accents, which in isolation are emotionally charged but in concert with other families of instruments sound jarring.

Shaftesbury complicated any notion of absolute mechanical design because each animal voice produced a unique sound from its internal cords, which were tuned to different temperaments. In Diderot's translation of Shaftesbury, *Principes de la philosophie morale; ou Essai de M. S***. sur le merite et la vertu*, the *philosophe* seizes on this notion in a lengthy discursive footnote in which he elaborates and modifies Shaftesbury's instrumental metaphor. Diderot anchors Shaftesbury's metaphor in a physical embodied presence: "Nous ressemblons à de vrais Instrumens dont les passions sont les cordes. Dans le fou, elles sont trop hautes, l'instrument crie; elles sont trop basses dans le stupide, l'instrument est sourd. Un homme sans passions est donc un instrument dont on a coupé les cordes qui n'en eut jamais."[44] (We are like true Instruments whose passions are the strings. In the madman, they are too high, the instrument shouts; they are too low in the stupid, the instrument is muffled. A man without passions is an instrument whose strings were cut.) Instrumental strings are not merely an analogy for the "fiber body"—the strings of the time were made from animal fibers. By imagining a person's affective profile through vibrating strings, Diderot situates the sentient voice within a matrix of interwoven fibers.

The voice, in this view, is a diagnostic tool. Sound can reveal the inner workings of a defective or monstrous being. Like an instrument without resonating strings, an impassive, unfeeling human lacks the capacity to intone emotions. The philosopher's ear, like a stethoscope, can also locate in a person's speech the high-pitched whine of insanity or the ponderous thuds of intellectual mediocrity. The voice's timbre thus becomes a sign of the fibrous composition: its elasticity, its weaknesses, and its resonance.

By reading Diderot's translations in dialogue with each other, the metaphorical tunings of a stringed instrument in Shaftesbury's essay are analogous to psychological effects that fibrous tissues in James's

Medicinal Dictionary have on human temperament. As if to reverse-engineer personality types, James even classified human personalities according to the qualities of their *fibres*. A cold temperament came from fortified *fibres* and a warm temperament from weakened filaments.[45] As Ishizuka notes, the "fibre body" explains in part differences in temperament based on age, sex, and social class.[46] As a calibrating metaphor, musical temperament represents the tension, strength, and elasticity of a person's fibers and makes audible the fibers that influence a person's physical constitution and emotional character.

In light of this context, scholars often interpret Diderot's references to the vibrating string in relation to medical theories of sensibility and irritability in which the vibrating *fibres* comprise the crisscrossing filaments of human anatomy. For instance, Veit Erlmann describes Diderot as a cordologist who interprets the physiology of Albrecht von Haller from the perspective of sensibility.[47] Diderot's physiological approach to vibrating strings, however, is not limited to sensibility. He also conceptualizes sound and harmony as aesthetic and moral objects, respectively. For instance, the *cri du fou* sounds a complex alarm of psychological disorganization. Through his discursive footnotes, Diderot explains how the *fibre* resonates at the frequency and timbre of the human machine. The resonant *fibre* is a malleable and dynamic model of human psychology that the *philosophe* attempts to understand musically and mathematically through harmonic ratios. In his early work, however, Diderot does not simply define the material, biological, and sentient qualities of the vitalist voice; he also devises strategies to translate these features across literary, philosophical, scientific, and musical discourses.

Diderot picks up the thread of the vibrating string a few years later and adds to its metaphorical meaning to include acoustical features. Specifically, in *Principes généraux d'acoustique* (1748), Diderot discusses sound's generation and movement as a moving string of propagated air particles, called a *fibre sonore*. When Diderot describes how music vibrates a character's *fibre* in his later works, the term *fibre* weaves together the internal resonant filaments of the human organism with a metaphor for sound propagated in air, like a string. From this aerial perspective, the *fibre* becomes a sound image that is an analogy for the speaker's internal organization. When Diderot discusses the *fibre sonore* in his mathematical treatise, he describes it as coming out of human mouths.[48] These sonorous fibers are merely filaments of sound that vibrate to the frequency of the voice's fibrous tissue. As a study of acoustics, the *Principes généraux d'acoustique* does not directly address the question of the voice. Instead, this treatise proposes a multidimensional understanding of air's acoustical properties.

In the first part of my analysis of the vibrating string, I have examined a dynamic approach to interpreting Diderot's work as a series of layered meanings that bring together multiple disciplinary understandings of an object. This approach to reading Diderot is a kind of vertical entanglement of simultaneously occurring meanings that interact with one another. On a metaphorical level, instrumental strings and their tuning serve as an analogy to human temperament. On a more literal level, the physical attributes of instrumental strings—created from the entrails of animals—can offer insight into the fibrous tissues that weave through the human body. By adopting this method of interpreting the vitalist voice, I expand the physiological space that it occupies. It is more than a simple organ. Through a deeper understanding of the vibrating string on a metaphorical and literal level, I interpret the vitalist voice as responsive to a network of fibrous tissue that weaves across the human body.

This interpretation of the vibrating string as both literal and metaphorical captures only its vertical layers. In the second part of my analysis, I shift to a horizontal approach. Here the string responds to and is acted upon by multiple competing forces. It is within this horizontal view of the vibrating string that I switch from a literary to a mathematical approach. Mathematical reasoning serves as an intellectual tool to calculate and weigh the various vitalist forces in and outside the human body.

This approach is unorthodox. By focusing on the mathematical reasoning behind Diderot's implicitly theorized vitalist voices, I question a well-worn narrative about Diderot's rejection of mathematical logic in favor of a Buffonian emphasis on history and analogy.[49] This narrative, however, ignores Diderot's continued engagement with mathematics in the 1760s.[50] Among his early philosophical and fictional works, mathematical reasoning is explicitly present.

This unorthodox approach is compelling when I apply both approaches: literary and mathematical. On the one hand, instrumental strings—in Diderot's early works—are a comparative and literal object associated with the voice. On the other, mathematical reasoning—ostensibly present only in Diderot's mathematical treatise—identifies the influence of variables on an object. For Diderot's translation of Shaftesbury, however, Diderot translates the metaphysical approach to emotions into mathematical theorems. Indeed, Diderot seizes upon Shaftesbury's references to harmony and proportion, and translates Shaftesbury's idea into an almost mathematical idiom. By defining affective animal forces as *equal to, proportional to*, or *against* each other, Diderot emphasizes the competing forces exerted within and across animal constitutions. Compare, for instance, Shaftesbury's metaphysical meandering with Diderot's translation, which distills a set of variables into a concise moral equation:

> That inward Deformity growing greater, by the Incouragement of unnatural Affection; there must be so much the more Subject for dissatisfactory Reflection, the more any false Principle of Honour, any false Religion, or Superstition prevails.[51]

> Mais la dépravation du caractere étant toujours proportionnelle à la foiblesse des affections naturelles & à l'*intensité* des penchans dénaturés; je conclus que, plus on aura de faux principes d'honneur & de Religion, plus on sera mécontent de soi-même & plus par conséquent on sera misérable.[52]

Diderot translates Shaftesbury almost mathematically: the variables of affections, depravity, superstition, and desire relate to each other as forces of proportionality and intensity. In Diderot's translation, affective communication results from a dynamic and mathematically inferred interaction subject to the competing influences of virtue, vice, superstition, and natural affection.

If we extend this notion of proportionality to Diderot's footnote on the strings of crazy and dispassionate individuals, we can appreciate Diderot's understanding of the vibrating string as more than a matrix of cohesive strings. Through mathematics, one can reverse-engineer the tension, mass, and material composition of the vibrating string. In other words, the *cri du fou*, which Diderot diagnoses as emanating from high-pitched strings, can be calculated through acoustic theories in which the *fibre sonore* (the sound) reveals the biomechanical features of the underlying matrix of fibrous tissue.

By following the parallel and complementary paths of music and mathematics, Diderot implicitly explores how the voice externalizes through sound the fibrous tension that weaves through the human body. This notion is the first step that leads to a form of embodied sentience whereby the body, with its fibrous tissue, glands, and organs, has a limited form of sensation that the voice externalizes through sound (timbre, hoarseness, register). Diderot explores this idea in more depth with his satirical novel *Les Bijoux indiscrets*, a novel about talking vaginas.

As I shift my analysis of the vitalist voice from its incarnation as a vibrating string to a sentient organ, I pause for a moment to consider how these two versions of the voice are interrelated within Diderot's early works. This implicit connection is most evident in a passage from *Bijoux* when the sultan Mangogul encounters a talking vagina with intimate geometric knowledge. The talking vagina

> s'est expliqué en termes d'une géométrie si profonde, que je ne l'ai point entendu, et peut-être ne s'entendait-il pas lui-même. Ce n'était que lignes droites, surfaces concaves, quantités données; longueur, largeur, profondeur, solides, forces vives, forces mortes, cône, cylindre, sections coniques, courbes, courbes élastiques, courbe rentrante en elle-même avec son point conjugué...[53]

> (spoke in terms of such sublime geometry, that I did not understand one word, nor perhaps did it understand its own language. It was nothing but right lines, concave surfaces, given quantities, longitude, latitude, profundity, solids, living forces, dead forces, cone, cylinder, conic sections, curves, elastic curves, curve re-entering into itself, with its point conjugated—)[54]

This passage, embedded in a satire partially critical of traditional scientific methods, reads at first as a critique of the mouthpieces of the French academy: scientists who employ terms whose meaning escapes their comprehension. By considering this passage, however, alongside

Diderot's mathematical treatise published the same year, I interpret it as an unsolvable riddle that nonetheless pays homage to mathematical reasoning. Here, the mathematical gibberish speaks to an abstracted understanding of the vitalist forces that course through the body and influence human physiology. The sublime geometric thinker alludes to theoretical approaches to the vibrating string with its discussion of lines, curvature, and elasticity. Then the embodied geometrician blends a mathematical approach with the vitalist concepts of living and dead forces, the *vis viva* as it were. This passage reveals—in its incoherent form—two important aspects of the vitalist voice. First, a network of glands, tissues, and organs have an obtuse form of sentience that the voice externalizes through unintelligible but emotionally inflected sounds. Second, since this embodied sentience cannot be articulated in rational language, it is impossible to understand how each tissue, gland, or organ influences the other's sentience.

Before continuing my analysis of *Bijoux*, I wish to acknowledge its problematic place in a post-#MeToo culture as well as point out its importance to my study of the vitalist voice. As a twenty-first-century reader, I attempt to analyze works that are several centuries removed from my own culture. Inhabiting the role of cultural translator, I recognize that *Bijoux* re-creates, satirizes, and parodies eighteenth-century French cultural norms surrounding sexual relationships that were—at the time—considered to be humorous but are currently antithetical to post-#Metoo approaches to sexuality and consent.[55] To ignore *Bijoux*, however, would overlook its importance to European discourses on sexuality and the voice. As Foucault notes in the first volume of his *Histoire de la sexualité*, *Bijoux* serves as an emblem of the confessional discourses that led to the "dispositif de sexualité."[56] Indeed, *Bijoux* formulates a discourse of sexuality that melds physiological knowledge with confessional narratives. In addition to contributing to discourses on sexuality, *Bijoux* extends our understanding of the vitalist voice insofar as Diderot situates the voice at the nexus of sexual passions (both desire and aversion) and reproductive organs.

In *Bijoux*, reproductive organs have a mind of their own to the degree that they appear to influence a person's temperament. For instance, the sultan's favorite concubine, Mirzoza, explains how the sentience of an organ modifies personality traits. Among Mirzoza's taxonomy of female temperament, she includes the sensible woman, the prude, the amorous, the sensual, the sycophant, and the coquette. Mirzoza then demonstrates a feedback loop between a person's reproductive organs and her temperament. For instance, Mirzoza includes two opposing personality types: "La prude, celle qui fait semblant de ne pas écouter son bijou ... la voluptueuse, celle qui écoute son bijou avec complaisance."[57] (The prude, she who pretends not to listen to her Toy ... the voluptuous, she who gives ear to her Toy with complaisance.)[58] Human temperament thus develops out of a complex relationship across the conflicting and contradictory desires of organs. With this example, the desires of reproductive organs are either in concert with or in conflict with the desire of a person's collective personality—which is the sum total of the desires and aversions of a person's organs, including their brain.

As I have mentioned, I interpret Diderot's literary texts on a continuum of literal and metaphorical (or allegorical) meaning. Even though Mirzoza's tongue-in-cheek theory is intended as an allegory for the vitalist body, Mirzoza's theory has elements that modify and reimagine ideas proposed in scientific studies of the voice and its relationship to reproductive organs. As such, talking vaginas give voice to a debate on the physiological relationship between the voice and human sexuality. Among works written or republished in the eighteenth century, we find references to sexually differentiated vocal organs. In reading through manuals on venereal disease, puberty, and sex, I have found three distinct categories of voices: a virile, a pubescent, and a diseased/surgically modified voice. The most modern approach is from Rousseau, who discusses the pubescent changes of men and women whose vocal organs transition from childhood to adulthood,[59] an approach that emerges earlier with the late seventeenth-century sexologist Nicolas Venette,[60] Then, there are mature masculine voices, associated with postpubescent men who attain virility. The natural philosophers who wrote on the mature masculine voice include such luminaries of midcentury science as Herman Boerhaave[61] and Charles Bonnet.[62] Lesser-known figures also wrote about it: the early eighteenth-century anatomist Joseph-Guichard Duverney,[63] and finally Jean-Baptiste Thibault de Chanvlon, the doctor.[64]

These natural philosophers, whose approaches to medicine differed, acknowledged transitions only among men whose vocal organs transformed to produce a deeper and more resonant sound, proving their virility. In considering the cause of this change, they identified seminal fluid as the biological agent responsible for modifying the resonance, timbre, and register of men's voices. For instance, Duverney described the production of seminal fluid, which then escaped into the body and increased its heat: "Pour lors la voix se change et se grossit" (Then the voice changes and becomes fuller).[65] Herman Boerhaave modified this logic slightly when he concluded that the male voice came into being thanks in equal parts to the production of sperm, changes in temperament, and the awakening of passions, a notion that Albrecht von Haller also espoused, arguing for the power of "semence" (semen) to change simultaneously the voice and the morals (*moeurs*).[66]

Jean-Baptiste Chanvlon de Thibault, holding onto Galenic tradition, explained vocal change as happening only among men: "Notre voix qui jusques-là ne différoit point de celle des femmes, change alors & baisse d'environ une octave; on éprouve dans le sang une plus vive chaleur; les forces augmentent."[67] (Our voice, which until up to that time did not differ from that of women, then changes register[,] lowering about one octave; we experience in the blood a warmer heat, vigor increases.) At the end of this androcentric turn, we find Charles Bonnet, who reported that sperm interacted with certain organs to make them "germer, croître, développer, meurir" (germinate, grow, develop, mature).[68] This maturation was "évident par la muë de la voix" (evident with the changing voice).[69] Across these approaches, the doctors shared a belief that the deep, resonant sound of a mature adult man served as audible proof of virility. These voices never existed in transition or gestured toward anxieties about fragile or unstable virility. Rather, they immediately produced the sounds of fully mature masculinity. By erasing the presence of the pubescent male voice and asserting the arrival of virile accents, these medical depictions suggest an anxiety about this moment of awkward becoming.

Finally, there are voices associated with monstrous forms of sexuality (the diseased, the castrated). In Diderot's late writings, the voice maintains an association with reproductive organs that *Bijoux* ostensibly parodies. In a chapter from *Éléments de physiologie* subtitled "Correspondance de la voix avec les organes de la generation" (Connection between the voice and reproductive organs), Diderot explains how modifications to genitals, regardless of biological sex, can modify the human voice.⁷⁰ According to Diderot, "La castration a un nombre infini d'effets qui constatent la liaison des parties de la bouche avec les parties génitales."⁷¹ (Castration has an infinite number of effects, which show the connection between the parts of the mouth and the genitals.) In recognizing this effect, Diderot acknowledges the physiological effects of castration, which include, according to Martha Feldman, an undescended larynx, a larger chest cavity, and a lengthening and thinning out of vocal folds.⁷² As discussed in chapters 1 and 5, the figure of the castrato haunts vitalist, sentimental, and uncanny voices. As I mentioned in chapter 1, the castrato goes against sentimental ideologies that promote traditional familial and marital bonds. For the vitalist voice, the castrato serves as proof of biological influences on the voice, especially reproductive organs.

In addition to castration, Diderot includes a series of modifications that could transform the sound of the voice, including venereal disease, the deflowering of a virgin, and excessive passion.⁷³ Omitted from this list, however, are the effects of puberty on male voices. This omission removes men's bodies from the construction of vocal physiology and instead focuses on two voices, which represent the dual poles of vitalism: one originating from nubile women and associated with female sexuality, and another originating from sterile men and associated with castration.⁷⁴ In Diderot's *Éléments*, the voices to which he refers evoke the binary aspects of vitalism: pleasure and aversion, the living and lifeless forces of matter.

Diderot even alludes to the physical effects of syphilis, namely the destruction of the soft palate, a deformity that severely affects the resonance and timbre of the voice. Diderot strategically chooses these particular vocal organs to embody vitalist forces. The voice of the deflowered virgin transforms the biological changes of puberty into a sexual act that draws attention to both desire and fertility. The diseased and castrati voices evoke both aversion and lifelessness.

After beginning to draft *Éléments de physiologie*, Diderot wrote the novel *La Religieuse*, which fictionalizes a correspondence between sexual gratification and the voice. For instance, the third Mother Superior—Madame ***—possesses a voice whose tones fluctuate according to her emotional and physical disposition. During moments of passion, Madame ***'s voice weakens and loses articulative control.

As Suzanne notes, "Elle m'exhortait en bégayant et d'une voix altérée et basse à redoubler mes caresses."[75] (She urged me with a stutter and a low, altered voice to increase my caresses.) Later on, Suzanne naively witnesses Madame ***'s erotic convulsions: "Elle avait un tremblement général dans tous les membres; elle voulait me parler, elle voulait s'approcher de moi, elle ne pouvait articuler, elle ne pouvait se remuer. Elle me disait à voix basse: Suzanne, mon amie, rapprochez-vous un peu..."[76] (She was trembling all over down to her limbs; she wanted to talk to me; she wanted to get closer to me; she couldn't articulate, she couldn't move. She said to me in a low voice: Suzanne, my friend, come a little closer...) In the final passage, the voice of Madame *** seems to be responding involuntarily to a pleasurably intense orgasm.

In the examples above, Diderot maps out a series of pleasurable and painful connections between the voice and a person's reproductive organs. In *Bijoux*, this vitalist duality—desire and aversion—exists as an allegorical dialogue between a woman's voice and her talking vagina. For instance, the character Monima swears by the sanctity of her "autel" (altar): "parle ou se taise, je ne crains rien."[77] (speak or be silent, I fear nothing from its talk.)[78] At that moment, Mangogul forces Monima's vagina to talk: "N'en croyez rien, elle ment."[79] (Do not believe her, she lies.)[80] Throughout the novel, the protagonist witnesses a similar scene. The voice and the talking vagina form a binary force of vitalism: the woman's voice publicly professes an aversion to sexual pleasure (shame, prudishness) while the talking vagina often confesses to varying degrees of interest (or disinterest) in carnal desire. On an allegorical level, it is a commentary on social conventions. Women (and men) are trapped in social conventions that require of them to silence (or make a show of) bodily desire, which solidifies through performance a socially acceptable gender role.

On a literal level, this duality further elucidates the way in which the body experiences sentience as a movement between aversion and desire. Although the voice in *Bijoux* serves as an allegorical figure for embodied sentience, I also interpret the voice of talking organs in relation to Diderot's physiological theories. Indeed, the narrator often calls the talking vaginas *organe*. The specific origin of this organ, however, is at times unclear. On the one hand, the talking *organe* is a reproductive organ, an interpretation that presages Diderot's later physiological work in which he describes a biological connection between reproductive organs and the voice. On the other, the narrator situates the talking *organe* in the abdominal region. At one point, the narrator even employs the word *engastrimuthe*, which means ventriloquist and derives from the Greek expression—words in the stomach.[81] In this chapter, I only gesture toward the physiological relationship between the voice and what *Bijoux*'s narrator locates in the stomach. In chapter 4, I will further develop the relationship between the diaphragm and the vitalist voice. It is a physiological relationship that is based on a physical and emotional reaction to pleasurable and painful sensations.

By adding confusion to the physiological origin of *Bijoux*'s talking *organes*, the narrator implicitly gestures toward an expansive view of the vitalist voice. The embodied, fleshy voice, which anatomical thinkers locate across a collection of organs (larynx, vocal cords, glottis, tongue, mouth, nose, lips) is too reductive. The vitalist voice extends out beyond the rigidly anatomical definition of the voice to include a constellation of organs, glands, and tissues whose sensitivity to pain and pleasure is transmitted to the physiological voice and turned into a sound that listeners can hear and even interpret. The vitalist voice thus is a physiological voice that involves the entire body.

IN THIS chapter, I have theorized that the vitalist voice, which is implicitly present in Diderot's early works, develops out of a physiological model in which interdependent organs connected by fibrous tissue interact with each other. To gain knowledge of this vitalist body, a reader must imagine human physiology in a way that goes beyond anatomy. I have proposed two interpretive methods. First, I developed an entangled understanding of words that shift between metaphorical and literal meanings. Next, I considered how a reader can transpose mathematical reasoning to enhance his knowledge of the vitalist body. By mathematical reasoning, I mean the notion that one can calculate and deduce the competing forces of vitalist energy across a constellation of organs. This method comes out of my interpretation of Diderot's scientific method.

For instance, in speculating on the future of experimental physics, Diderot imagines a life force, or *vis viva*, of affection. He asserts, "Tous les phénomènes, ou de la pesanteur, ou de l'élasticité, ou de l'attraction, ou du magnétisme, ou de l'éléctricité, ne sont que des faces différentes de la même affection."[82] (All phenomena—from gravity, elasticity, attraction, magnetism to electricity—are but different faces of the same affection.) The term *affection* has mathematical, physical, and emotional meanings, and its ambiguity contributes to a vitalist interpretation. The life force of affection crosses between inert matter and organic molecules. Diderot returns to the term *affection* in the first volume of the *Encyclopédie* when he defines its physiological meaning as "l'impression que les êtres qui sont ou au-dedans de nous, ou hors de nous, exercent sur notre ame. Mais l'*affection* se prend plus communément pour ce sentiment vif de plaisir ou d'aversion que les objets, quels qu'ils soient, occasionnent en nous."[83] (the impression that beings who are either inside, or outside of us, exercise on our soul. But *affection* is more commonly taken for that lively feeling of pleasure or aversion that objects, whatever they are, cause in us.) With this definition of affection, Diderot reformulates the mathematical and moral theory of affection that he first articulates in *Essai sur le mérite et la vertu*. Underneath the natural forces of Diderot's 1750s vitalism, we can hear the faint echo of the *fibre sonore*, with its desirable consonance and unpleasant dissonances, the sound image of moral, musical, and mathematical interactions, that appears in Diderot's early work.

4

Sound and Sensibility

Music in *Le Neveu de Rameau*

♪

In the years following the 1748 editions of *Les Bijoux indiscrets* and *Principes généraux d'acoustique*, Diderot's published and unpublished work reexamined how the voice related to physiology, emotion, sentience, and perception. By 1756, Diderot had even established himself as an authority on vocal performance, so much so that Jean Blanchet, the doctor who claimed authorship of Jean-Antoine Bérard's singing treatise of the year prior,[1] included Diderot among the "people of talent," including famous singers and established composers, with whom he had consulted.[2]

Diderot's philosophical expertise in the voice and vocal physiology is evident in his work. For instance, in a passage from *Lettre sur les aveugles*, the narrator meets a blind man from Puisaux, a small town in the province of Gâtinais. The narrator then explains how a person deprived of sight evaluates aesthetic beauty through touch: "Il juge de la beauté par le toucher, cela se comprend; mais ce qui n'est pas si facile à saisir, c'est qu'il fait entrer dans ce jugement la prononciation et le son de la voix. C'est aux Anatomistes à nous apprendre, s'il y a quelque rapport entre les parties de la bouche & du palais, et la forme extérieure du visage."[3] (He judges beauty by touch, that is understandable; but what is not so easy to grasp is that he incorporates into this judgment the pronunciation and the sound of the voice. The Anatomists must teach us whether there is any relation between the parts of the mouth and the palate, and the external form of the face.) Remarkably, the narrator describes a sort of echograph from which a blind listener reconstructs a speaker's vocal physiology and facial structure. By imagining touch as the sense through which a blind person not only identifies beauty but also senses physiological structures, the narrator implicitly refers to a voice whose vibrations externalize the internal tension of a speaker's fibrous anatomy.

A metaphorical version of this physiological voice returns in many iterations throughout Diderot's published and unpublished works: two noteworthy examples, respectively from *Lettres sur les sourds et muets* (1751) and *Entretien entre d'Alembert et Diderot* (written in 1769 and published in the *Correspondance littéraire* in 1782), are the musician in a cuckoo clock orchestrating sound, and a metaphorical harpsichord whose fibrous construction represents the human body. At the crossroads between these two metaphorical musicians stands the nephew from Diderot's philosophical dialogue *Le Neveu de Rameau*, written or conceived around 1760–62 and revised around 1773–74.[4] Diderot based the nephew character on a historical figure, the real nephew of the composer Jean-Philippe Rameau, named Jean-François (1716–1777). In fact, Jacques Cazotte, a contemporary of Diderot, published an anonymous poem on the vagabond meanderings of Jean-François.[5] This minor figure started in the military, which he later left to enter a religious order. By the 1760s, he was writing harpsichord pieces.[6] In *Neveu*, the nephew performs musical interludes that serve as more than mere entertainment. They enact another version of the vitalist voice, one that is reactive to the diaphragm.

My reading of *Neveu* reexamines this text as an experimental manuscript that engages the reader's imagination. The unpublished manuscript of *Neveu*, also entitled *Satire II*, experiments with a method of eliciting from readers an imaginative re-creation of vocal performance. As an experimental dialogue, the *Neveu* manuscript invites its readers to imagine and enact the nephew's vocal performance. Diderot's musical interludes give musical and sonic context to his dialogue. This chapter argues that music in *Neveu* becomes part of a discourse on human sensibility, converting the philosophical dialogue into a hybrid musical-narrative text that communicates emotions and ideas through the full range of a reader's sensibility.

THE SENSIBILITY to which the *Neveu* refers is intimately linked to theories developed in Diderot's late works, including *Le Rêve de d'Alembert* (written in 1769, published in *Correspondance littéraire* in 1782), *Réfutations d'Helvétius* (written around 1773–74), and *Éléments de physiologie* (begun around 1765). Diderot revised *Le Neveu* around the time he was in Holland writing *Réfutations d'Helvétius*.[7] While the dialogue's setting dates the encounter to the early 1760s, many of the philosophical questions resonate with ones that Diderot posed in *Réfutations d'Helvétius*, namely about the inherent originality and inequality of human beings, whose moral disposition is attributable in part to a person's *sensibilité physique*.

In *Neveu*, when the narrator describes how music vibrates a character's *fibre*, the nephew relies on music to demonstrate this physiological process. His voice externalizes through sound the physiological tensions of the human body and translates them into melodic formulas. To define this internal tension, I use the versatile concept of *sensibility*. This term, in Diderot's works, builds on a medical conception of human sentience.[8] His preoccupation with bodily reactions derives in part from the Enlightenment notions of *sensibilité* and *irritabilité*, developed by physicians such as Herman Boerhaave and championed by Robert James and Albrecht von Haller. In chapter 3, I explored how Diderot translated from Robert James a theory of the fibrous body that had been assimilated from the work of Boerhaave. In this chapter, I expand the *fibre* theory to include the notion of a *fibre* network. In short, *irritabilité* refers to an "involuntary and unconscious reaction" to a stimulus, and *sensibilité* refers to the transmission of sensations via nerves, "lead[ing] to perceived sensation."[9] In his works, Diderot integrated *sensibilité* and *irritabilité* into a unified theory of life. Within medical theories of sensibility, the *molécule sensibile* attaches to and forms the matrix of more complex social and biological organisms, which in turn combine into aggregated beings (beehive swarms) or continuous beings (multicelled organisms).[10] In multicelled organisms, sensibility becomes a matrix (*faisceau*) with a network of vibrating *fibres* that connect tiny *polypes* (cells or organs, as discussed in what follows) to a continuous organism. At the heart of this physiological model, the materialist soul receives sensations from multiple parts of the body and then translates those sensations into comprehensible expressions, ideas, and thoughts. The voice, as part of the fibrous network, calls upon memory to translate raw sensations into ideas, thoughts, and emotions, because memory allows us to compare our present sensations to those of the past.

Diderot used multiple names to describe this internal faculty: "sens interne" in *Lettre sur les aveugles;* "l'origine du faisceau" in *Le Rêve de d'Alembert;* a musician in a cuckoo clock (*horloge ambulante*) in *Lettre sur les sourds et muets;* and a *philosophe-clavecin* in *Entretien entre d'Alembert et Diderot,* where *philosophe* refers to a materialist soul and *clavecin* to the physiological network of human sensibility.[11] In this chapter, I focus on a slightly different version of the materialist soul, which I call the interpreter. By referring to the interpreter instead of the soul, I wish to emphasize how the voice externalizes the complex thoughts and feelings that accompany sentience. Importantly, this interpreter does not have a specific embodied location. Instead, it is similar to the *origine* from *origine du faisceau,* which refers to a metaphorical hub through which mental and physiological information (memories and sensory information) combines in a network of vibrating fibers to create thoughts, ideas, and judgments.[12]

These vibrating fibers connected to tiny fibers, however, tell only part of the story about the nephew's musical performance. The nephew's voice is a disruptive presence that irreverently elevates the function of the body as a tool of philosophical inquiry. His physical voice is a remarkable organ that the nephew traces back to the "famous Stentor," an exceptionally loud-voiced character from Greek mythology.[13] To project so forcefully, the nephew must exert an impressive amount of diaphragmatic control, which he reduces to three constituent parts: "des poumons; un grand organe; un volume d'air" (lungs, a large organ, a volume of air).[14] Diaphragmatic control is essential to vocal performance, and it can only be mastered with a great deal of training and practice. It requires a firm yet untensed breath control, and the exercise can leave a singer physically exhausted. Jean Blanchet's singing manual from 1756 describes diaphragmatic control in terms similar to the way I learned to sing Western music: "To inhale properly, it is necessary to raise and widen the chest, in such a way that the stomach inflates: through this artifice, one will fill all the lung's cavity with air. To exhale properly, it is necessary to let out the internal air with more or less force, with more or less volume, according to the character of the song."[15] In practice, this exercise translates into a unique type of breath control. Without making much noise, a singer needs to inhale a large volume of air between musical phrases. Depending on the song, he may have less than a second to fill his lungs, and he must then slowly and evenly release air over the length of the following musical phrase. With a sufficient amount of air and diaphragmatic control, a singer is able to shape the phrase, increasing or decreasing the volume, in part through the controlled release of air.

Although the nephew is silent on the importance of diaphragmatic control, the diaphragm itself features prominently in Diderot's late theories of sensibility, and it appears in works that Diderot drafted, revised, or wrote before, during, and after the 1773–74 period to which Henri Coulet dates the final version of *Neveu*.[16] According to *Réfutations d'Helvétius*, a person with an overactive diaphragm is either drawn to or repulsed by tragic scenes—an apt description of the ever-mercurial nephew.[17] The nephew, called LUI, exhibits a very active, even volatile, version of diaphragmatic sensibility.

Across Diderot's late works, the *sensibilité du diaphragme* refers to the "seat of all our pleasure and pain,"[18] which is reminiscent of the voices in *Bijoux* that are forced to talk about their feelings of gratification and discomfort. The diaphragm, in eighteenth-century medical literature, is an intermediary organ between vocal and reproductive organs. To be sure, its upward movement increases air pressure against the glottis, or vocal cords. It was also thought to respond to sensations emanating from reproductive organs. According to a popular treatise on vitalist medicine, *Idée de l'homme physique et moral* (1755), the diaphragm makes the breath "shorter, and consequently faster" after an orgasm, which is a symptom of its role in moving and releasing seminal fluids, both male and female.[19] In addition to its association with the pleasures of orgasm, diaphragmatic pressure is related to menstruation.[20] Given this medical background, the vitalist voices in *Bijoux* personify a medical conception of the voice's diaphragmatic sensibility, which is deeply connected to reproductive organs and consequently reactive to the pleasure and pain of said organs.

By the 1750s, doctors from the Montpellier school of medicine, those who were in part responsible for the vitalist movement in France, were speculating on the diaphragm's role in the body. As Ann Thomson notes, the diaphragm was associated in vitalist medicine with the center of phrenic forces in the body.[21] In *Idée de l'homme physique et moral*, La Caze notes that the fibers form the diaphragm in the fetus in such a way as to connect it to other parts of the body, including the head, the reproductive organs, and an "external organ."[22] As a result, the diaphragm reacts to sensations in other parts of the body.

Across Diderot's late works, the author refers to the diaphragm's role in the perception of and reaction to pleasure and pain. It is through sensation that the diaphragm has an intimate and sympathetic link to other parts of the body, including the brain—a fact to which Diderot returns in *Réfutations* and *Éléments de physiologie*: "Il y a une sympathie très marquée entre le diaphragme, et le cerveau. Si le diaphragme se crispe violemment, l'homme souffre et s'attriste: si l'homme souffre et s'attriste, le diaphragme se crispe violemment."[23] (There is a strong sympathy between the diaphragm and the brain. If the diaphragm tenses violently, the man suffers and saddens: if the man suffers and saddens, the diaphragm tenses violently.) In Diderot's aesthetic and moral theories, the diaphragm plays a crucial role in the development of an individual's talent and moral disposition.

The nephew brings to life the erratic performance style of sensibility that Diderot references in the *Paradoxe sur le comédien*. In his theory on acting, Diderot claims: "C'est l'extrême sensibilité qui fait les acteurs médiocres; c'est la sensibilité médiocre qui fait la multitude des mauvais acteurs, et c'est le manque absolu de sensibilité qui prépare les acteurs sublimes."[24] (It is extreme sensibility that causes an actor to be lackluster; it is weak sensibility that fashions the multitude of bad actors, and it is the absolute lack of sensibility that prepares sublime actors.) On the surface, the sublime actor that Diderot describes appears to have similarities to the nephew. This actor does not feel emotions; instead, he performs emotions as if they were notes on a score: "Les cris de sa douleur sont notés dans son oreille."[25] (The cries of his pain are recorded in his ear.) Upon further study, I consider the nephew's performance to be similar to the actor of sensibility. As Diderot observes of these actors, "Ne vous attendez de leur part à aucune unité; leur jeu est alternativement fort et faible, chaud et froid, plat et sublime."[26] (Do not expect any uniformity from them; their performance is alternately strong and weak, hot and cold, flat and sublime.)

This distinction becomes clearer through a physiological reading of the sublime actor and the performer of sensibility. Whereas the sublime actor performs from the brain, the sensitive one feels emotion from the heart and gut. Diderot specifically targets the abdomen for its troubling effect on acting: "Ce sont les entrailles qui troublent sans mesure la tête de l'homme sensible."[27] (The guts disproportionately bother the head of a sensitive man.) In an anecdote that resembles the convivial atmosphere of the *Neveu*, a character from the *Paradoxe* states: "Je vous entends: vous faites un récit en société: vos entrailles s'émeuvent, votre voix s'entrecoupe, vous pleurez."[28] (I can hear you: you tell a story among company: your bowels move, your voice cuts out, you weep.)

The erratic style that characterizes the actor of sensibility is more reminiscent of the nephew's wildly uneven performance, which is at times sublime and at others repulsive. I attribute this difference to the physiological source of the nephew's talent. He is not performing from the head. He admits to his mediocrity and compares his inadequacy to the genius of his uncle. In the *Paradoxe*, the actor of genius, also called the "comédien de nature," derives his talent from his brain.[29] What's more, a great actor, according to the *Paradoxe*, is neither "un piano-forte, ni une harpe, ni un clavecin, ni un violon, ni un violoncelle; il n'a point d'accord qui lui soit propre, mail il prend l'accord et le ton qui convient à sa partie" (a piano-forte, nor a harpsichord, nor a violin, nor a cello: he does not have his own unique chord [*accord*], but he takes the harmony [*accord*] and pitch [*ton*] that suits his part).[30] In drawing a distinction between the great actor and a mediocre one, the *Paradoxe* cites the metaphorical instrument, which is often an analogy of the vitalist body. In this regard, the vitalist body does not influence the performance of a great actor. Instead, he controls and recalibrates his body to perform different emotional accents. The nephew, by contrast, is reactive to his guts along with his sensitive and defective paternal fiber.

The nephew's performance, however, cannot be reduced to an acting theory. His artistic production makes visible and audible a broader influence of the vitalist body on artistic talent and moral temperament. A central node of this physiological influence is the diaphragm, or gut. This idea is only comprehensible in relation to Diderot's broader debate with Helvétius. As Roland Desné notes, Diderot criticizes in Helvétius's philosophy an overreliance on experience, such that a good education is thought to be enough to eliminate personal failings and dramatically improve a person's intellect.[31] In other words, human beings have no innate capacity that is determined or restricted by biological difference. What's more, for Helvétius, biological difference does not fundamentally change the ways human beings react to events. Everyone responds to and is influenced by events in the same way.[32] The case of morality is particularly relevant to my discussion of *Neveu*. For Helvétius, morality arises from a reaction to physical sensation. A person chooses to be generous to those less fortunate for selfish rather than altruistic reasons. Moral desire is constructed through self-love (*amour de soi*): the generous party feels pleasure when he sees the recipient's gratitude. Conversely, it is through generosity that a person avoids the painful sight of misery. As Desné argues, Helvétius understands virtue as the product of a desire for our own well-being.[33]

In *Réfutations d'Helvétius*, Diderot first mentions the diaphragm within a commentary on human experience. Although Helvétius concedes that every person "does not feel the same sensations," he does believe that "everyone feels objects in a proportion always the same."[34] Diderot begins his objections with the metaphor of the instrument, which compares human physiology to the tension, elasticity, and acoustics of musical instruments. Each individual is tuned differently to "thirds, fourths or fifths," and each producing sounds "more or less dull, more or less shrill."[35] Shifting from this musical metaphor into a more explicit commentary on physical sensibility, he describes the role of the diaphragm as a seat of pleasure and pain, which is to say a center of the sensations underlying a materialist conception of morality. Diderot then goes on to discuss the diaphragm's capacity to shape personalities.

In this discussion, the "oscillations" and "tensions" of this "thin and sinewy membrane" play a vital role in constructing human identity, including the relative "weakness" or "strength" of a person's "soul."[36] Attributing a host of affective responses to the diaphragm, Diderot then differentiates between the intellectual faculties of the mind and the emotional properties of the diaphragm: "La tête fait les hommes sages; le diaphragme les hommes compatissants et moraux."[37] (The head makes wise men; the diaphragm compassionate and moral men.) This distinction between a person's intellect and moral fiber aligns well with *Neveu*'s narrative in which artistic genius often does not correspond with moral goodness. In *Neveu*, LUI demonstrates through song how intellectual and artistic genius are decoupled from a person's moral fiber. Returning to the *Réfutations*, this distinction is intended to dispute Helvétius's notion of equality. By highlighting the diaphragm's role in an individual's sensibility, Diderot argues that the relative flexibility of this organ partly explains personality differences. Not only does each person perceive sensations differently, but variations in the diaphragm determine how people respond to pleasure and pain. Since the diaphragm helps construct a moral identity, its fibrous construction is a determining factor in a person's emotional and moral disposition.

The diaphragm brings together many of the properties and organs of the vitalist voice. The vitalist voice in Diderot's work envelops all of the organs of the voice, including the diaphragm. The elasticity of an individual's *fibres* affects the relative mobility of the diaphragm, and by extension, the moral disposition and artistic talents of an individual. As an independent and interconnected organ, it exhibits sentience with its capacity to perceive pain and pleasure, and it even forms sympathetic relationships with other organs, including the brain. In *Neveu*, the nephew engages his *sensibilité du diaphragme* in part through singing, and in the process, he demonstrates how the diaphragm engenders sympathetic movement between physical sensibility and emotional reactions through two complementary pathways. On a physical level, air acts as a physical stimulant, which gives his fibrous tissue elasticity.[38] On an emotional level, songs, through their marriage of melody with lyrics, elicit in the singer an affective response. By singing, a person can experiment with feeling the *sensibilité du diaphragme* and learn how it relates to other organs.

WHEN THE nephew suggests that we set to music "les *Maximes de La Rochefoucaut, ou les Pensées de Pascal*" (La Rochefoucauld's *Maximes* or Pascal's *Thoughts*),[39] he is inviting the readers to marry their reading of the moralist's texts with singing. The nephew's suggestion was not novel for its time. Between the early and the mid-eighteenth century, artists had published a series of song volumes that did exactly what the nephew proposes.[40] They created anthologies of famous aphorisms from ancient and modern writers and set them to well-known tunes, called vaudevilles.[41] A 1749 volume of "chansons morales" included passages from ancient writers such as Seneca, Horace, Pliny, Aristotle, and Ovid as well as modern ones such as La Bruyère, La Rochefoucauld, and Pascal. Above each textual fragment, the author cited a popular tune whose melody the reader could find in the appendix of the volume. For instance, figure 5 shows how the author sets a passage of La Bruyère, numbered with the roman numeral VII, to the popular tune "De la Samaritaine," indexed as song 118. The reader could either remember or refer to the melody, and then sing la Bruyère's aphorism.

Throughout the *Neveu*, the nephew borrows from well-known melodies, similar to the vaudeville in figure 5. Vaudevilles are traditionally

FIG. 5. *Nouvelles étrennes utiles et agréables, recueil de chansons morales et d'emblèmes sur de petits airs en vaudevilles connus* (Paris, 1749), appendix pp. 4–5. (Bibliothèque Nationale de France)

associated with early to mid-eighteenth-century fair theater plays and are often cited as a source of pleasure and entertainment for the readers of published plays. For instance, Alain-René Lesage, a famous playwright from the fair theater, commented on this style of reading: "Il faut chanter & ne pas lire simplement nos Couplets. Regardez-les comme les vers des Divertissemens d'Opera. . . . Le chant vous inspirera une gayeté indulgente."[42] (We inform you that you must sing and not simply read our couplets. Look at them like the poetic lines of opera. . . . Song will inspire in you indulgent happiness.) In the anonymously published volume of "chansons morales," the vaudevilles serve to "brighten" the reader's "spirit" and "relax the mind."[43] Vaudevilles, as musical paratexts within a published work, entertain the readers and engage them in the experience of song.

In practice, vaudevilles provided the reader with more than simple amusement. They were a popular form of mnemonic that crossed over into oral culture.[44] The short and catchy tunes were highly adaptable, often reused and set to completely different types of lyrics.[45] Since the songs were recycled so often, they often lost any association with the affective or semantic meaning of previous works.[46] Occasionally, however, a song retained a specific extramusical connotation.[47] For instance, the vaudeville "Or écoutez, petits et grands" became associated with the comic demise of a character, just as Chopin's *Funeral March* (Piano Sonata no. 2 in B♭ minor) often serves as comic shorthand in modern films and cartoons.[48]

In *Neveu*, the nephew cites popular vaudevilles of the day, such as "Va t'en-voir s'ils viennent, Jean."[49] Instead of adapting popular songs from the fair theater, he employs this borrowing technique to incorporate well-known songs from French lyric theater. To illustrate music's capacity to activate emotional memory, the nephew chooses songs emblematic of emotional extremes: specifically, two popular midcentury *opéras comiques*, *Isle des fous* by Egidio Duni and Carlo Goldoni and *Maréchal ferrant* by François André Philidor and François-Antoine Quétant.[50] His examples are overwrought caricatures of passionate feelings: love in "Monseigneur, laissez-moi tranquille" and avarice in "O terre reçois mon or." The nephew finally quotes a song from *Maréchal ferrant*, "Mon coeur s'en va," as a melodic expression of death. In its original context, the character Colin sings this tune after he unwittingly drinks a sleeping draught and mistakes its effect for poison. Colin's song, according to the nephew, imitates the sound of a dying man: "Allez, Allez entendre le morceau où le jeune homme qui se sent mourir, s'écrie, Mon cœur s'en va. Ecoutez le chant; écoutez la symphonie, et vous me direz après quelle différence il y a, entre les vraies voies d'un moribond et le tour de ce chant."[51] (Go, go listen to the musical passage where the young man, upon feeling death, cries out, 'My heart is faltering.' Listen to the melody, listen to the accompaniment, and afterwards you will tell me how the true path of a dying man differs from the contour and movement of this melody.) The nephew invites a reader, with knowledge of 1760s music culture, to associate the melodic expression of dying with the dramatic situation. (see example 2).

As James Johnson notes, Diderot's work bears traces of the broader aesthetic theory of the time, in which music allegedly imitated passions.[52] The nephew is not merely performing a melodic imitation. He sings as an exercise that activates his diaphragmatic sensibility. In other words, vaudevilles, instead of simply imitating passions, activate the diaphragmatic sensibility when they are sung aloud: the acts of breathing and of singing the melody stimulate physical sensibility, and the lyrics associate this physical sensibility with an emotional disposition. Vaudevilles essentially operate as vibratory agents, connecting the *sensibilité du diaphragme* with the mind.[53]

Furthermore, the nephew intones the melodic snippet to engage the reader's aural memory and to elicit an emotional association. Colin's air is not necessarily a sonic example of death but rather a vibrating force that activates the fibers of human sensibility. Eighteenth-century theater attendees might have remembered Colin's melody in its original theatrical context. Colin's predicament may have elicited feelings of sympathy tinged with ridicule. The melodic and rhythmic vibrations would have provoked a well-versed reader's

EXAMPLE 2. François-André Danican Philidor, "Mon coeur s'en va," *Le Maréchal ferrant* (1762), act I, scene 10, mm. 1–4.

memory to experience physical sensations, intended to elicit an emotional response.[54]

The nephew's illustration of musical mnemonics demonstrates sensibility's circuit, from aural memory to physical sensation (imagined listening) to emotional response. This mnemonic circuit, however, represents only one way of eliciting a listener-reader's response. In essence, the text both engages a reader's sensibility and describes the physical responses of human sensibility within its narrative universe. Indeed, the narrator recounts how listeners respond to the nephew's performance. In these passages, the narrator describes the nephew's singing voice and gestures (aural and visual sensations), which then either elicit emotional responses or produce a physical reaction from his audience. The passages locate the origin of musical aesthetics in human sensibility instead of in music itself. Human sensibility is no mere reaction to musical aesthetics; it is, instead, the instigator and progenitor of such aesthetics.[55]

Musical passages in *Neveu* are more than an illustration of the dialogue's philosophical commentary on human sensibility and musical aesthetics. These passages serve to exercise the reader's body and mind. The nephew follows an example that Diderot the author proposed to readers for his essay *Interprétation de la nature:* "Je me suis moins proposé de t'instruire que de t'exercer."[56] (I was less willing to instruct you than to make you exercise or practice.) *Exercer* here implies a dual form of readerly training that is embodied and mental insofar as it refers to bodily movement as well as mental operations, intended to improve a person's performance in a particular activity. As such, one can "s'exercer à chanter" (practice singing) and also "exercer sa mémoire" (exercise one's memory).

As an example of this experiential approach to teaching, musical passages in *Neveu* offer readers a lesson that activates both mental and physical exercises. *Neveu*, as a parody of didactic dialogues, imitates a particular type of literary genre, associated with this form of practical pedagogy. From the Renaissance to the eighteenth century, music theorists published didactic dialogues that included musical examples. As Cristle Collins Judd notes, musical examples in didactic dialogues are presented in the narrative as singing and composition exercises, first demonstrated by the master and then practiced by the student.[57]

The reader then can follow along with the fictional student, performing the excerpts that the fictional teacher glosses.

Judd points out, however, that musical examples are only sometimes intended as "notation ... to be 'read' and heard."[58] They also serve two supplementary purposes as iconic illustrations of music, or as an acknowledgment of music's sonic medium.[59] Diderot was well-versed in this genre. For instance, the *Leçons de clavecin* illustrates Diderot's familiarity with and willingness to experiment with the didactic music dialogue.[60] The musical examples in *Neveu* are best understood as a continuation and transformation of this long-standing genre. *Neveu* integrates musical examples in ways that modify their traditional functions.

In fact, *Neveu* expands on what such examples normally serve to illustrate. Scholars have astutely noted that *Neveu* contributes to an ongoing debate on the relative merits of French and Italian music. For instance, the nephew comments on and proposes changes to musical elements, including harmony, melody, and rhythm, that integrate aspects of French and Italian music.[61] These musical examples also go beyond a purely aesthetic discussion of music to become iconic illustrations of a debate on communication in which the music structures the dialogue while also commenting on the affective limits of language.[62] Finally, the nephew relies on music to illustrate the vitalist workings of the body's fibrous tissues and their connection to the physical voice. Although scholars have noted that the nephew's musical performance and pantomime represent the character's sensibility,[63] they have not examined how musical examples are intended to be heard and performed by readers.[64] The nephew has a particular temperament that the reader can hear through a reconstruction of his musical references. The innovation of *Neveu*'s musical examples is not only due to their function as physiological illustrations of the nephew's moral tuning. They also activate the reader's sensibility through song. By engaging their diaphragm, and remembering the melody, readers exercise their physical sensibility along with their mental faculties. In so doing, they can reflect on their own moral tuning.

By interpreting musical examples as both an illustration and a reenactment of the nephew's diaphragmatic sensibility, it becomes possible to view these examples as an active meditation on physical and moral sensibility. In a particularly compelling example of this function, the nephew performs a braying rendition of two popular Rameau arias: "Tristes apprêts" from *Castor et Pollux* (1737) and "Profonds abîmes" from *Temple de la gloire* (1745). The nephew's medley begins with Telaïre's mournful aria "Tristes apprêts" (E♭ major), in which she renounces the light of day. To this solemn song the nephew adds a malevolent tone with Envy's "Profonds abîmes" (E minor), in which the character of Envy calls on demons to eclipse the light of day in her fight against the sun god Apollo.[65]

In *Neveu*, the audience's reaction to "Tristes apprêts" is striking. Among audiences of the eighteenth century, the song usually elicited pathos-filled reactions. The nephew's voice, however, is so loud and atrocious that listeners reflexively move away and plug their ears:[66] "Pâles flambeaux, nuit plus affreuse que les ténèbres ... Dieux du Tartare, Dieu de l'oubli ... Là, il enflait sa voix; il soutenait ses sons; les voisins se mettaient aux fenêtres; nous mettions nos doigts dans nos oreilles. Il ajoutait, C'est ici qu'il faut des poumons; un grand organe; un volume d'air."[67] (Pale torches, night more ghastly than darkness ... Gods of Tartarus, God of oblivion ... Here his voice swelled, sustaining the notes; those closest to him moved toward the windows and we stuck our fingers in our ears. He added: "Here's where good lungs are required, a mighty voice, plenty of air.") In this medley, the nephew reveals the unique and unpleasant sound of his diaphragmatic sensibility. Indeed, the narrator describes the nephew's performance as peculiarly unpleasant.

Although the audience's reaction may comport with the second air (Envy's malevolent rant), the composer himself asserted that the first song should elicit a teary response.[68] To explain the audience's response in relation to auditory sensations, I propose a melodic reconstruction of this medley. To guide my reconstruction, I draw inspiration from both the sung-spoken dialogue style of the *opéra comique* and the nephew's comments on the arrangement and rearrangement of melodic fragments.[69] The resulting reconstruction aligns the nephew's borrowed lyrics with Rameau's melody. As examples 3 and 4 illustrate with numbered boxes, LUI fragments and transposes Rameau's melodies into the following order: (1) Pâles flambeaux, nuit plus affreuse que les ténèbres ... (2) Dieu du Tartare, (3) Dieu de l'oubli. Example 3

EXAMPLE 3. Jean-Philippe Rameau, "Tristes apprêts," *Castor et Pollux* (1754), act 2, scene 2, mm. 13–25.

highlights the cuts the nephew makes to the beginning and the end of Telaïre's opening phrase. Without the final six bars, the nephew eliminates sonically and semantically the mournful rising sun. In sections 2 and 3, the nephew adds another layer of parodic technique. In addition to fragmenting the song, LUI transposes the melodic order. As example 4 shows, the nephew inverts the order of the original melody, intoning "Dieu du Tartare" before "Dieu de l'oubli."

My proposed reconstruction (ex. 5) combines these two fragmented and inverted melodies, separated by blank spaces, with intentional incompleteness. The nephew's medley represents what resonates in the text. Readers can imagine a variety of acoustic and musical events that the narrator merely evokes. My reconstructions are intended to be spliced extracts of a *vaudeville*-style performance in which many competing sounds intermingle (crowd noise, the nephew singing). The nephew may continue singing more of "Tristes apprêts," or the café's noise may drown out his singing. This melodic reconstruction offers a fragmentary record of the nephew's medley, to which the reader's memory and senses respond.

These musical snippets, while limited, have an associative quality intended to elicit in listeners ideas, thoughts, and sensations. Two musical figures help explain why the café-goers are so repulsed by the nephew's singing. Instead of resolving his medley, the nephew ends with a jarring tritone interval, which should provoke feelings of discomfort in the listeners. Moreover, the two fragments are related enharmonically. As example 5 shows, the first fragment begins and ends on A♭, a pitch enharmonically associated with the final melody's concluding G♯. In modern equal temperament, enharmonic pitches are similar. In alternate tuning systems, like mean-tone temperament, there is a quarter-tone difference between enharmonic pitches. The

EXAMPLE 4. Jean-Philippe Rameau, "Profonds abîmes," *Temple de la gloire* (1786 edition), Prologue, scene 1, mm. 6–20.

use of this intervallic relationship is not a coincidence: Diderot believed an infinitesimal pitch variation was ideal for declaiming passionate discourses and described these microintervals as smaller than the *quart de ton*.[70] The nephew's rendition represents a specific type of passionate discourse that expresses horror. Indeed, eighteenth-century music commentators imagined the affective power of enharmonicism.[71] As Alexander Rehding has noted, Rameau and Rousseau hotly debated the question of how enharmonicism provoked horror, situating its power in melody and harmony, respectively.[72]

Rameau even attempted to experiment with enharmonicism in his opera *Hippolyte et Aricie*. At the moment when Theseus descends into hell, the fates were to sing a trio that was intended to provoke horror in the spectators. The experiment failed, however, because the singers refused to perform this particularly challenging trio.[73] Unlike Rameau's failed performance, which relied on the technical skills of the singers, the nephew's performance is a fictional rendition of the enharmonic genre, intended to awaken in the reader's imagination this horror-inducing interval.[74] In this passage, the enharmonic interval retains a strong cultural (mnemonic) association with the forces of vitalism: namely, feelings of repulsion, aversion, and horror. By plugging their ears and walking toward the windows, the café-goers show that they sense horror in the nephew's barely perceptible enharmonic interval. As Wilda Anderson notes, Diderotian horror "begins at the edges of perception" and "has the potential to yield a form of intuitive understanding or a form of cognitive induction that operates from initial dissonance."[75]

The nephew's horror-inducing medley illustrates a broader theme to which the nephew returns throughout *Neveu*. His diaphragmatic

EXAMPLE 5. A reconstruction of the nephew's Jean-Philippe Rameau medley of "Tristes apprêts" and "Profonds abîmes."

sensibility is tuned at times to the accents, sounds, and pantomimic gestures of horror, revulsion, and aversion. For instance, with the story of the Avignon renegade, the nephew thoroughly disgusts the narrator, who retorts that he cannot tell what "me fait le plus d'horreur, ou de la scélératesse de votre renégat, ou du ton dont vous en parlez" (gives me the most horror, either the villainy of your renegade, or the tone that you use to talk about him).[76] Even before this passage, the nephew reveals the diaphragmatic power of his stentorian voice to annoy, unsettle, and disperse crowds. After commenting on the power of his voice, the nephew demonstrates it with a cough: "Il se mit à tousser d'une violence à ébranler les vitres du café, et à suspender l'attention des joueurs."[77] (He began to cough so violently that it shook the café windows, and interrupted the players' state of immersion.) He then explains his talent as a concussive sound, like a "comminge" (a large mortar) or "tonnerre" (thunder) that erupts in the middle of a debate.[78] This concussive power comes from his *sensibilité du diaphragme*, which is directly linked in Diderot's physiology to the moral disposition of an individual.

When the narrator hears the nephew's stentorian voice, he can detect, through the nephew's cough, accents, and even enharmonic intervals, a defect in his diaphragmatic sensibility, a monstrosity at the heart of his vitalist organization. If we transpose this fibrous defect to another version of Diderot's metaphor of harpsichord strings, we discover an alternate way of imagining how the vitalist voice in Diderot's writings is somewhat limited by its physiology.

When the narrator, called MOI, asks the nephew why his capacity to see moral goodness does not equal his artistic sensibility, the nephew blames "une fibre qui ne m'a point été donnée, une fibre lâche qu'on a beau pincer et qui ne vibre pas" (a fiber that wasn't given to me, a loose fiber that one tries to pluck, and does not vibrate).[79] The nephew's singing voice combines physiology, morality, aesthetics, and physics to produce an atrocious-sounding, horror-inducing medley. His diaphragmatic sensibility reveals a flaw in his paternal *fibres*, which intone their defects through musical example. As he claims, "la molécule paternelle ... dure et obtuse ... cette maudite molécule première s'est assimilé tout le reste" (the hard and obtuse ... paternal molecule ... this damn first molecule assimilated all the rest).[80] His musical performance, responding to an overly mobile diaphragm, gives voice to a monstrous physiology.

Monstrosity only partially characterizes his singing voice because the nephew has a mercurial performance style that floats between accents of horror and divine sonorities.[81] The nephew modulates his accents as he passes from one emotional register to another such that his voice moves between revolting and pleasant tones that reveal the extremes of musical and emotional expression: it is "tantôt grave et pleine de majesté; tantôt légère et folâtre" (sometimes deep and majestic, sometimes light and amusing).[82]

In *Neveu*, musical examples paired with narrative descriptions of the nephew's performance invite the reader to imagine and reenact the nephew's diaphragmatic sensibility. This version of the vitalist voice is deeply connected to physical sensibility, to the perception of pain and pleasure, and by extension, to the creation of a moral identity. As a representation of Diderot's vitalist voice, the nephew's vocal performance is a product of the nephew's unique human physiology. Its accents, tuned to his particular body, at times sound painfully dissonant and at others, surprisingly consonant.

THIS DIAPHRAGMATIC voice is an integral organ in a constellation of physiological systems and intellectual faculties that cooperate to create the vitalist voice. The physiological voice is connected to the body's fibrous tissue—with its elastic sinews, tendons, and nerves—as well as the diaphragm, which connects the body with the mind. As Diderot mentions in *Éléments*, the diaphragm and the brain have a singular relationship. It is in part through the diaphragm that the voice maintains a sympathetic connection to the brain. This sympathetic relationship provides a physiological explanation for the unique position of the vitalist voice between the body and the brain. For instance, in *Éléments de physiologie*, the voice is both a physiological organ and a metaphorical intermediary that serves as a *truchement* (interpreter) of physical sensations and mental thoughts.

The *vitalist voice* is an umbrella term for the physiological connection across a constellation of organs—fibrous tissues, diaphragm, larynx, lips, nose. The metaphorical interpreter, in turn, controls vocal organs to externalize thoughts, emotions, and physical sensations. These two operations are essential to understanding certain musical passages in *Neveu*. Specifically, there is a moment when the nephew performs a medley that represents through music the sympathetic link between a diaphragmatic voice, which feels physical pleasure and pain, and the brain, which conceives of ideas. The nephew's medley represents through music how the metaphorical interpreter brings together the intermediary organs of the vitalist voice. The metaphorical interpreter differs from the vitalist voice because it translates a person's unique bodily sensations into a language that listeners can understand. A similar yet slightly different version of this voice is found in *Lettre sur les sourds et muets*, in which a figurine in a cuckoo clock transforms the chaotic movement inside the clock into cogent and pleasing music.[83] During the *pantomime de l'homme orchestre*, the nephew experimentally brings to life the vitalist voice that reveals his internal temperament and translates his sensations into language.

The passage from *Neveu* in question begins with an extended medley of opera airs and ends with Niccolò Jommelli's *Lamentations*. This pivotal scene invites the reader to feel, listen to, and experience the process of human sensibility: from the physiological and emotional model of the *clavecin*, in which vibrating organs and fibers interact and respond to physiological and emotional sensations that cause the vitalist voice to produce involuntary sounds, and then to the metaphorical interpreter (*truchement*), which translates a chaotic sensory experience into comprehensible ideas, thoughts, and language. This performance represents the imperceptible sympathy that exists between the diaphragm and the brain.

The models of perception and cognition in *Neveu*, *Éléments*, and *Lettre sur les sourds et muets* have something in common: each one represents a slightly different version of the metaphorical interpreter. In each, a musical instrument (voice, cuckoo clock, harpsichord) represents human sentience—with its physical sensations and thoughts—through melody, harmony, or lyrics. In Diderot's philosophy of sensibility, the metaphorical interpreter translates into language sensations that occurs initially in sensitive molecules and travel via fibers. As Andrew Clark notes, the musician in the *Lettre sur les sourds et muets* represents the importance of judgment, first in differentiating "natural order" from "harmony," and then "transmit[ting] . . . ideas to an auditor."[84] Meanwhile, the metaphorical interpreter—represented as a *clavecin-philosophe*—evokes the harpsichord as a metaphorical instrument of perception. On the one hand, the harpsichord reveals the "simultaneity of sensation."[85] On the other, the tactile memory of a plucked string represents the importance of memory in a listener's ability to evaluate music.[86] These musical metaphors represent different processes through which the human body and mind incorporate and judge sensations.

Sensations, however, vibrate through the human body in a jumbled mess before the mind organizes them into an intelligible form. According to Sophia Rosenfeld, "Diderot attempted to demonstrate that in all modern languages there is always, already, a fundamental discontinuity between verbal signs and thought or between language and sensation."[87] A particularly compelling musical example of discontinuity appears in the figure of the *clavecin-philosophe* from the *Entretien*. According to this dialogue, fibers are comparable to instrumental strings for at least two reasons. First, a vibrating string resonates long after it has been plucked. Its sustained resonance suggests an embodied form of memory in which our organs are capable of retaining the sensible qualities from an object even after said object has gone. Second, a vibrating string creates a cascade of resonances among other strings: "Cet instrument a des sauts étonnants, et une idée réveillée va faire quelquefois frémir une harmonique qui en est à un intervalle incompréhensible."[88] (This instrument can perform shocking and unexpected leaps, and one recalled idea will sometimes trigger harmonic vibrations of incomprehensible intervals.) Diderot imagines that a subject's sensitive *fibres* set off a chain reaction of vibration, thereby generating both overlapping and unrelated ideas.

To these different versions of the materialist soul, the nephew adds a malleable version that translates the mechanisms of human sentience into melodic fragments. To suggest this jumble of sensations, the nephew borrows from the compositional style of *opéra comique*: *vaudeville* couplets possess an associative power that imitates sensibility's vibrating and resonating *fibres*. The parody practice of *opéra comique* also mirrors the nephew's description of musical composition: "C'est au cri animal de la passion, à dicter la ligne qui nous convient[.] Il faut que ces expressions soient pressées les unes sur les autres; il faut que la phrase soit courte; que le sens soit coupé, suspendu; que le musicien puisse disposer du tout et de chacune de ses parties; en omettre un mot, ou le répéter; y en ajouter un qui lui manque; la tourner et retourner, comme un polype, sans la détruire."[89] (The animal cry of passion should dictate the contour of the melodic line. Expressions of passions should be crowded together in a rapid string of phrases one after the other; the phrase should be short; the meaning fragmented, delayed so that the musician can manipulate the whole as well as each part; omit a word, repeat it, and add to it a missing word, turn the phrase upside down and inside out, like a polyp, without destroying it.) The nephew's melodic *polypes* resemble the detached vaudeville couplets of *opéra comique* texts, in which writers sewed together pastiche dialogues that combined famous verses and melodies. Their dialogues blend song with verse. When the nephew describes the process of *polype* composition, he maintains that each *polype* (borrowed lines of text and melodic phrases) can be rearranged without losing its meaning. The nephew's strategy involves more than recycling melodic and textual *polypes*.[90] His parodic strategy also reintegrates these *polypes* into a new creation, inserting their original meaning into a new context.

The nephew's melodic *polypes* intone through sound the discontinuity between language and sensation, between the mind and the chaotic matrix of the body's sensitive molecules. He transforms Diderot's figurative model of simultaneous resonance (or rather, our jumble of sensations) into a performance medley of emotional extremes. His improvisation conveys the aural memory of emotion through a series of popular tunes, and specifically songs from the famous Italian intermezzo *La Serva padrona* and the French *opéra comique L'Isle des fous*. The narrator describes this moment of musical invention as a paroxysm of passion: "Il commençait à entrer en passion, et à chanter tout bas. Il élevait le ton, à mesure qu'il se passionnait davantage; vinrent ensuite, les gestes, les grimaces du visage et les contorsions du corps; et je dis, Bon; voilà la tête qui se perd, et quelque scène nouvelle qui se prépare; en effet, il part d'un éclat de voix.... Tous les pousse-bois avaient quitté leurs échiquiers et s'étaient rassemblés autour de lui. Les fenêtres du café étaient occupées, en dehors, par les passants qui s'étaient arrêtés au bruit."[91] (He began working himself into a frenzy while singing softly. As he became more impassioned, he raised his voice. Then came the gestures, grimaces and bodily contortions, and I said, Okay, now he's going to lose his head, and start some new scene. And indeed, he started to raise his voice.... All the players left their chessboards and gathered around him. Outside, passersby, transfixed by the noise, crowded in front of the café windows.) The narrator characterizes LUI's performance as overwhelming, with references to passion and madness. He draws attention to his gestures, facial expressions, and his intonation. However, MOI barely describes the nephew's voice and instead conveys a sense of the performance with visual and gestural descriptions. Highlighting LUI's success, MOI notices that the café-goers have returned to listen, and a sidewalk crowd is gaping through the windows around him.

The medley begins with tunes from *Isle des fous* and ends with snippets from *La Serva padrona*.[92] These musical snippets supplement the narrator's visual description with sonic material. In example 6, I have reconstructed how the nephew alternates vocal extremes between bass and soprano, intoning melodic figures emblematic of passionate feelings: these tunes fall within an emotional gamut that ranges from anger to love through avarice, coquettishness, belligerence, and guile.

LUI weaves these unrelated couplets into a melody of fragmentation and extremes. As with the Rameau medley reconstruction, I have aligned LUI's lyrics with their corresponding melodies."Je suis un pauvre misérable ... monseigneur, monseigneur, laissez-moi partir ... ô terre, reçois mon or; conserve bien mon trésor ... mon âme, mon âme, ma vie! ô terre! ... le voilà le petit ami; le voilà le petit ami! ... aspettare e non venire ... a Zerbina penserete ... sempre in contrasti con te si sta."[93] (I am a worthless wretch ... my lord, my lord, let me leave ... oh earth, receive my gold; protect my treasure well ... my soul, my soul, my life! Oh earth! ... here is my precious, here is my precious! ... [in Italian:] wait and don't come ... think of Zerbina ... It's constant conflict with you!) (see ex. 6). For the following reconstructed improvisation, I created an aggregation of melodic *polypes* that represent

EXAMPLE 6. The nephew's medley of *L'Isle des fous* and *La Serva padrona*.

the sonic memory of emotional extremes. Given that the narrator describes this medley as the jumbling together of thirty melodies, this reconstruction could never be an exhaustive recording of the nephew's entire musical performance; rather, it evokes sonic passages intended to reverberate through the text and activate a reader's aural memory. Example 6 suggestively presents the structure of a duet between LUI and his listener in which the reader–listener can retain the aural memory of a melody, marked in brackets in example 6, even after the nephew interrupts himself with a new song.[94] Consequently, although the nephew performs each melodic snippet unaccompanied, the listener can experience it as an experimental and barely perceptible duet. This duet translates into music the dynamic matrix of sensibility. Fragmentation, transposition, and alternation comprise the nephew's primary improvisational techniques. This medley, moreover, represents the vibrating *fibres*, which harmonize the internal and external senses (that is, memory and hearing) and in turn engender competing and contradictory feelings and ideas. The nephew's improvisation triggers a chain reaction in which one vibrating melodic *polype* resonates and starts to oscillate with a contradictory one. He thus transmits an aural collage of his diaphragmatic sensibility with its resonant fibers and oscillating organs: bass and soprano registers, conjunct motion and triadic movement, fast and slow tempi, duple and triple meters, and finally major and minor keys. The nephew's extreme vocal range (bass and soprano) intones his sensibility's cacophony of simultaneous sensations, memories, and thoughts in a linear progression. His melodic versatility (fast, slow, major, minor) spells out the associative power of contrasting and dissonant ideas rhythmically. Finally, LUI even evokes the unique resonances of our atomistic organs with a timbred imitation of symphonic color: raspy and dark oboes, brassy and nasal horns, sibilant piccolos, and warm strings.[95] In short, a thought can vibrate within the matrix of sensibility and awaken an entirely unrelated and dissimilar idea. His improvisation represents an aesthetic in which music imitates the competing forces of sensibility: external and internal sensations (that is, embodied cognition), memory, and ideas.

The nephew's dramatic vocal range, moreover, delineates the extreme poles of human sensibility, from the *sensibilité du diaphragme* to the mind. From the heights of a tightened falsetto, the nephew performs in the soprano register, and then quickly descends into a chesty voice for the bass line: "Tantôt avec une voix de basse-taille, il descendait jusqu'aux enfers; tantôt s'égosillant, et contrefaisant le fausset, il déchirait le haut des airs."[96] (Sometimes, with a bass voice, he'd descend into the depths of hell; sometimes, screeching and imitating a falsetto, he'd rip through high notes.) If these tunes were performed in their original key, the nephew's medley would be physically impossible for one singer to perform. In fact, the nephew's register extends far beyond the range of the eighteenth-century French high tenor, or *haute-contre* (see ex. 7). Indeed, if we compare the nephew's range to that of the *haute-contre* in Jean-Jacques Rousseau's *Dictionnaire de musique* and Michel Corrette's *Le parfait maître à chanter*, the nephew's register surpasses by an octave that of the *haute-contre*.[97] He appears to be performing a virtual melody that intones the full spectrum of human sensibility.[98]

This performance of sublime buffoonery, which the narrator describes as a moment of madness, seems to translate into sound the chaotic and disorganized matrix of sensibility.[99] The performance even echoes a passage from the *Entretien* in which Diderot's character compares madness to the *clavecin* metaphor: "Il y a un moment de délire où le clavecin sensible a pensé qu'il était le seul clavecin qu'il y eût au monde, et que toute l'harmonie de l'univers se passait en lui."[100] (There is a moment of madness when the *clavecin sensible* believes that it is the only harpsichord that has ever existed in the world, and that all the harmony in the universe has flowed out of it.) LUI's performance instantiates through sound *Entretien*'s isolated *clavecin* and its vibrating human *fibres*, which lose themselves in pure sensations and even imagine with their momentary form of consciousness that all the harmony of the universe is passing through their fibrous body. The nephew's performance essentially removes the metaphorical interpreter so that

EXAMPLE 7. Comparison of the nephew's and the *haute-contre*'s vocal range.

when he performs the chaotic and incomprehensible sensations of the fibrous body, listeners cannot understand its meaning.

In other words, the nephew eliminates the metaphorical interpreter, which allows a feeling being to become a thinking and social being. Example 6 captures both the sequence and the simultaneity of embodied sensations (musical vibrations), which occur in the matrix of sensibility. LUI's performance imitates the simultaneous interplay between the diaphragmatic voice, which involuntarily intones sensations, and the metaphorical interpreter (*truchement*) of the *Éléments*, which expresses those ideas cogently. The café-goers fail to comprehend the nephew's medley because he gives voice to the multiple vibrations of our sensitive organs and the cacophony of sonorities (sensations, memories, and ideas) that the mind later organizes into an intelligible whole. On the surface, the listeners respond to his raucous performance with laughter and ridicule because of his comic style. The nephew indeed performs each snippet as a sequence of melodies that he renders with special attention to tempo, pitch, and meaning.[101] On a deeper level, MOI's inability to comprehend the nephew's music can be attributed to the music's expressive format. Unlike language, which filters out extraneous embodied sensations, the nephew's music—an experimental duet between performer and listener—revels in the overlapping, chaotic, and incomprehensible vibrations of the feeling harpsichord body.

Shortly after this virtuoso performance, the nephew pairs his imitation of an unmediated materialist sensibility with a dynamic musical model of the metaphorical interpreter. The nephew's performance of a passage from Niccolò Jommelli's *Lamentatione prima* (1751) demonstrates the metaphorical interpreter's ability to integrate sensation into an intelligible whole. For this passage, LUI abandons his fragmentary improvisational style for a more fluid rendition: "S'il quittait la partie du chant, c'était pour prendre celle des instruments qu'il laissait subitement pour revenir à la voix, entrelaçant l'une à l'autre de manière à conserver les liaisons, et l'unité du tout."[102] (If he left the vocal part, it was to take up the instrumental one, which he'd suddenly drop to come back to the vocal section, intertwining one with the other in such a way to preserve the connection [between parts] and the unity of the whole.) In knitting together the melodic lines of voice and instrument, LUI preserves musical continuity and unity. For one brief moment, this touching passage elevates the narrator's soul and moves him to tears.

The musician who performs *Lamentations* can be read as a lyrical version of the metaphorical interpreter who, similar to the musician in the cuckoo clock in *Lettre sur les sourds et muets*, judges and compares the proper sonorities, ignoring certain sounds and allowing others to follow in succession. In this way, it translates simultaneous and contradictory sensations into comprehensible ideas, thoughts, and experiences. The nephew demonstrates a similarly discerning ear. He ignores his surroundings (the café-goers' laughter) and chooses only the most beautiful sections from Jommelli's *Lamentations*.

The narrator depicts the nephew's performance differently from the previous interludes. Instead of deconstructing his performance into fragmented melodies or visual descriptions with no logical connection, the narrator characterizes the recitative as a comprehensible whole that touches listeners.[103] The nephew alternates between vocal and instrumental sections in a moving display of *pathos*.[104] The selection of a *récitatif obligé* seems strategically aligned to Rousseau's and Diderot's praise of the genre's capacity to convey the complexity of human experience, including passions and sensations. According to Rousseau's *Dictionnaire de musique* (written in 1764 and published in 1768), the *récitatif obligé* allows a singer to become silently overwhelmed with feeling while the orchestra expresses the singer's emotional turmoil.[105] Furthermore, Diderot's *Entretiens sur le fils naturel* (1757) explains how a recitative combines the arts (music, gesture, dance, and visual art) to imitate different aspects of the same action.[106]

The *récitatif obligé* offers a linear medium that translates the simultaneity of embodied cognition (including sensations, thoughts, and emotions). The *récitatif obligé*, however, offers a third mode of communication: linear multiplicity. In essence, it translates the complex experience of sensations, emotions, and thoughts into a linear musical, visual, and verbal pantomime.[107] The recitative's melody, which migrates between the orchestral accompaniment and the singer, thus imitates the communication between physical sensibility and the mind. The nephew performs the coordination and interdependence of diaphragmatic sensibility and the metaphorical interpreter.

The *Lamentations* performance, however, blends sublime music with the nephew's shifty character. Noticing in the nephew's performance a hint of ridicule, the narrator equivocates: "Admirais-je?" (Did I admire it?).[108] His reaction attests to the nephew's molecular improvisational style, which depicts suffering (*douleur*) with a mixture of exalted singing and grotesque instrumental imitations. MOI's ambivalence captures the narrator's physical and mental reactions to the nephew's performance. In similar fashion, the nephew intones suffering as a complex combination of human sensibilities. The nephew's performance—a *polype* mixture of human experience with melodies and gestures, sounds and noises, the ridiculous and the grave—combine into a sonic imitation of suffering. The nephew improvises a version of his atomistic self in which sympathetic and contradictory sensations combine to become thoughts.

The nephew's cacophonous performance is surprising in part because it transgresses the rules of the performance space. The Café de la Régence was a popular meeting place that hosted lively debates, including those of the Querelle des Bouffons. It was most famous for its legendary chess games. Such games typically took place in near silence. Indeed, in a novel by Jean-Baptiste Louvey de Couvray, the narrator speaks of the silence that reigns over the Café de la Régence and the admonition he receives from a player who yells, "Hé! Messieurs, dans le *café de la régence*, on ne doit pas crier, on ne doit pas parler."[109] (Hey! In the Café de la Régence, we should not shout, we should not speak.) The chess players represent thought as a silent, meditative activity. The sporadic staccato of wooden pieces hitting the board, imitating short synaptic bursts, interrupts long stretches of silent contemplation.

The raucous nephew shatters this silence. Indeed, the nephew's final words ("Rira bien qui rira le dernier" [He who laughs best, laughs last]) evoke the sound of a body in spasms, of a pulsating diaphragm with a unique timbre.[110] A vocal performance, whose infinite variety remains outside a purely symbolic representation, carries a variety of discrete meanings, ranging from irony and mockery to joy and happiness. In the café setting, we see how the medley can introduce the body into philosophical inquiry. By performing an irreverently raucous and sublimely lyrical rendition of his atomistic self, the nephew draws attention to the discourses that are welcomed and discouraged within philosophical inquiry. As a social being and a performer, he uses more than language—he dares to translate the vibrations of his defective paternal *fibre* and his overly labile diaphragm into a delightfully repulsive medley of music and bodily noises.

5

The Haunted Listener

VOICES OF POSSESSION IN *LE DIABLE AMOUREUX*

♪

Among the voices that I described as vitalist, I have highlighted those voices whose articulations alternate between sublime melismas and repulsive noises. As I noted in chapters 3 and 4, Diderot's exceptionally mercurial characters, such as the nephew and Madame *** from *La Religieuse*, perform beautifully appealing music while also giving voice to their bodies' more visceral, pleasurable, and at times repulsive needs. Their voices are emblematic of a vitalist duality that animates the sentience of the body. Within a vitalist body, the most obtuse cells of the body express a limited sentience that hovers between desire and aversion, pleasure and horror.

In this final chapter, I examine the emergence of uncanny voices whose tones reconfigure characteristics of sentimental and vitalist voices in such a way that disarticulates the voice from the body. Unlike vitalist and sentimental voices, the uncanny does not serve as a guarantor of the speaker's physiological temperament. Instead, the uncanny voice unhinges the listener's epistemological certainty in the physiological truth that a listener came to expect from hearing the speaker's voice. The story of the uncanny voice begins with a curious novel written by Jacques Cazotte entitled *Le Diable amoureux* (1772, 1776).

Cazotte's novel reexamines the physiological connection between the voice and the body in part through its deployment of supernatural voices. *Supernatural* here refers to voices that originate in the spiritual realm or whose incantation crosses the veil separating the spiritual and material realms; *uncanny* refers to voices that seem out of sync with a being's physiological temperament. Before and after writing *Diable*, Cazotte had several encounters with the supernatural. As an author, he adapted and translated into French the *Arabian Nights*, a collection of Orientalist supernatural tales. During the Querelle des Bouffons, the midcentury debate on the relative merits of French and Italian opera, Cazotte penned a pamphlet that defended the French *Tragédie en musique* and its deployment of the supernatural. Finally, as a colonial administrator in Martinique from 1747 to 1760, he might have become familiar with Martinism, a sect of Freemasonry that was practiced in the Caribbean. With certain Martinist chapters, their members even incorporated Caribbean beliefs into their version of the supernatural.[1] Cazotte's encounters with the supernatural hint at the complex and varied terrain covered by practitioners of and believers in the occult. Their work constituted more than a lighthearted literary current; it had important religious and political implications. *Diable* is one such work: in it, the supernatural is part of a critique of occult practices that rely on the voice to cross over from the material to spiritual realm. In *Diable*, the supernatural emerges through the novel's representation of voices. Indeed, the narrator fills his novel with occult chanting, spirit invocations, ghoulish wailing, and lyrical spell casting. The voices contained by the text are powerful and often musical forces that direct action and reaction in the novel's fantastical universe, granting the space its own peculiar operating laws of cause and effect.

In the story's opening, the protagonist, Dom Alvare, learns from his master, Soberano, about the supernatural force behind incantations. Standing in the middle of a pentagram, Alvare intones a conjuring spell that will enable him to summon and control spirits. Once his incantation brings forth the supernatural being Béelzébuth, however, the demon bellows a terrifying yawl that momentarily paralyzes Alvare with fear. Eventually, he composes himself and commands the creature to take a series of more pleasant forms: a spaniel, a valet, an opera singer, and finally a beautiful woman, Biondetta, who dresses like the valet, called Biondetto. After this fateful séance, the conjured spirit Biondetta/o persuades Alvare to enter into a demonic pact whose binding power is sealed once Alvare recites its words. After pledging fealty to Biondetta, Alvare has trouble seeing Biondetta as a disguise of Béelzébuth. Then, when he hears Biondetta sing a touching solo, he begins to doubt that Béelzébuth ever existed. Biondetta's performance marks a transition from supernatural voices to uncanny ones because her song nearly erases Alvare's memory of her formerly monstrous appearance. This lyrical moment also represents a turning point that further destabilizes Alvare's perception of the creature. Only at the end of the first edition (1772) does Alvare realize, in a surprising moment of clarity, that Biondetta is Béelzébuth. Finally resolving this temptation story, Alvare relies on his supernatural voice to cast the malevolent spirit away with a forcefully intoned magical incantation.[2]

Through its representation of the voice, *Diable* offers two versions of this tale. The first edition differs from the canonical second edition (1776) in both format and content, insofar as the original version contains engravings, musical scores, and written passages that showcase a whole range of voices: demonic yawls, siren songs, and magical incantations. The denouement of the first version also differs from the ambiguous ending of the second one.[3] In the canonical version, Alvare never resolves the riddle of Biondetta's supernatural provenance. In contrast, the first edition offers the protagonist a clear resolution in the form of a vocalized disenchantment, a magical incantation whose force casts out the demon.

Unlike Alvare's supernatural voice, which establishes a connection between the material and supernatural realm, Biondetta's voice destabilizes the voice's relationship with the material world. In so doing, it has an uncanny effect on the protagonist. This elusive and polysemous term has been used to refer to many aspects of demonic and haunting voices.[4] Theorists have traced the perception of uncanniness to a belief in animism, which is to say the belief that inert objects have life. From this belief flows the Freudian notion of the *unheimlich*, in which a familiar object becomes unfamiliar.[5] The Freudian notion of the uncanny helps to explain what makes the voices in *Diable* so unsettling: lovable and alluring beings are represented as apparitions of the demon Béelzébuth. Moreover, the narrative action often reframes recognizable scenes in ways that destabilize the protagonist. For instance, when Biondetta performs music, she takes a familiar scene (a love scene) and makes it unfamiliar (a scene about demonic possession). A Freudian interpretation of the text, however, does not highlight the eighteenth-century influences that made the modern uncanny possible.

Terry Castle argues that the uncanny arises from a confrontation and overcoming of belief in supernatural and animistic ideologies.[6] The uncanny arises when fantastic literature parodies this eighteenth-century theory of life science and transforms it from a scientific intuition, a rational explanation that exceeds the limits of human understanding, into a feeling of uncanniness, a strange sense that familiar objects are no longer governed by rational laws.

We find yet another version of the uncanny in music studies, where scholars have situated its emergence in the late eighteenth century and associated the operatic voice with an uncanny form of subjectivity. As Gary Tomlinson argues, the operatic voice became uncanny around the late eighteenth century, "when supersensible realms and human access to them were reshaped."[7] While "the voice of the Cartesian subject ... pointed beyond itself to a transhuman harmony," the modern voice reveals that "mystery points not out, but inward, toward the center of human knowledge that now encompasses its own supersensible realm. This voice exists, like the modern subject it describes, in a doubling over on itself of empirical and transcendental fields."[8] In *Diable*, we find uncanny voices that fill the gap between the Cartesian subject and the modern voice that Gary Tomlinson analyzes. Given that these analyses define the uncanny in opposition to Cartesian dualism, they do not account for the influence that vitalism and sentimentalism, and by extension theories of embodied sentience, had on the creation of uncanny voices.

The uncanny voice emerges from a rejection of the embodied, physiological voice. To believe in the vitalist voice is to have faith in the body's capacity to externalize through sound its physiological temperament. When Cazotte penned *Diable*, he was a staunch rival of the French *philosophes*. In his correspondence, Cazotte criticized Enlightenment science, including the secular approaches developed by the *philosophes* and the more religiously inflected approaches that married science to a belief in God. Commenting on *Diable*'s literary reception, Cazotte complained that a great scientist of the day—possibly François Rozier, the editor of the *Journal de Physique et d'Histoire naturelle*—had read the *Diable* and believed that Cazotte was well versed in occult sciences.[9] The supernatural and uncanny voices in *Diable* present a direct attack on the beliefs of the *philosophes*. Biondetta's uncanny voice attacks the secular belief in human sensibility, which idealized the moral influence of vocal expressions: the supernatural ones remind the reader that the origin of these secular beliefs, the *philosophes*, have a demonic origin. From this critique of the Enlightenment, we discover a new version of the voice, an uncanny one that is paradoxically created from the vitalist and sentimental forces that it was intended to undermine.

BOTH *DIABLE* and Cazotte had a storied past with occult history.[10] The author was rumored to be a practitioner of the occult arts and had earned a reputation as a prophet by the late 1780s. While he was initiated into a Martinist order around 1777, the Cazotte of the Revolutionary period was careful to present *Diable* as a critique of occult practices.[11] In a 1790 letter, Cazotte linked the emergence of occult orders to his creative inspiration. Specifically mentioning a 1773 Freemasonry Lodge called the "Grand Orient," Cazotte explained, "Je me trouvai à portée d'entendre leur rapsodie, et profitant de leurs contes, dans un instant de gaieté, je fis le *Diable amoureux*, ne me doutant pas que je cassois bien des vitres."[12] (I found myself within earshot of their rhapsody, and taking advantage of their tales in a moment of playfulness, I completed *Le Diable amoureux* without suspecting that I would make waves.) Ever the storyteller, Cazotte in this recollection simplified the messy genesis of *Diable*, which was written in three versions: the 1772 version, with engravings and a musical score; a 1774 version that he recited to friends; and finally the canonical 1776 version, published in a larger collection of stories without the first edition's engravings.[13]

In this postrevolutionary letter, Cazotte forgot (perhaps deliberately) his first version, which, according to his own account, contemporaneous readers found lacking in its "dénouement trop brusque" (too abrupt ending).[14] His postrevolutionary account, however, still expresses something true about the first version: that occult voices (and their rhapsody) performed the role of muse in his creative process. Indeed, a reader of the first version cannot escape the occult's influence on the novel, in which demonic voices cross between the supernatural realm and fictional reality.

Cazotte's 1790 letter not only reveals the importance accorded to occult voices in *Diable* but also brings to light a compelling insight into superstitious beliefs. His tract apparently condemns only occult orders and specifically rails against "all those ramblers ending in–ist," such as the Martinistes, Convulsionnistes, Mesmerists, and Cagliostrotists.[15] Surprisingly, however, this laundry list subsumes under the same heading radically different belief systems and rituals: faith in spirits is grouped with the medical science of magnetism, and Martinist ritual incantations with Cagliostrist's magical spells. Dubbing Freemasonry "the antechamber of the frauds of the human species," Cazotte next discusses the zealotry of eighteenth-century scientific inquiry.[16] Using a natural philosopher turned mystic, Emanuel Swedenborg, as an emblem of enlightened zealotry, Cazotte rhetorically asks whether Swedenborg has become "le plus extravagant des visionnaires" (the most fantastical of false prophets).[17] In so doing, Cazotte connects occult beliefs with the scientific and philosophical inquiries of "leur siècle ... lumineux" (their enlightened ... century).[18]

As Fabienne Moore notes, spiritual and rational poets shared a desire "to search, understand and admire" the secrets of the universes,[19] and their poetic meditations often required a new form of typography, which could "amplify the voice on the page" and "introduce a clear vibration in the text intended to alert readers."[20] Here I return to a thread that starts in the introduction and runs through chapter 4. The use of print to make a character's voice audible (and possibly even reproducible through performance) to the reader. Certain eighteenth-century figures believed that the printed text could become a recording technology for the voice of feeling. In Baculard d'Arnaud's preface to his sentimental drama *Euphémie* (1768), the writer explains that typographical expressions of exuberance such as recurring ellipses convey "l'accent ... du sentiment" (the accent ... of emotion) and animate "le langage de la passion" (the language of passion)[21] While few writers proposed or even imagined a solution to the ephemeral nature of vocal inflection, Baculard d'Arnaud's experiments with typography reflect a trend, which I discussed in chapter 2, of using print to record and re-create vocal inflections.[22] *Diable* is part of this trend. As a printed record of supernatural voices, Cazotte's lesser-known first edition offers invaluable insights into what Brian Kane calls the *techne* of the voice:[23] here I am referring to eighteenth-century experiments intended to record voices in print.

As I discussed in chapter 2 the sentimental text is pedagogical in the sense that it cultivates the reader's ability to feel compassion by inviting him or her to imagine a character's suffering. As part of this pedagogical approach, musical scenes inserted into novels transform a moral lesson into an embodied one, in which the reader shares with the protagonist his lyrical expression of suffering. Chapter 2 analyzed a novelistic expression of this idea in which musical performance moderates the passions and replaces them with moral reflection. In the present chapter, I argue that *Diable* articulates a counterargument to the notion of moral awakening. Specifically, *Diable*'s musical paratext critiques the idea that music represents and awakens different forms of moral consciousness. Far from cultivating our moral consciousness, the human voice poses a grave danger to the Catholic soul. In fact, after publishing both versions of *Diable*, Cazotte explicitly criticized eighteenth-century humanist ideas by grouping them together. He imagined them to be antipodal and even dangerous to Catholic faith, and even attributed the secular and philosophical writings of the *philosophes* to "the work of the Devil."[24]

Cazotte's antiphilosophical argument reverses the outcome of the age of reason. In this view, instead of ridding humanity of superstition, Enlightenment philosophers replaced superstition with a spurious belief in the Promethean power of science. Indeed, Cazotte condemned Enlightenment as a form of superstition and pitted against it a rational form of Catholic faith based on common sense and sound reason. Whereas the popular science of the day shared superstitious tendencies with explicitly occult belief systems, according to Cazotte, religious belief (and specifically Catholic faith) was possible only through reason. We find the seeds of Cazotte's postrevolutionary letters in the 1772 version of *Diable*. As a literary expression of this religious perspective, the 1772 version draws a fine distinction between "rational" characters who believe that life is divinely ordered and "irrational" characters who promote embodied and vocally intoned passions.

In the previous chapters, we encountered versions of the voice that serve as tools of humanistic discovery. The vitalist voices in Diderot's work reveal the different tunings of human temperament. They also translate into language the sensations of the body and the thoughts of the mind. The sentimental voices that I discussed in Rousseau's,

Richardson's, and Baculard d'Arnaud's works serve as moral guides that moderate physical desires and promote social cohesion. They become part of a sonic regime that the protagonists create to regulate emotions. As counterarguments to the vitalist and sentimental voices, uncanny voices exist between the sonic and acousmatic regimes discussed in chapter 2. In *Diable*, the protagonist experiences voices that construct seductive and vulnerable female identities as uncanny because these alluring voices disguise a monstrous physiology. The uncanny voices, moreover, raise epistemological doubts concerning the vitalist and sentimental voices.[25] In vitalism, vocal accents are tuned to, and modulate according to, the tensions within a person's fibrous physiology. In the sentimental scenes that I analyzed in chapter 2, singing serves as a moral exercise that modifies a person's moral fiber, or his emotional disposition and physiology. Uncanny voices, however, undermine the belief that the voice is an audible signature of a person's moral temperament and physiology.

To CONTEXTUALIZE the vitalist voices of chapters 3 and 4, I discussed materialism; in chapters 1 and 2, I related the sentimental voice to the theory of moral hygiene. *Diable*'s voices emerged from a different intellectual context. To appreciate these supernatural voices, we can return to the Ansacq sound event discussed in the introduction. The first explanation for Ansacq's sound event came from an anonymous Burgundian priest who blended science with spirituality. Although he at first ascribed the event to an "effet Physique" (phenomenon of physics) due to the "dispositions de l'air" (arrangement of air), he then shifted to a theological perspective.[26] Citing Saint Paul's letter to the Ephesians, the anonymous writer echoed the apostle's assertion that "L'air est rempli de démons" (air is filled with demons).[27] He also likened the demons to "esprits aëriens" (aerial spirits) and "choses *spirituelles*" (*spiritual* things), calling them "*Princes de ténebres*" (Princes of darkness).[28] According to the anonymous writer, "Dieu permet peut-être la réalité du fait d'Ansacq pour obliger les Philosophes de convenir qu'il y a des esprits aëriens."[29] (God possibly permits the reality of the Ansacq event in order to compel the *philosophe* to admit that aerial spirits exist.)

The anonymous Burgundian priest ended his letter with a seemingly paradoxical request: "J'attends une explication Physique de ce prodige par quelqu'un de ceux qui croyent difficilement les choses *spirituelles*" (italics in original).[30] (I am waiting for a physical explanation of this miracle from someone who has difficulty believing in *spiritual* things.) Although it seems counterintuitive that a devout Catholic priest should have eagerly awaited a purely scientific explanation for a miracle, his faith allowed him to believe that spiritual entities such as demons could influence matter. According to his thaumatological perspective, a scientific explanation would complement his own supernatural explanation, because miracles occur when spiritual beings interact with and influence the material world.

The Burgundian's letter left unspoken a series of theist assumptions that Descartes and his followers explicitly articulated. One assumption involved the interaction between material space and spiritual beings. This notion is clearly implied in Descartes's theory of matter. In 1649, Descartes explained in a letter to Henry More that God could extend power to the material world: "In God and angels and in our mind I understand there to be no extension of substance, but only extension of power. An angel can exercise power now on a greater and now on a lesser part of corporeal substance; but if there were no bodies, I could not conceive of any space with which an angel or God would be coextensive."[31] In other words, spiritual beings do not *occupy* physical space; instead, they harness their power to *transform* material space. Theologians continued to promote this theist position throughout the eighteenth century. The Benedictine scholar Antoine Augustin Calmet explained how angels and demons interacted with the material world in his popular *Dissertations sur les apparitions des anges, des demons et des esprits* (1746). The Jesuit Claude-François Nonnotte similarly espoused a theist perspective in his *Dictionnaire philosophique de la religion* (1772) and included many articles that offered a full-throated defense of theism, or the belief that God continues to intervene in the physical world.

According to Calmet's writings, spiritual entities resided in the air and may even have been made of a similar substance. The aerial location of angels is relevant to discussions of sound generally, and specifically to acousmatic events, because by the early eighteenth century, there was a partial consensus that sound moved through air. Given that aerial particles are involved in sound's propagation, the composition of air could provide explanations for acoustical phenomena. For acousmatic events, air along with its spiritual properties become the origin of a sound that an unknown and unseen agent produces.

To explain unseen sound, natural philosophers with a theistic perspective emphasized air as a medium both for sound's movement and for spiritual involvement with the material world. In 1730, the year of the Ansacq event, Calmet republished his biblical *Dictionnaire historique, critique, chronologique, géographique et littéral de la Bible*, to which he added a definition for air. From a theological perspective, "*Les puissances de l'air* . . . sont les Démons qui exercent principalement leur puissance dans l'air, en y excitant des tempêtes, des vents, des orages."[32] (*The powers of the air* . . . are demons who principally exercise their power in air, by creating storms, winds and thunderstorms [italics in the original].) As Calmet explains, demons have airy bodies that move through the sky and produce meteorological phenomena. Spiritual beings interact with the material world much as the soul does with the human body. For instance, Claude-François Nonnotte's 1772 *Dictionnaire philosophique de la religion* defines miracles as a spiritual process that resembles the operation of the Cartesian soul. In Nonnotte's article on miracles, a fictional *philosophe* squares off with a fictional theologian. In considering how a spiritual being could influence the physical world, the naïve philosopher asks "comment un pur esprit, un démon peut agit sur la matiere, sur les corps" (how a pure spirit or demon can act on matter or a body).[33] The theologian replies, "Cela n'est pas plus difficile, que de concevoir comment notre ame agit sur notre corps, & met en mouvement les fibres, les nerfs, les différentes parties de notre corps. Nous le faisons très-naturellement."[34] (It is no more difficult than to conceive how our soul acts upon our bodies, and sets in motion the fibers, the nerves, the different parts of our body. We do it very naturally.) By comparing the influence of angels and demons on matter to the way our immaterial, spiritual soul interfaces with organic matter, Calmet and Nonnotte extended Cartesian dualism into a two-layered universe, in which spiritual beings could influence, move, and modify objects in the physical world.

The examples of spiritual-material interactions also reimagined Cartesian-style scientific explanations. According to Calmet, angels and demons could move, thicken, and condense air.[35] It may not come as a surprise that the scientific explanations for the Ansacq event were almost identical to Calmet's spiritual explanations. The scientifically minded respondents described how the air had condensed, became thinner, or fermented a variety of aerial and terrestrial particles.[36] These mechanical movements had in turn produced Ansacq's sound event. In light of this theological context, the anonymous Burgundian could plausibly accept the scientific explanation as long as a spiritual entity had caused movement in air particles, which had in turn produced sound.

The responsible party, however, was not solely demons in the air. As the anonymous Burgundian notes, it was in fact God who gave the demons permission to act. Calmet and Nonnotte adopted a similar line of reasoning in their discussions of miracles: angels and demons may only interact with matter if and when God grants them permission. Indeed, divine interference is at the heart of a theist approach to miraculous sound. As the anonymous writer explained, Ansacq's diabolical music was only possible because God allowed aerial spirits to interact with the physical world. God's permission had a persuasive function; the purpose was to convince philosophically minded readers that angels and demons existed.

The theist perspectives of Calmet and Nonnotte reveal that sound could retain a spiritual aura. Even as acoustical science began to uncover the mechanisms of sound, Calmet and Nonnotte held onto a belief in miracles. Their thaumatological contribution incorporated scientific explanations within a theist cosmology. Their perspective, moreover, provides important context for my discussion of the uncanny voices in *Diable*. Certain natural philosophers maintained a fascination with the invisibility of sound, and its invisibility allowed it to straddle materialist and spiritual conceptions of the voice. With his distinction between the materiality of visual phenomena and the spirituality of acousmate, Calmet situated sound in a hybrid position somewhere between the spiritual and physical dimensions. Sound produced in the air could come from demons that inhabit, manipulate, and interact with air particles.

At the same time, sound could be more than a purely mechanical movement of air particles. It could also retain an immaterial, spiritual presence completely detached from matter. Calmet distinguished between mechanisms that produce a visual phenomenon and those that cause an acousmatic event. Although Calmet contended that angels and demons could modify matter to produce visual phenomena, audible miracles were of a different order: "Il ne faut pas s'étonner s'ils peuvent former des corps aëriens, qui seront visibles par l'opacité qu'ils leur donneront. A l'égard des organes nécessaires à ces corps aëriens pour former des sons, & se faire entendre; sans avoir recours à la disposition de la matière, il les faut attribuer entièrement au miracle."[37] (It is not surprising that [souls, angels and demons] may transform into aerial bodies, which will be visible by the opacity which they give to [air particles]. With regard to the organs necessary to form sounds, and to be heard; without having recourse to the disposition of matter, we must attribute them entirely to miracles.) To create illusions, spiritual entities change the material properties of light (reflection, opacity, transparency) because they increase the density of air. Angels and demons, however, are not made of flesh, and so they lack the *organ to form sounds*. As Calmet speculates, angelic choirs and demonic howls require a purely spiritual intervention. It is as if Calmet realizes that spiritual sounds communicate more than just noise. Angels and demons express thought and manipulate a spiritual voice rather than a material instrument.

Diable's first edition articulates a similar thaumatological perspective on sight and sound. The demonic creature Béelzébuth appears out of thin air and performs amazing visual illusions, transforming its own appearance and the décor of its surroundings. The voice, however, enters the novel as an invisible supernatural power that also crosses the barrier between the material and spiritual realms. This characterization of the voice is evident not only in the first edition's plot but also in its fascinating paratext (engravings, a musical score) and editorial elements (italicization), all of which give prominence to the novel's supernatural voices. In particular, the second engraving depicts Dom Alvare reciting a chant in a pentagram, a practice that resembles a cult ritual, much like the rituals of Martinism, in which believers stood in the middle of a protective circle and recited magical words to conjure benevolent spirits (see fig. 6).[38]

For the moment, let us consider the outcome of Alvare's occult ritual. Instead of conjuring a benevolent spirit, Alvare's incantation misfires and brings forth Béelzébuth, a demonic spirit with a well-established

Fig. 6. Alvare's séance scene. Jacques Cazotte, *Le Diable amoureux* (Naples [Paris]: Le Jay, 1772), 14. (Beinecke Rare Book & Manuscript Library, Yale University Library)

lore in Europe. Calmet's *Dictionnaire historique* even references "Béelsébub" in its definition of "Demon." According to Calmet, "Le Prince des Demons est nommé Béelsébub, Sammaël, Asmodée, Bélial, Satan, Dragon, Ange exterminateur, Prince des puissances de l'air."[39] (The Prince of Demons is called Beelzebub, Samael, Asmodeus, Satan, Dragon, exterminating angel, *Prince of the powers of the air* [italics added for emphasis].) Calmet's definition follows a Christian tradition that gives the Devil the alternate name Beelzebub.

During the sixteenth and seventeenth centuries, the malevolent spirit Beelzebub appeared in a number of French possession stories. In 1610, the Dominican witch-hunter Sébastien Michaelis, reporting on the demonic possession of Madeleine Demandols de la Palud, paid particular attention to Madeleine's voice. As Michaelis states, "Beelzebub sortit par la bouche de la fille faisant un bruit comme d'un rot."[40]

(Beelzebub came out of the girl's mouth producing a sound like a belch.) Most famously, in the winter of 1565–66, Beelzebub entered Nicole Obry, the young daughter of a butcher. In accounts of Obry's public exorcism, those present witnessed the effect of the consecrated host on the possessed girl and reported that she "hideusement esgarouillé" (hideously gurgled) and made "horribles & espouentable criz & hurelementz" (horrible and frightening cries and screams).[41] During a later encounter, Obry unleashed "une merueilleusemet horrible voix ... comme trois doigts abbaissant les marches, ouvroyent le vent à trois tuyaux d'Orgues ensemblement sonnans" (a marvelously horrible voice ... like three fingers holding down organ stops).[42] Her voice sounded like "Le cry ou grongnement d'vn gros Pourceau, l'abboy d'vn gros Chien, & le Muglemét d'vn gros Taureau eschauffé" (the snorting of a large pig, the barking of a big dog, and the bellowing of an enraged bull).[43] As Olivia Bloechl shows in her study on early modern exorcism, the signs of demonic possession included a range of vocal utterances that included yells, animal cries, and tawdry singing.[44]

As if borrowing from Beelzebub's rich anecdotal history, the narrator characterizes the demon's voice with similar monstrous and supernatural effects. For example, the preface describes the dark lord's first utterance as "le caverneux *che vuoi*" (the cavernous *what do you want*).[45] The editor then visually translates Béelzébuth's demonic voice through print and illustration. While the italicized print calls attention to the camel's question, the engraving spatially emphasizes "*Che vuoi?*" on a speech scroll located near its center, a prominent position that also dominates Alvare's upside-down incantation. The narrator first draws attention to Béelzébuth's demonic appearance with a description of the camel's "oreilles démesurées" (disproportionately large ears) and gaping mouth.[46] With "un ton assorti au reste de l'apparition" (a tone of voice well-matched to its appearance), the camel responds with a question whose sound terrifies Alvare.[47] It is as if the camel's question visually screams from the page. The narrator complements the visualized roar with a simple sonic description: it was an "effrayant tableau" (frightening image) combined with a "bruit plus effrayant" (more terrifying noise) that "retentissait" (resonated) in his ears.[48] The narrator's choice of words helps portray the "caverneux *che vuoi*" as the space of a "cavernous" mouth, and also the rumbling sound of a deep, hollow bass. As the narrator attests, the rumbling *Che vuoi* shakes the reflective stone surfaces of the Portici vaults.

The narrator's sonic and spatial description re-creates previous accounts of demonic possession. In Jean Boulaese's account of Nicole Obry's possessed voice, Boulaese notes that Obry's "voix sentoit come le muglement d'un gros Taureau eschauffé. La bouche se ouuroit quelques fois (principalement le vingt septiéme de Ianuier, & le second de Feurier) tellement demesuréement, que l'on voyoit fort auant en la gorge" (voice resembled the deep bellowing of an enraged bull. Her mouth opened sometimes [principally January 27th and February 2nd] so excessively that one could see far back into her throat).[49] However, unlike Obry's disproportionately large mouth, the camel's voice performs an expansion beyond measure by engulfing the entire space in sound: "Toutes les voûtes, tous les caveaux des environs retentissent à l'envi du terrible *Che vuoi?*"[50] (All the arches and burial vaults in the vicinity reverberate emulating the terrifying *Che vuoi?*) The camel's surroundings vibrate and resonate as an extension of its voice. *Che vuoi* melds sound, sight, and touch into a combined vocal force that envelops Alvare.

In *Diable*, the camel's voice echoes off the walls of the vaulted room and modifies its sound. In this way, the room replaces the voice box as the instrument. The camel's yawl then transforms its sepulchral surroundings into a cavernous mouth that swallows Alvare whole. Béelzébuth's "terrifying noise" passes through Alvare and troubles his mind: "une multitude de sentimens, d'idées, de réflexions touchent mon cœur, passent dans mon esprit, & font leur impression toutes à la fois."[51] (Many feelings, ideas, and thoughts touch my heart, pass through my mind and simultaneously make their impression.) Béelzébuth's voice even elicits cold sweats, a physical symptom found frequently in descriptions of early modern exorcisms.[52] Similar to the vocal characteristics of demonic possession in exorcism tales that Olivia Bloechl analyzes, *Diable* represents "the presence of a non-rational" and invisible "force"—such as Béelzébuth's demonic voice or Alvare's incantation— "that had power to alter the embodiment and with it the identity of its listeners."[53]

IN *DIABLE*, the voice as an invisible, spiritual force occupies a sphere of occult activities that range from possession to incantation. For instance,

Alvare's incantation breaks an invisible barrier between the natural and supernatural worlds. Moreover, the narrator recalls this moment in the present tense, which conveys a sense of immediacy, increasing the tonal tension. It is at this moment that the narrator focuses on his voice, because by summoning a demonic spirit, his voice performs a magical act: "je prononce l'évocation d'une voix claire & soutenue, & en grossissant le son, j'appelle à trois reprises & à très-courts intervalles, *Béelzébuth*" (italics in original).[54] (I pronounce the incantation with a clear and sustained voice, crescendoing. I call, three times in rapid succession, *Béelzébuth*). Even the invocation, "*Béelzébuth*," has a distinct phonetic (foreign) sound, with its repeated *b*s and its odd consonant marriage of *l* and *z*. Alvare's repetition of this foreign-sounding word adds a chanting quality to his conjuration. Furthermore, the narrator prepares the reader for Alvare's transformative incantation, much as he did with Béelzébuth's roar. This preparation uses multiple textual and narrative techniques and strategies: italicization, narrative description, and finally an illustration, with Alvare's incantation depicted in an upside-down speech scroll.

The engraver positions Alvare's speech scroll in such a way that Béelzébuth is addressed instead of the viewers. The orientation of the scroll also represents a form of magical attraction wherein Alvare's incantation is drawn toward the source of its power, Béelzébuth. When we interpret Alvare's incantation according to the rules governing summoning spells, we discover where Alvare's incantation goes awry. For instance, the theologian Edme-François Mallet explains in the *Encyclopédie* how summoning spells are intended to control demonic spirits: "Dans la *conjuration*, on agit par des prières, par l'invocation des saints, & au nom de Dieu, pour forcer les diables à obéir. Le ministre qui conjure par la fonction sainte qu'il exerce, commande au diable, & l'esprit malin agit alors par pure contrainte: au lieu que dans le sortilège on agit en s'adressant au diable, que l'on suppose répondre favorablement en vertu de quelque pacte fait avec lui, en sorte que le magicien & le diable n'ont entre eux aucune opposition."[55] (With *conjuration*, one acts through prayers, by invoking saints, and in the name of God, in order to force evil spirits [*les diables*] to obey. The clergyman, exercising his sacred duty to conjure, commands the devil—and the malevolent spirit is forced to act. For spells, one acts by addressing oneself to the devil, whom one supposes to answer favorably by virtue of some pact made with him, that the magician and the devil have no opposition between them.) Since the term *diable* could refer not only to the Devil but also to malevolent spirits, demons, and fallen angels, the magician in the article conjures, somewhat facetiously, a lesser demon.

Diable, which represents the Enlightenment as a form of diabolic power, changes the conjurer's role from one of command to one of subservience.[56] His incantation, moreover, does not portray a *sortilège* in which the magician works in concert with the devil. Instead, the text and illustration represent Alvare's invocation as a subordinate style of conjuration, insofar as his speech does not project a commanding tone.

His compromised incantation nevertheless possesses a magical force that unleashes a powerful spiritual substance. The nineteenth-century occult historian Jacques Matter sheds light on Alvare's incantation *Béelzébuth*. Comparing Alvare's ritual to those performed by the eighteenth-century occult order of Martinism, Matter sees the *Béelzébuth* ceremony as "une pneumatologie si piquante" (a very racy pneumatology).[57] Echoing Saint-Martin's belief that certain words possessed supernatural properties, Alvare intones *Béelzébuth* as a magical word. According to Matter's analysis of Martinism, only certain spiritual words—such as *Jésus*—possess such power when a conjurer pronounces them in the correct way. Matter further hypothesizes that humanity has forgotten the correct pronunciation for these words and therefore has lost the ability to unleash their spiritual and magical properties.[58] Matter's emphasis on pronunciation partially explains why Alvare, the narrator, takes note of his inflection. If vocal delivery could influence a spell's outcome, a conjurer's recitation style might intone as much meaning as the recited words.

Speculating on the importance of pronunciation, Matter goes on to propose a theory about the way speech can transform into a substance: "En effet, comment peut-on dire que chaque mot prononcé devient substantiel? Est-ce à dire qu'il en résulte une substance? L'émission de nos idées traduites en mouvements qui frappent l'air y enfante des vibrations, les vibrations produisent des sons, les sons des idées, les idées des sentiments, les sentiments des volitions, les volitions des œuvres, et les œuvres sont les unes des créations, les autres des transformations."[59] (Indeed, how can we say that every spoken word becomes substantial?

Is that to say that the result of speech is substance? The transmission of our ideas translated into movement that hits the air engenders vibrations, which produce sounds, then ideas, then feelings, then volitions, then acts, and the acts are either creations or transformations.) Matter extends a vibrant occult tradition from the eighteenth century and imagines a process in which a voice's sound, vibration, and movement attach to words the speaker's ideas, feelings, and volition.

Matter's second hypothesis is productive for this analysis because it demonstrates how closely occult beliefs could resemble mid-eighteenth-century medical treatises on sensation. From the chief surgeon at the Hôtel–Dieu in Rouen, Claude-Nicolas Le Cat, to the Montpellier-trained doctor Joseph-Louis Roger, scientists published medical treatises that examined the curative properties of music.[60] At the boundary between adherents of supernatural powers and scientists stood the Mesmerists, who believed that music "reinforced" the magnetic "fluid's action on the internal sense."[61] These different perspectives on music show that certain figures located musical and vocal sound in a liminal space between physical vibrations and invisible forces. Together, Matter's two hypotheses uncover the potentially magical forces behind Alvare's ritual incantation: the words and the vocal inflection. Alvare's incantation inhabits a middle ground between these hypotheses. Although only certain words, like *Béelzélbuth*, possess supernatural properties, Alvare's vocal inflection infuses this word with magical power, which modifies his séance's outcome.

But to interpret Alvare's enchantment in relation to Martinist "pneumatology," one must pay close attention to *three* aspects of the incantation: Alvare's words, his vocal inflection, and his state of mind. The author best depicts Alvare's state of mind with the felicitous expression "imagination libertine" (libertine imagination).[62] These two words, intended in the preface as an explanation for Alvare's gullible nature, transform the irreverent, domineering, and womanizing libertine into a fanciful and passionate ingénue. As a libertine novice, Alvare describes the séance as a much-anticipated tryst, a "rendez-vous galant."[63] Using a sentimental and impassioned register, he spouts metaphors of desire ("Il me brûle") and speaks in desperate tones ("j'abandonne," "je mourrois d'impatience").[64] The narrator then represents Alvare's impatient interruptions and dramatic sighs with a preponderance of ellipses, twelve in the span of a page and a half. The sheer number of ellipses transforms this common typographical style—typically associated with sentimental prose—into a comical scene. His incantation parodies the involuntary vocal signs commonly associated with the sentimental voice.

Given that Alvare is performing a Martinist-style incantation and that the pronunciation of magical spells could influence their supernatural outcome, his excessively sentimental style seems inappropriate for a conjurer, who, according to the *Encyclopédie*, is supposed to command spirits. Instead of a calm, firm incantation, Alvare's voice recites "Béelzébuth" with passion, perhaps intoning this word with a heavy staccato that betrays his desire. This incantation would sound more like a proposal of love than a command of servitude. Alvare's tone may partly explain the outcome of his incantation: he conjures the devil in love, and the devil's driving motivation is to seduce Alvare.

While Alvare's voice performs visible tasks (conjuring and later banishing spirits), his thoughts and feelings have a tangible influence on the outcome of his occult performance. Alvare essentially intones a rhetorical style, blending authority with passionate expressions, and thus opens a space in which his incantation, inflected with passion, extends a magical invitation to love.[65] While the above explanation elucidates primarily the narrative consequence of Alvare's impassioned incantation, my attention to Alvare's voice as words, intention, and inflection reveals a counterexample against which to read Clarissa's and Lorezzo's performances, discussed in chapter 2. Whereas Clarissa's and Lorezzo's voices moderate their passions, Alvare's incantation represents a sentimental voice that is passive and dangerously close to sexual desire.

By performing his incantation with this passive, sentimental voice, Alvare prepares the reader for Béelzébuth's subsequent transformation into impassioned female singers. This transformation is at the root of *Diable*'s uncanny vocality. In the sentimental and vitalist vocal types, physiology impacts the accent, timbre, inflection, and turbulence of organs. Accordingly, Alvare has difficulty understanding the incongruence between Biondetta's feminine voices and the demonic yawl of Béelzébuth. Throughout his tale, Alvare describes Béelzébuth's female voices as a cause of his mental disorientation and emotional upheaval.

From his recollection of Fiorentina's "voix ravissante" (ravishing voice) and "chant mélodieux" (melodious song) that entered his heart, to Biondetta's voice, song, and lyrics that "jettent" (throw) him "dans un désordre" (into a disorder), these feminine voices are an invisible force that affects Alvare's physical and mental well-being.[66]

Alvare even describes his experience with Biondetta as an *obsession*. His choice of the word *obsession* (or haunting) refers to a specific type of demonic victimization. According to the *Encyclopédie* (1765), the location of the demon relative to its victim distinguishes haunting (*obsession du démon*) from possession.[67] Whereas possession means that a demon enters a human host, haunting refers to a process of external torment and harassment. Within the demonology of *Diable*, Fiorentina's and Biondetta's songs haunt the listeners. That the demons sing as part of their haunting is not surprising because tawdry songs were a common refrain in exorcism stories of the time.[68] These feminine apparitions, however, sing standard Italian melodies. Fiorentina, as an opera diva, performs a *récitatif obligé*, an Italian operatic number whose melody alternates between the singer and the orchestra. Midway through the story, Biondetta sings folksy Italian tunes. She first *improvises*, a term that retains an Italian inflection in Rousseau's *Dictionnaire de musique* (1768): according to Rousseau, "c'est faire & chanter impromptu des Chansons, Airs & paroles" (to create & to sing impromptu songs, tunes and lyrics).[69] Finally, Biondetta sings a popular *barcarolle*, a genre that Rousseau associated with Italian commoners from Venice: specifically, gondoliers sang *barcarolles* in the Venetian dialect. Informed listeners of the period as Rousseau's or Burney's would not have associated the supernatural with *barcarolles* or Italian improvisations. By singing in Italian, the language that Rousseau recommended to express emotion, Biondetta emulates a specific construction of Rousseau's sentimental voice.

The banquet that follows Alvare's incantation performs a similar function: it reconfigures a French cultural trope that equated Italian music with the natural expression of emotion. Fiorentina's performance gestures toward the artifice and even unnaturalness of Italian singing. She first performs virtuosic vocalizations that highlight the artifice of melismas. What's more, her transformation—from camel to spaniel, to valet, and finally to diva—evokes the monstrous otherness of Italian castrati.[70] Although the French considered castrati to be monstrous, Fiorentina's performance is more than monstrous because her singing destabilizes the vitalist and sentimental belief in the voice as a privileged organ that reveals the singer's physiology, and by extension his or her moral temperament.

The uncanniness of *Diable*'s voices is closest to the terrifying strangeness of the actor's voice in Diderot's *Paradoxe*. As I mentioned in chapter 4, only the actor of genius, a rare individual, disarticulates his embodied sentience and mentally controls his vocal articulations. This rare actor essentially suppresses and controls the articulations of the vitalist voice. As the interlocutor *Le Premier* states, the actor of genius is a terrifying figure because he inhabits a mannequin that he "meut ... d'une manière effrayante" (moves ... in a terrifying manner).[71] *Le Premier* precedes to paint a haunting image: "Il nous épouvante ... ainsi que les enfants s'épouvantent les uns les autres en tenant leurs petits pourpoints courts élevés au-dessus de leur tête, en s'agitant, et en imitant de leur mieux la voix rauque et lugubre d'un fantôme qu'ils contrefont."[72] (He scares us ... much like children terrify each other by holding their doublets over their heads, while acting and imitating as best they can the hoarse, lugubrious voice of a phantom that they impersonate.) The actor of the paradox exists at the threshold of uncanniness: a performer whose impersonation of a fictional character can leave spectators with a sense of terror.

Whereas the performer of genius is able to ignore the impulses of his physiological sensibility, and impersonate the ghostly appearance of a fictional character, the mediocre actor fails to inhabit his role fully. He differs from the performer of genius because he is reactive to his physiological sensibility and thus allows his vitalist voice to interfere with his performance. The mediocre actor is marked by an uneven performance style because his vitalist and sensitive body interrupts his performance.

Among Diderotian characters who share a monstrous form of sensibility, we should not confuse them with Biondetta. For instance, Madame *** in *La Religieuse* possesses a voice whose tones may appear to veil her moral temperament. I would argue, however, that her voice fluctuates according to changes in her fibrous tensions. Throughout her encounters with Suzanne, her voice betrays feelings of desire and frustration through subtle changes in dynamics and sudden losses in articulative control. As I mentioned in chapter 3, the narrator of *La Religieuse* makes note of a sudden drop in volume when the voice of Madame *** suddenly quiets down as it accompanies her pleasurable convulsions.[73]

Both the vitalist and sentimental theories of the voice are inherently bound to the physiological temperament of the human body. For instance, within sentimentalism, and even in Albrecht von Haller's version of vitalism, certain behaviors can generate physiological transformations. We encounter the most full-throated expression of this idea in Johann Caspar Lavater's medical essays, where he defines physiognomy as "*le talent de connoître l'intérieur de l'Homme par son extérieur*" (the talent to know the interior of human beings from their exterior).[74] Among the external signs, Lavater considers whether a voice can reveal a person's moral character: "Il est presqu'impossible qu'un ton déguisé puisse échapper à une oreille délicate, ou s'il m'est permis d'employer cette expression, à une *oreille physiognomique*"[75] (It is nearly impossible for a disguised tone to escape a delicate ear, or if I may be permitted to use the expression, a *physiognomic ear.*) Lavater goes so far as to conclude that "quand mon oreille est frappée de ce ton simple et naturel qui n'appartient qu'à la plus exacte probitée ... mon cœur tresaille de joie, & je suis tenté de m'écrier: *ceci est la voix de Dieu*" (when my ear is struck by that simple and natural tone that only belongs to the most exact probity ... my heart is full of joy, and I am tempted to cry out: *this is the voice of God*).[76] Within this haptic, sensationalist approach to human morality, scientists and moral philosophers observe the voice's capacity to provide the listener with audible evidence of a person's moral fiber.[77]

Uncanny vocality arises when the listener encounters a paradox in his epistemological assumptions. While the voice normally reveals the hidden tuning of a being's physiological temperament, it becomes uncanny when its timbre and accents are out of sync with the speaker/singer's material body or spiritual essence. In *Diable*, this hybrid creature—part demon, part opera singer—possesses an uncanny voice for the protagonist because it is no longer in sync with the demon's hidden essence. To be sure, its soft accents imitate the sound of a sentimental heroine and seem well-suited to Biondetta's appearance. The voice becomes uncanny when Alvare realizes that it serves to veil Biondetta's demonic essence. Indeed, Biondetta's voice is most unsettling to Alvare in a scene in which he gazes at her back through a keyhole as she performs pathos-filled songs (see fig. 7). At this pivotal moment of the narrative, he asks rhetorically, "Peut-on mieux emprunter les traits de la vérité & de la nature?" (Can one better emulate the features of truth and nature?).[78] Alvare's question suggests that Biondetta's expression of passion imitates the "natural" accents of moral sentiment. Since Alvare experiences Biondetta's features of truth and nature primarily as aural sensation, his question suggests confusion about a sentimental voice whose accents should be an audible guarantor of her moral fiber.

Indeed, Biondetta imitates signs of sincere emotion with a pastiche of sentimental topoi—*larmes, mouchoir, emporter, suffoquer* (tears, handkerchief, to get carried away, to suffocate)—that Alvare hears but can only partially see through the keyhole. The narrator also conveys

FIG. 7. Engraving of Biondetta's improvisation. Jacques Cazotte, *Le Diable amoureux* (Paris, 1772), 78. (Beinecke Rare Book & Manuscript Library, Yale University Library)

the sighing sentimentality in her speech with frequent ellipses. With Biondetta's *silence*, her *rêverie*, her back hunched over the harpsichord, her *chant à demi-voix* (song at half-voice), and the muffled closed-door venue, her performance could even be considered a sonic representation of sensibility, with the qualities of softness and inwardness that the musicologist Elisabeth Le Guin associates with musical sensibility in Boccherini's cello music.[79]

Alvare responds to Biondetta's voice in a way that parodies a growing trend among opera listeners of the time. As James Johnson notes, the emergence of a cult of sensibility had begun to influence how people listened to opera: "What later generations might have called hysteria—more humanely called a *bouleversement* by these sensitive spectators—occasionally seized women and the young during performances."[80] Spectators' hearts were subject to any number of violent sensations: "Tears, *sanglots*, crises, palpitations, *bouleversements*, convulsions, and *frissons* of every sort agitated hearts in the 1770s."[81] Like many sensitive listeners of eighteenth-century opera, Alvare experiences a moment of hysteria. As the narrator notes, "Le son de la voix, le chant, le sens des vers, leur tournure, me jette dans un désordre que je ne puis exprimer."[82] (The sound of the voice, the meaning of the verses, their turn of phrases, throw me into a disorder that I cannot describe.) Biondetta's voice, the melody, the lyrics, and her style disorient Alvare to such an extent that he cannot express the full impact of her performance. Alvare's enraptured listening, however, carries him from the aesthetics of sensibility into the supernatural realm of demonic haunting.

Cazotte's novel reveals a porous boundary separating the *frissons* of sensibility from occult practices, a discovery shared by several of his contemporaries. Fanny de Behaurnais's posthumous comedy *Les Illuminés* (1786), for instance, includes a mesmerist character, Cléante, who finds an affinity between sentimental language and mesmerist magnetism: "Ce langage sentimental . . . nous fait communiquer nos pensées d'un pôle à l'autre."[83] (This sentimental language . . . lets us communicate our ideas from one pole to the other.) As a critique of sensibility, Cazotte's novel reveals the true danger of this emotional cult: a misguided trust in the expression and cultivation of passion, especially through the voice.

Diable's vocality sets aural forms of demonic haunting apart from other sensory experiences. In particular, Cazotte portrays music as a spiritually dangerous activity, an idea to which he returned throughout his writing career. Pure music, he suggests, is a physical language of desire. A listener of pure music who ignores his sense of sight puts himself in moral, and even mortal, danger. *Le Lord Impromptu* (1767), a novel by Cazotte set in England, contains another keyhole performance in which two female characters repeatedly listen to the male protagonist as he plays a harpsichord behind a closed door. Like Biondetta's songs, the keyhole performances inspire a dangerous passion in the women.[84] From his novels to his pamphlets, Cazotte's work represents music as an unadulterated language of passion, a language that threatens bachelors with the moral danger of extramarital passion because it ambiguously melds love with seductive passion.[85]

According to Cazotte's pamphlet on opera, French audiences similarly experienced Italian song as a form of pure music. In his *Lettre à une dame* (1753), a contribution to the Querelle des Bouffons, Cazotte mentions that for French audiences, Italian opera delights the ears to the detriment of other senses.[86] In relation to Cazotte's notions of music, *Diable*'s musical score serves as a form of pure music, which the reader is invited to enjoy alongside the protagonist (see fig. 8). Biondetta's performance combines two elements of pure musical delight: first, Italian melodies, and second, their performance through a keyhole. These two elements together intensify the expression of unbridled passion that would be dangerous for almost any listener, but especially for a young, impressionable bachelor like Alvare.

Indeed, Biondetta's songs deeply disturb him in a way that Fiorentina's song does not. Upon hearing Biondetta, Alvare is so troubled that he decides to escape the dulcet tones of the keyhole: "Que je suis heureux de n'avoir connu que d'aujourd'hui le trou de cette serrure, comme je serois venu m'enyvrer, combien j'aurois aidé à me tromper moi-même! Sortons d'ici. Allons sur la Brente, dès demain. Allons-y ce soir."[87] (I am happy to not have known until today this keyhole, since I would have come to intoxicate myself. How much I would have helped myself to this deceit! Let's leave here. Go to la Brente as soon as tomorrow. Let's go tonight.) The narrator reveals the effect of this event as a sensation, for the verb "to know" can mean "to experience" or "to feel."[88]

FIG. 8. Biondetta's "Barcarolle" score. Jacques Cazotte, *Le Diable amoureux* (Paris, 1772), 80. (Beinecke Rare Book & Manuscript Library, Yale University Library)

Given that Alvare sees Biondetta's back through a keyhole, he is free to imagine her appearance. Her voice, muffled as it may be, distorts his perception of Biondetta to such a degree that he almost forgets Biondetta's demonic identity.

His disorientation comes in part from the obscurity through which he hears and sees Biondetta. While her dulcet tones construct the identity of a sentimental heroine, her silhouette provides Alvare enough visual input on which to imagine Biondetta's feminine form. Biondetta's performance subverts the conventions on which music listening developed. As Nina Eidsheim notes, operatic and symphonic listening is a multisensory experience: "The collective inner ear that we have developed to listen to music is tied to the visual/sonic image or situation of statically facing the orchestra while seeing and hearing the instruments in front of us. . . . Thus, this sonic/visual/visceral combination is inseparable from the sound, and sound is experienced within this spatial-relational acoustic package."[89]

Alvare loses his mental faculties in part because he first trusts the sonic/visual/visceral paradigm on which listeners decipher music. In the context of sentimental and vitalist voices, Alvare hears and sees a partially obscured Biondetta and interprets her song as sonic, visual, and haptic proof of her physiological temperament—a vulnerable woman in love. The narrator even alludes to Alvare's loss of reason with the metaphorical usage of *s'enyvrer*. According to the *Encyclopédie* (1765) article on metaphor, *s'enyvrer* means "to make one lose reason."[90] Alvare here loses the intellectual capacity to question the veracity of his senses, which in turn leads to his inability to recognize Biondetta's demonic essence. Biondetta clouds Alvare's reason through vocal and gestural expressions that imitate a sentimental heroine.

In analyzing the aural forms of haunting that Biondetta deploys, I have focused on the way she crafts, through sound and images, a particular version of an Italian sentimental singer. But if we pause for a moment to consider the sentimentality of her voice, we can also identify the influence of English sentimentality. For educated, well-read, Anglophilic French readers, Béelzébuth would have conjured the image of the vilest bachelor of English literature, Lovelace, whose resemblance to Cazotte's demon is twofold. First, Anna Howe refers to Lovelace as "Beelzebub," a moniker Lovelace intercepts while surreptitiously reading Clarissa's correspondence.[91] Second, as I discussed in chapter 2, Lovelace is also known for imitating the vocal and written tones of genuine sentimentality. His performance of pathos and sincerity convinces Clarissa to trust his feigned love over the cruel austerity of her family.

The plot of *Diable* even resembles a waking dream that Lovelace has. As Terry Castle notes, Lovelace's dream involves "the transformation of things into their opposite."[92] Indeed, Lovelace describes a series of events wherein identity becomes fluid and transsexual transformations serve as plot twists that lure Clarissa into a trap of sexual predation. Lovelace's dream climaxes with a series of vocal utterances: "Scenes perpetually shifting; now nothing heard from the Lady, but sighs, groans, exclamations, faintings, dyings—From the gentlemen, but vows, promises, protestations, *disclaimers of purposes pursued*."[93] Here the sentimental voice of Clarissa, described as a series of involuntary sighs and exclamations, conveys ambiguous meaning. Are her vocal expressions a sign of protest, of sexual desire, or of death? With Lovelace, his "vows, promises, [and] protestations" overdetermine the sincerity of his speech and seek to undo the taint of his unscrupulous behavior. If we interpret Lovelace's dream from an anti-British, antisentimental perspective, Lovelace's dream serves as a warning to the reader wherein the sincerity of the sentimental voice suddenly changes its tune and instead expresses the allure of perilous seduction. *Diable*'s plot enacts the waking dream of Lovelace, who, in *Clarissa*, is known as the unchained Beelzebub. Similar to Lovelace's waking dream, Biondetta/Béelzébuth relies on a fluid identity as part of her/their seduction ploy. For instance, when Alvare listens to Biondetta, the protagonist is confronted with an entity whose voice and appearance transform a monstrous being of horror into a beautiful woman in love. As the sentimental Italian version of Béelzébuth, Biondetta incarnates two foreign expressions of desire: the intoxicating charm of the Italian singer and the allure of English sentimentality.

Through its plot and paratext, *Diable* critiques these two foreign incarnations of the sentimental voice, English sentimentality and Italian operatic lyricism, and transforms this voice into an uncanny one. While Biondetta's voice constructs the identity of a touching and powerless victim, underneath her disguise, the narrative implicitly represents her as the embodiment of two monstrous figures: the libertine Lovelace, called Beelzebub, and the Italian castrato.

In fact, Biondetta impersonates a vocal style that for Rousseau was diametrically opposed to the castrato. As Martha Feldman points out, Rousseau criticized in castrati a virtuosic style that lacked "warmth and passion": "it was these very oppositions—sensible/pathetic versus ostentatious/bizarre—that lurked in Rousseau's condemnations of castration and castrati."[94] Feldman also shows that eighteenth-century thinkers, partially inspired by Rousseau's critique of unnaturalness, began to associate the castrati with a lack of warmth or passion whose virtuosic style became an emblem of ancien régime decadence, an "antifamilial," immodest, and "unmanly" personage.[95]

Biondetta's voice becomes uncanny when her pathos-filled singing constructs a sentimental gender identity that disguises her monstrous spiritual essence. The protagonist experiences her uncanny identity when he hears her voice and sees her partially veiled appearance. In this regard, the uncanny in *Diable* subverts the visual/sonic image that listeners rely on to interpret the moral and physiological temperament of a person.

By comparing Biondetta's performance to an earlier one by Fiorentina, we discover that sensory experience influences Alvare's reaction to his demonic antagonist. Both the feminine incarnations of the page Biondetto and the transdimensional Béelzébuth character sing to Alvare. While he panics at Biondetta's voice, he displays more emotional control during Fiorentina's performance. This control is related to the manner in which he observes Fiorentina. Instead of attending to her voice, he watches the Italian diva with rapt yet calm fascination. He notes her manner of dress—"déshabillé étoffé et modeste; un chapeau de voyage et un crêpe très clair sur les yeux" (a modest and elaborate negligee; a travel hat, a very light crepe over the eyes).[96] When she plays the harp, he focuses on the movement of her fingers: "Elle prélude avec une petite main longuette, potelée, tout à la fois blanche et purpurine, dont les doigts insensiblement arrondis par le bout, étaient terminés par un ongle dont la forme et la grâce étaient inconcevable."[97] (She preludes with a long, chubby little hand, at once white and purplish, whose fingers, imperceptibly rounded at the tip, were terminated by a nail whose shape and grace were inconceivable.) Even when she sings, his eyes are drawn to her throat.[98] The narrator distinguishes a dual temporality that bifurcates the sonic/visual image into a present that is visible and an audible performance believed to be in the past. As he visually observes her performance in present tense, he recounts in the past tense an impression of her performance's sonic qualities: "Nous crûmes entendre le plus délicieux concert."[99] (We thought we were hearing the most delicious concert.)

As the narrator listens to Fiorentina, he learns how to decipher her visual illusion. Unlike Biondetta's voice, which disguises her transdimensional origins, Fiorentina's appearance allows Alvare to pierce her veil, which disguises her supernatural monstrosity in a woman's body. Describing Fiorentina's harp performance in terms more visual than aural, Alvare devotes less attention to her voice than to the parts of her body.

To be sure, the erotic imagery partly explains why Fiorentina's seductive pose (possibly straddling a harp) distracts him to the point that he ignores the song. Alvare's fascination with Fiorentina's hands, however, veers into strange descriptions that meld traditional feminine qualities (*petite, potelée, blanche* [small, plump, white]) with slightly more idiosyncratic terms (*longuette, purpurine* [longish, purplish]). This confusing imagery reflects Alvare's wandering mind, which alternates between Fiorentina's hands and his fleeting thoughts of seduction. Tantalized by Fiorentina, he fetishizes parts of her body and even the form and grace of her fingernails.

Through his description, Alvare reconfigures her beauty into a grotesque sensuality. As he focuses on specific body parts—fingernails and throat (*gosier*)—Alvare's erotic imagery becomes desexualized and mildly comical: "La Dame chante. On n'a pas, avec plus de gosier, plus d'âme, plus d'expression: on ne sçauroit rendre plus, en chargeant moins."[100] (The lady sings. One does not have more throat, more soul, more expression: one would not be able to express more, by adding less.) The third-person neutral pronoun *on* reinforces Fiorentina's gender ambiguity. Alvare's description also presents the key to Fiorentina's illusion: her feminine identity is synecdochally constructed. Alvare first observes her hands, fingers, fingernails, throat, and finally eyes. Her clothing (*déshabillé, crêpe*) simultaneously covers and reveals her body, shaping her figure to create a patchwork of feminine attributes.

As long as Alvare directs his attention to the fetishized parts of Fiorentina's body, her appearance draws him in and deceives him. Alvare, however, need only gaze on the whole to dispel the illusion, a process that begins when he observes her eyes: "Le feu de ses regards perçoit à travers le voile: il étoit d'un pénétrant, d'une douceur inconcevable; ces yeux ne m'étoient pas inconnus. Enfin, en assemblant les traits tels que le voile me les laissoit apercevoir, je reconnus dans Fiorentina le fripon de Biondetto."[101] (The fire of her gaze pierced through the veil; it had a penetrating, soft and inconceivable quality; these eyes weren't unfamiliar. Finally, by assembling the traits as the veil allowed me to see them, I recognized in Fiorentina the rascal Biondetto.) Alvare sees beyond the barrier that Fiorentina has constructed and recognizes Béelzébuth's demonic presence beneath Fiorentina's disguise.[102] Even though the veil obscures her body and accentuates her feminine attributes, Alvare reassembles her parts in his mind's eye and, in so doing, recognizes the page Biondetto. This brief moment of recognition follows a pattern that is threaded throughout *Diable*. Whenever Biondetta's uncanny vocality is disregarded, Alvare attains a level of mental and visual acuity that allows him to break through the beguiling devil's illusions and see them laid bare in a transdimensional form.

THE UNCANNY voice in *Diable* reimagines vitalist and sentimental voices. The vitalist, sentimental, and uncanny voices all express sensations, passions, and emotions, and they all do so in ways that modify the identities and relationships of the vocalizing and listening subjects. The vitalist voice reveals to the listening subject the hidden temperament of the vocalizing subject. The sentimental voice constructs a social identity for the vocalizing subject and guides that subject into a morally acceptable gender role. With the uncanny voice, the vocalizing subject constructs a sentimental identity that disguises his/her moral fiber. The uncanny voice thus departs from the previous versions of the voice because it diverts the listening subject away from human discovery. Instead, the uncanny voice is out of sync with the speaker or singer's internal essence and, as such, causes the listener to feel uneasy about the speaker or singer's identity. In chapters 1 through 4, the voice offered insights into consciousness, morality, and sociability. The uncanny voice, however, subverts the listener's expectations. It drives the listener to search for an object that exists only as invisible, intangible, and immaterial sound. In other words, the uncanny voice is not socially useful, as the other voices are; it offers only unhealthy temptation.

Finally, the voices of *Diable* are uncanny because they unravel the connection between vocal physiology and the sound of the voice. In chapters 1 and 2, sentimental voices were organs through which it was possible to modify and improve a person's mental and emotional wellbeing. In chapters 3 and 4, we considered the vitalist voice as an audible fingerprint of a person's physiological temperament. By hearing a person's voice, the listener could judge his or her emotional and mental state. In both versions of the voice, the connection between the body and the voice remained intact. In chapter 5, however, we have seen that the uncanny voice disarticulates the sound of the voice and a person's physiological temperament, and so causes the listener to doubt phenomenal knowledge.

Although literary scholars such as Todorov have often attributed the importance of *Diable* to its representation of phenomenal doubt, I consider this doubt to be the consequence of a deeper issue connected to *Diable*'s critique of Enlightenment philosophy. In *Diable*, uncanny voices parody the forces that vitalist thinkers attributed to all matter: aversion and desire. Indeed, we encounter these dual forces in the figure of Béelzébuth/Biondetta. Below the surface of *Diable*'s uncanny voices, we can still hear the accents of vitalism. The origin of these vitalist forces, however, shifts between the first and the final editions. In the first edition, the protagonist feels the forces of vitalism personified in the haunting figure of Biondetta/Béelzébuth. In the canonical version, the protagonist is left thinking that he may have dreamed this horrifyingly seductive tale. The uncanny voices in the final version of *Diable*, then, sublimate the material forces of vitalism, desire, and aversion into imaginary forces of the listening subjects' mind. In the epilogue, we will consider the legacy of this approach to the uncanny in which a female singer's voice arouses in a male listener the conflicting sensations of desire and aversion.

Epilogue
Talking Heads

♪

In 1779, the Académie impériale de Saint-Petersbourg opened a competition to create a mechanical reproduction of the human voice. Among the entrants was a French machinist, Abbé Mical. According to French scientists and journalists of the time, his machine, the *Têtes parlantes*, was more impressive than the winning entry because Mical's mechanical heads literally spoke. The *Têtes parlantes*, consisting of two heads set above bellows and artificial glottises, approximated vocal sounds (see fig. 9).[1]

In the fall of 1783, Mical granted access to members of the Académie royale des sciences, who wrote a report on the machine's value to science. The anatomist Félix Vicq d'Azyr, who later penned a treatise on the voice, wrote a positive review.[2] For Vicq d'Azyr, the value of Mical's invention lay in its capacity to bring to light the mechanism of the voice.

Despite this report, the Académie royale des sciences members did not purchase Mical's invention. To recoup the cost of his work, Mical decided to display it to a paying public, beginning on April 12, 1784. According to an advertisement in the *Journal de Paris*, Parisians could see and listen to his mechanical voices at "rue de Marivaux, près de la Comédie Italienne, vis-à-vis l'entrée de la Reine, ouvert au Public tous les jours, excepté le Mercredi & le Samedi, depuis cinq heures après-midi jusqu'à huit" (Marivaux Street, next to the *Comédie Italienne*, across from the Queen's entrance, open to the Public every day except Wednesdays & Saturdays, from 5 in the afternoon until 8).[3] In other words, the *Têtes parlantes*, displayed near the theater, lost its scientific gravitas and became a sideshow curiosity.

At these séances, the audience heard the *Têtes parlantes* perform a dialogue in praise of Louis XVI. Voice one would begin by saying, "Le Roi donne la Paix à l'Europe" (The King gives peace to Europe), to

FIG. 9. *Têtes parlantes*, anonymous, 1784. Michel Hennin Collection, vol. 115. (Bibliothèque nationale de France, département Estampes et photographie, https://gallica.bnf.fr/ark:/12148/btv1b8410437r)

which the second voice would reply, "La Paix fait le Bonheur des Peuples" (Peace is the happiness of the people).[4] The first voice would then conclude with the following statements: "Et la Paix couronne le Roi de gloire ... O Roi adorable, Pere de vos Peuples, leur bonheur fait voir à l'Europe la gloire de votre Trône."[5] (And peace crowns the King with glory ... O King worthy of adoration, father of your people, their goodness shows Europe the glory of your throne.)

The public reception was mixed—in part because Mical's mechanical voices did not sound human enough. A review in the *Journal* *de Paris*, published on April 11, described the voice as "sur-humaine" (superhuman) and consequently not an "organe flatteur" (agreeable organ).[6] A month later, the anonymous reviewer, who took the pseudonym Comte de ***, enumerated the ways Mical's voices disappointed a public composed of "simples Curieux" (naïve spectators).[7] According to reviews in the *Journal de Paris* and the *Mercure de France*, its timbre was "désagréable" (disagreeable), "rauque" (hoarse), "âpre" (raspy), and "sauvage" (feral).[8]

In the same *Journal* article, Le Comte de *** explained how the "gosier d'airain" (brass throat) enunciated vowels and consonants in a confused jumble of sound.[9] Its imperfect articulation, unlike a human voice, was followed by "[une] vibration, [un] retentissement, [un] tintement qui nuit à la voyelle suivante, en occupant l'oreille de ce son prolongé" (a vibration, a resonance, a ringing that interferes with the next vowel, by occupying the ear with this prolonged sound).[10] The resonance of Mical's mechanical voice interfered with clear enunciation: "En général il règne sur tout le langage de ces Automates un bourdonnement qui enveloppe & qui voile leur articulation."[11] (Generally, a buzz, which envelops and covers their articulation, reigns over all the language of these Automata.) The artificial voices were superhuman because the metallic buzzing overshadowed the phrases they spoke. The April 11 reviewer compared this prolonged, imperfect articulation to that of a "muet qui commence à prononcer, qui n'a point encore la liberté de l'articulation & l'habitude de l'inflexion" (mute who begins to pronounce, who does not yet have the natural disposition for articulation, nor practice with vocal inflection).[12] In the account of the April 11 reviewer, the voice is not mechanical and superhuman but rather imperfect in the ears of ableist spectators.

While the sound of the voice disappointed naïve spectators, the Comte de *** also presented the opinion of a second public of *connoisseurs*, who expected Mical's *Têtes parlantes* to function like a "clavier général de la langue" (general harpsichord of language).[13] This concept gained traction among other reviewers. For instance, the journalist, writer, and translator Antoine Rivarol explained in detail how such a language keyboard would work. According to Rivarol, Mical's *Têtes parlantes* could include two keyboards, one for prosody and the other for "tous les *sons* et tous les *tons* de la langue française" (every *sound* and every *tone* of the French language).[14] Rivarol dreamed of a day when foreigners could perform Voltaire's *La Henriade* at Mical's keyboard. He imagined Mical's invention as a method for performing language, similar to the way one performs an opera at the harpsichord.[15] In a letter on Mical's invention, Rivarol even speculated that the *Têtes parlantes* could give voice to those deprived of speech.[16] With this comment, which may have been made in response to the negative press cited above, Rivarol reenvisioned the less than human aspect of Mical's voice as a tool to benefit humanity.

Rivarol includes Mical's *Têtes parlantes* among the long list of French accomplishments that he cites as proof of the French language's global dominance. Specifically tracing the rise of French intellectual prestige across the European continent and throughout the world, Rivarol lists famous works of the period, including Montesquieu's *L'Esprit des lois*, Voltaire's prodigious corpus, Diderot and D'Alembert's *Encyclopédie*, and finally Abbé Raynal's *Histoire des deux Indes*. Rivarol claims to elevate the status of French language because it serves as a repository for the immortal patrimony of famous intellectuals:[17] "Les grands écrivains ont tout fait. Si la France cessoit d'en produire, la langue de Racine et de Voltaire deviendroit une langue morte."[18] (Great writers have done everything. If France ceased to produce them, the language of Racine and of Voltaire would become a dead language.) Rivarol situates the source of a language's genius first in its writers and then proposes that Mical's invention can preserve more than merely its words. Unlike ancient languages, which survive only in written form, Mical's *Têtes parlantes* can record for posterity the sound of the French language. Rivarol even compares the *Têtes parlantes* to Gutenberg's invention: "On peut dire que si les Allemands ont inventé l'imprimerie des caractères, un Français a trouvé celle des sons."[19] (It may be said that if the Germans invented the printing of characters, a Frenchman found that of sounds.)

The results of Mical's experiment, however, fell short of its promise. As the Comte de *** explained, the *connoisseurs* group, who may have been a set of intellectuals that included members of the Académie, were disappointed with Mical's invention because it failed to deliver the "general harpsichord of language."[20] In an article in the *Mercure de France* by the writer Jacques Mallet du Pan, the harpsichord emerges again as a model for the voice. Here it is proposed that unlike the harpsichord evoked in Diderot, which served as a model for his early *vitalist* voice that revealed the tensions beneath human consciousness, Mical's harpsichord of language could marry vocal sounds with linguistic expression.

In this article, Mallet du Pan touches on two significant issues, one involving the intellectual response and the other the popular reaction to Mical's *Têtes parlantes*. Although he praises the genius of this invention, Mallet explains that the vocal execution in the *Têtes parlantes* lacks the panache that Parisians seek in their entertainment. Instead of fully evaluating the scientific import of the *Têtes parlantes*, Mallet du Pan criticizes it for its lack of spectacular effects. He also articulates why the lack of intonation caused spectators to undervalue Mical's invention: in re-creating the voice, the organ of human sentience, Mical's automata attempted to animate inert matter. As Mallet explains: "L'extrême des efforts de l'art paroît donc se réduire à organiser la matière de manière à en tirer des sons articulés. Cette faculté réservée, ainsi que le rire, à l'espèce humaine, résultante d'une construction d'organes très-compliqués & très-délicats, peut cependant être transmises à des corps inanimés, il s'agit de les transformer eux-mêmes en instrument vocal."[21] (The extreme efforts of [this] art thus seem to be reduced to organizing matter so as to produce articulated sounds. This ability, along with that of laughter, restricted to the human species, resulting from a construction of very complicated and delicate organs, can, however, be transmitted to inanimate bodies, and it is a question of re-fashioning them into a vocal instrument.) With this explanation, Mallet elevated the standards by which one should evaluate a mechanical voice. It was not enough that Mical's invention could approximate phrases. A successful artificial voice should also produce the sentient sounds of human existence, including that of laughter. Evaluated according to this lofty goal, Mical's bronze voices fell well short of the target. "Il nous est impossible," Mallet acknowledges, "d'animaliser la matière; nos forces sont réduites à lui faire imiter les mouvements extérieurs des êtres sensibles & intelligens: le sentiment ni la pensée ne sortiront jamais des ateliers du Mécanicien; c'est le *feu créateur*, aucun Prométhée ne le dérobera."[22] (It is impossible for us to animalize [i.e., animate] matter; our forces are reduced to imitating the external motions of sentient and intelligent beings; neither sentiment nor thought will ever come out of the Mechanic's workshops; it is the *creational fire*, no Prometheus will steal it.) In describing a mechanical voice as an attempt to "animalize matter," Mallet evokes the fascination with vitalism to which Diderot contributed. In other words, Mical's voice would have been of great interest if it had managed to transform a mechanical voice into a vitalist one—an animated voice whose accents imitated the human voice.

While Mical's automata could not "animalize" matter, it did accomplish what the natural philosophers Denis Dodart, Antoine Ferrein, and François David Hérissant had declined or failed to do: it approximated the mechanics of vocal physiology. To return to the 1730 Ansacq sound event described in this book's introduction, the natural philosophers who responded to the curé Ptoncour's article attempted to explain the haunting acousmatic voices heard in Ansacq by incorporating the phenomenon into a mechanical understanding of acoustics. Half a century later, this scientific project—of providing a scientific and mechanical explanation for the mystery of speech—reached a conclusion with Mical's invention. The *Têtes parlantes* brought into being a voice that was mechanical and programmatic.

Indeed, the predictable, mechanical qualities of Mical's invention, which at the time were constructed and programmed to celebrate the French monarch, later became an emblem of the pro forma—and programmatic—role of the constitutional monarch. After the revolution, the national assembly member Nicolas de Condorcet cited Mical's *Têtes parlantes* in his "Lettre d'un jeune mécanicien" (1791) as a model for replacing the flesh-and-blood king with an unfeeling and unthinking automaton that could perform the vacuous rituals of a constitutional monarchy.[23] Mical's creation, intended to praise the king through its mastery of nature, came to signify an empty system divorced from a supernatural power. As Mallet explains, Mical's invention, like its inventor, laid bare the mystery of speech for all to decipher: "Puis l'inventeur est sans emphase comme sa machine sans mystère: les ressorts sont à découvert: On voit un assemblage mécanique qui ne laisse rien à dire à l'imagination."[24] (Then the inventor is without guile, like his machine without mystery: the springs are uncovered: We see a mechanical assembly that leaves nothing for the imagination to contribute.) Once the mechanical voice became a practical reality, its prosaic form left the Parisian public uninterested.

Why did Mical's bronze voices fail to captivate the ears of 1784 Paris? A central problem, according to Mallet, was that Abbé Mical lacked a flair for show business: "Sa candeur & sa modestie ont nui à ses succès. Ce n'étoit pas le tout d'être Mécanicien habile, il falloit encore être charlatan audacieux."[25] (His candor and modesty have detracted from his success. It was not enough be a skillful machinist, he still needed to be a daring charlatan.) Mallet suspected that Mical's automata only half-interested Parisians because of their paradoxical love for the *merveilleux*. In Mallet's view, this love was a veritable "maladie d'un siècle où l'on prétend ne plus croire au merveilleux" (sickness of a century when people pretend to believe no longer in the supernatural).[26] While Mical lost part of his audience because he did not completely animate the mechanisms of the voice, his automata's "âpre" (raspy) and "sauvage" (feral) tone also contributed to the audience's tepid response. Its rough timbre merely "surprised" the ear instead of pleasing it.[27] An anonymous observer, whom Mallet cites, asks why Mical's voices do not produce "les sons harmonieux d'une Cantatrice" (the harmonious sounds of a diva) or why "la voix humaine ... sort de ces lèvres colossales sur lesquelles nous ne voyons ni les grâces ni le coloris de l'expression" (the human voice ... does not leave those colossal lips on which we see neither the charm, nor the color of expression).[28] It is revealing that this observer brings up the diva's voice in the context of mechanical sound reproduction. The diva's voice emerges in Mallet's review as a harmonious, delightful sound whose accents could transform Mical's invention into an alluring attraction for Parisian audiences.

Beneath the surface of Mallet's review, we see traces of different versions of eighteenth-century voices. Mallet identifies the mechanical voice in Mical's bronze organs, and he even speculates that Diderot, who "désiroit, dans ses Opuscules Mathématiques, une machine sur laquelle on pût jouer un Sermon comme une pièce de musique ... ne s'attendoit guères [sic] à voir ce souhait réalisé de son vivant" (desired, in his mathematical opuscules, a machine on which one could play a sermon like a piece of music ... never expected his wish to be realized during his lifetime).[29] In Mallet's review, Mical's success is cast as an achievement that a leader of the Enlightenment would celebrate. In this way, Mical realized one of the goals of the period: to uncover the hidden mechanisms of the voice.

Furthermore, when Mallet raises the possibility of animalizing matter, he gestures to the vitalist voices that I explored in chapters 3 and 4. Collectively, these vitalist voices lead to a material understanding of human sentience in which the silent parts of the body either have a voice or are forced to talk. In other words, the vitalist voice animalizes our bodily organs and allows them to express their sentience through sound.

The reception of Mical's invention is emblematic of my study of the voice in that the reviewers evaluated the invention in relation to its ability to reproduce the varied tones, accents, and sounds of human sentience. Throughout each chapter, I have investigated how writers incorporated scientific, medical, and acoustical theories into their literary representations of the voice. In so doing, I have argued that the vitalist and sentimental voices emerged out of and in opposition to a mechanical, rational understanding of the voice. I have paused on Mallet's review because what he found lacking in Mical's voices echoes a similar critique proposed by Diderot and Rousseau. According to this critique, the purely mechanical understanding of the voice, forwarded by scientists such as Ferrein and Hérissant, failed to account for the vitalist sounds or sentimental accents that the human voice could produce.

Despite these differences, the authors of the mechanical, vitalist, and sentimental voices shared a goal: to explain the mystery of human expression. The mechanical voices of Dodart, Ferrein, and, finally, Mical follow a path toward an anatomical human voice. The vitalist and sentimental voices in turn transform this voice into an object of discovery—a discovery not about human anatomy but about human temperament and morality. With Diderot's *vitalist* voices, studied in chapters 3 and 4, we saw how the voice translates a person's unique temperament into a vitalist sound. Chapters 1 and 2 investigate how vocal sounds produce sentimental accents. Across these three versions of the voice, writers investigate how different voices produce intelligible sounds.

Mallet's critique is revealing because it presages a turn toward the uncanny voice. To represent uncanny and spectacular sounds, Mallet proposes an alternative talking head that would produce an alluring diva's voice, which would "animalize" matter and elicit desire in the listener.

This move from vitalism to the uncanny is crucial because it transforms the voice once again: from an object of discovery, it becomes one of desire. The diva robot differs from the voices described above because it transforms inanimate matter into a seductive being. Its beautiful accents baffle the listener's senses and give him a false perception of the singer. This hybrid voice—part diva, part machine—echoes the uncanny voice that I analyzed in chapter 5. The uncanny voice differs from mechanical, vitalist, and sentimental voices because it both seduces the listener and distracts him from discovering the voice's identity. With Cazotte's *Diable amoureux*, vocal oddness is still grounded in the voice as a flesh-and-blood organ; the voice of the demon Béelzébuth rumbles beneath the dulcet tones of Biondetta. However, in Mallet du Pan's review, we encounter the uncanny voice as a manufactured simulacrum.

The suggestion in Mallet's review—that a mechanical voice should sound like a diva—is prescient because French writers soon began to depict uncanny female voices. Instead of describing female voices as flesh-and-blood organs, many of these writers began to allude to a manufactured simulacrum of a female voice. Among the many fictional singers in nineteenth-century French literature, three—Zambinella in Balzac's *Sarrasine* (1830), Halady in Villiers de l'Isle-Adam's *L'Ève future* (1886), and La Stila in Jules Verne's *Le Château des Carpathes* (1892)—evoke and develop the uncanny voice encountered in Cazotte's *Le Diable amoureux*. Across these three examples, we encounter the same essential story: a bachelor falls in love with a simulacrum of feminine beauty. The simulated voice constructs a female identity whose seductive accent masks the embodied condition of the singer: namely, the castrato voice of Zambinella, the android voice of Halady, and the phonographic voice of La Stila. Representing a fetishized Platonic ideal of feminine beauty, these singers star in a modern version of the Pygmalion myth wherein men fashion or imagine a feminine ideal in part because the feminine-sounding voice becomes an incorporeal metonymy of beauty's essence and mechanical vitality.

The original Pygmalion is not uncanny but merely a supernatural creation whose physical appearance conforms to the physiological constraints of the human body. In contrast, the nineteenth-century versions of Pygmalion are uncanny because their voices construct identities that disguise their physiological or technological temperaments. This hidden, transcendental identity does not preclude a post-Kantian interpretation of these nineteenth-century voices. To be sure, they represent the construction of a modern subject that emerges at the nexus of a transcendental and empirical understanding of the voice. Nevertheless, these modern voices reconfigure and parody the limited sentience of vitalist bodies who pass between the opposing forces of aversion and desire. This is not to say that aversion and desire are exclusively a figure of vitalism. Rather, the uncanny voice meets the vitalist at the intersection of this duality.

With uncanny voices, they also configure the sentimental gender dynamic of passion and desire. Their voices elicit in male listeners an intense desire for physical contact. Once the male protagonists attempt to consummate their desire, however, they experience a strong aversion. From the perspective of these male protagonists, the material manifestations of the singers are not capable of satisfying male desire.

With this brief overview of the rise of uncanny voices in the nineteenth century, I return to the notion of "voices from beyond." The uncanny voice brings new meaning to "voices from beyond." The sentimental and vitalist voices are *from beyond* because they exist outside a mechanical understanding of the body. The vitalist voices arise from the invisible life force that animates matter, the sentimental from the circulation and exchange of emotion. The uncanny voice, however, is *from beyond* because its intangible beauty becomes an ephemeral object of desire. It is a voice that the listener attempts to capture, master, and record, but without success. It elicits desire but is beyond the listener's control. It is a voice that is neither constrained by the human body nor tethered to material existence.

In tracing different versions of the voice, I have argued that writers theorized the voice through textual strategies that represented the voice as both a physiological organ and a sound. Previous scholarship has distinguished between physiological studies of the voice and reproductions of the voice:[30] while physiological studies analyze vocal sound through anatomy, reproductions of the voice eliminate the effects of vocal anatomy on acoustical production. By investigating premechanical forms of recording, specifically print technologies and literary genres, I show that reproductions of the voice do not necessarily divorce vocal sound from its anatomy. Indeed, the writers at the center of this study represented the voice as both an embodied organ and a vocal accent. I also demonstrate that it was not reproduction alone that led to the disarticulation of vocal sound and anatomy. Although mechanical reproduction certainly contributed to the separation of anatomy from sound, the advent of uncanny voices in literary texts disarticulated vocal sound from physiology long before the introduction of phonographs.

By examining interactions across a variety of texts—imprints of vocal physiology, literary texts, and philosophical essays—I have shown that the distinction between representations of vocal sound and studies of vocal physiology has a history. The works that I analyzed attempted to preserve, adapt, and invent powers of the voice through a dynamic interaction that crisscrosses print technologies, literary genres, and readers' reenactments. In this regard, these texts do more than represent the voice. Those representing sentimental and vitalist voices ask the reader to conceive of vocal expression as an embodied action whose sounds are intimately connected to human physiology and moral sentiment. By separating vocal sound from its physiology, the uncanny voice subverts these paradigms and examines the unknowable, immaterial qualities of the voice. Well before the advent of the phonographic reproduction of the voice, French literary works were investigating—through textual representations—paradigms that understood vocal sound either as an extension of the material, physiological forces that animate the voice or as a confirmation of its ethereal, uncanny qualities.

NOTES

Introduction

1. Louis de Cahusac, "Chant," in *Encyclopédie, ou dictionnaire raisonné des sciences, des arts et des métiers, etc.*, ed. Denis Diderot and Jean le Rond d'Alembert (Chicago: University of Chicago: ARTFL Encyclopédie Project [Autumn 2017 Edition], ed. Robert Morrissey and Glenn Roe), 3:141, http://encyclopedie.uchicago.edu.dartmouth.idm.oclc.org/.
2. Claude Perrault, *Oeuvres diverses de physique et de méchanique de MM C. & P. Perrault, [. . .] divisées en 2 volumes [. . .]*, vol. 1 (Leiden: chez Pierre Van der Aa, 1721), 397.
3. Antoine Ferrein, "De la formation de la voix de l'homme," *Histoire de l'Académie royale des sciences* (Paris: De l'Imprimerie royale, 1741), 417.
4. François David Hérissant, "Recherches sur les organes de la voix des quadrupedes, et de celle des oiseaux," in *Histoire de l'Académie royale des sciences* (Paris: De l'Imprimerie royale, 1753), 279–95.
5. Leigh Eric Schmidt, *Hearing Things: Religion, Illusion, and the American Enlightenment* (Cambridge, MA: Harvard University Press, 2000), 8.
6. David Appelbaum, *Voice* (Albany: State University of New York Press, 1990), 6.
7. Downing A. Thomas, *Music and the Origins of Language: Theories from the French Enlightenment* (Cambridge: Cambridge University Press, 1995); Tili Boon Cuillé, *Narrative Interludes: Musical Tableaux in Eighteenth-Century French Texts* (Toronto: University of Toronto Press, 2006).
8. Thomas, *Music and the Origins of Language*, 85–89.
9. Cuillé, *Narrative Interludes*, 5–6.
10. Martha Feldman, "The Interstitial Voice: An Opening," in "Colloquy: Why Voice Now?," *Journal of the American Musicological Society* 68, no. 3 (2015): 653–59, https://doi.org/10.1525/jams.2015.68.3.653.
11. See Jacques Derrida, *De la grammatologie* (Paris: Minuit, 1967); Philippe Lacoue-Labarthe, "L'Echo du sujet," in *Le sujet de la philosophie: (typographies 1)* (Paris: Aubier-Flammarion, 1979), 217–303; Michel Poizat, *L'opéra ou Le cri de l'ange: Essai sur la jouissance de l'amateur d'opéra* (Paris: Métailié, 2001); Mladen Dolar, *A Voice and Nothing More* (Cambridge, MA: MIT Press, 2006); Adriana Cavarero, *For More Than One Voice: Toward a*

Philosophy of Vocal Expression, trans. Paul Kottman (Stanford, CA: Stanford University Press, 2005); and Michel Chion, *The Voice in Cinema*, trans. Claudia Gorbman (New York: Columbia University Press, 1999).

12. Roland Barthes, "Le grain de la voix," *Musique en jeu* 9 (1972): 57–63.
13. Naomi Adele André, *Voicing Gender: Castrati, Travesti, and the Second Woman in Early-Nineteenth-Century Italian Opera* (Bloomington: Indiana University Press, 2006); Katherine Bergeron, *Voice Lessons: French Mélodie in the Belle Epoque* (Oxford: Oxford University Press, 2010); Steven Connor, *Dumbstruck: A Cultural History of Ventriloquism* (Oxford: Oxford University Press, 2000); Feldman, "The Interstitial Voice"; Martha Feldman, *The Castrato: Reflections on Natures and Kinds* (Berkeley: University of California Press, 2015); Aaron A. Fox, *Real Country: Music and Language in Working-Class Culture* (Durham, NC: Duke University Press, 2004); Nicholas Harkness, *Songs of Seoul: An Ethnography of Voice and Voicing in Christian South Korea* (Berkeley: University of California Press, 2014); Steven Rings, "Analyzing the Popular Singing Voice: Sense and Surplus," in "Colloquy: Why Voice Now?," *Journal of the American Musicological Society* 68, no. 3 (2015): 667.
14. Nina Sun Eidsheim, *Sensing Sound: Singing and Listening as Vibrational Practice* (Durham, NC: Duke University Press, 2015), 139, http://libcat.dartmouth.edu/record=b6280719~S1.
15. Eidsheim, *Sensing Sound*, 139.
16. This "howling gibberish" was reported as "jargon clapissant." I am assuming this is a typo and should be "jargon glapissant." Abbé Treüillot de Ptoncour, "Lettre de M. Treüillot de Ptoncour, curé d'Ansacq, à Madame la Princesse de Conty, troisième Doüairiere, & relation d'un phénomene très extraordinaire, &c.," *Mercure de France*, vol. 2, December 1730, 2813.
17. Treüillot de Ptoncour, "Lettre de M. Treüillot de Ptoncour," 2820.
18. Treüillot de Ptoncour, "Lettre de M. Treüillot de Ptoncour," 2815.
19. Treüillot de Ptoncour, "Lettre de M. Treüillot de Ptoncour," 2819.
20. Treüillot de Ptoncour, "Lettre de M. Treüillot de Ptoncour," 2808.
21. Treüillot de Ptoncour, "Lettre de M. Treüillot de Ptoncour," 2831.
22. Treüillot de Ptoncour, "Lettre de M. Treüillot de Ptoncour," 2832.
23. Treüillot de Ptoncour, "Lettre de M. Treüillot de Ptoncour," 2832.
24. For a historical discussion of acousmatic sound, see Brian Kane, "The Baptism of the Acousmate," in *Sound Unseen: Acousmatic Sound in Theory and Practice* (New York: Oxford University Press, 2014), 73–94.
25. "Lettre sur les bruits aëriens entendus près le village d'Ansacq, Écrite de Paris ce 15 février 1731," *Mercure de France*, March 1731, 448.

26. "Lettre sur les bruits aëriens entendus près le village d'Ansacq," 450–53.
27. "Extrait d'une lettre Écrite de Bourgogne à M. D. L. R. Le 4 février 1731, contenant quelques reflexions sur l'Akousmate d'Ansacq, dont il est parlé dans le second volume du Mercure de décembre dernier," *Mercure de France*, February 1731, 333–37.
28. See Laloüat de Solaines, "Lettre de M. Laloüat de Soulaines, écrite à M. L. B. C. D. au sujet de l'Akousmate d'Ansacq, et d'un autre pareil dont il a été le témoin," *Mercure de France*, vol. 2, June 1731, 1516–31; and "Réfléxions sur l'explication physique, donnée Par M. Capperon, ancien doyen de S. Maixent, de l'Akousmate d'Ansacq, inserée dans le Mercure de France, du Mois d'aoust 1731," *Mercure de France*, November 1731, 2572–80. See also Nicolas Capperon, "Explication physique des bruits entendus en l'air dans la paroisse d'Ansacq, Diocèse de Beauvais, dont il est parlé dans le second volume du Mercure de France du mois de décembre 1730. Par M. Capperon, Ancien Doyen de Saint Maxent," *Mercure de France*, August 1731, 1841–54.
29. Treüillot de Ptoncour, "Lettre de M. Treüillot de Ptoncour," 2828–32.
30. Downing A. Thomas, *Music and the Origins of Language: Theories from the French Enlightenment* (Cambridge: Cambridge University Press, 1995), 82–142; Jean Starobinski, *Jean-Jacques Rousseau: La transparence et l'obstacle: Suivi de Sept essais sur Rousseau* (Paris: Gallimard, 1971), 356–79.
31. Derrida, *De la grammatologie*.
32. Diane Hoeveler, *Gothic Riffs: Secularizing the Uncanny in the European Imaginary, 1780–1820* (Columbus: Ohio State University Press, 2015), 59.
33. The closest modern example of this voice is found among Lacanian scholars such as Michel Poizat and Mladen Dolar. Poizat, in particular, examines the operatic voice as a Lacanian *objet-voix*, which gives the opera lover pleasure in the moments when its sounds cease to carry meaning. As he argues, the female voice begins to replace the castrati, and with this substitution, the female voice becomes the *objet-voix* of desire (Dolar, *A Voice and Nothing More*; Poizat, *L'opéra ou Le cri de l'ange*).

1. The Physiology of Accent

1. David Hume to Charlotte-Françoise Du Mesnildot de Vierville, marquise de Barbentane, Lisle Street, Leicester Fields, February 16, 1766, in Jean Jacques Rousseau, *Correspondance complète de Jean Jacques Rousseau: Décembre 1765–février 1766*, ed. R. A. Leigh, vol. 28 (Oxford: Voltaire Foundation, 1977), 308.

2. Rousseau, *Correspondance complète*, 28:308.
3. See Jacques Derrida, *De la grammatologie* (Paris: Minuit, 1967); Michael O'Dea, introduction to *Jean-Jacques Rousseau: Music, Illusion and Desire* (New York: St. Martin's, 1995), 1–6; Downing A. Thomas, "Music and Original Loss in Rousseau's *Essai sur l'origine des langues*," in *Music and the Origins of Language: Theories from the French Enlightenment* (Cambridge: Cambridge University Press, 1995), 82–142; and Cynthia Verba, "Music as Expressive Art: Rameau versus Rousseau on Expressive Means and Content," in *Music and the French Enlightenment: Rameau and the Philosophes in Dialogue*, 2nd ed. (Oxford: Oxford University Press, 2016), 34–55.
4. Jean Jacques Rousseau, *Correspondance complète de Jean Jacques Rousseau: Janvier 1769–avril 1770*, ed. R. A. Leigh, vol. 37 (Oxford: Voltaire Foundation, 1980), 57.
5. Jean Jacques Rousseau, *Correspondance complète de Jean Jacques Rousseau: 1768*, ed. R. A. Leigh, vol. 36 (Oxford: Voltaire Foundation, 1980), 196.
6. Rousseau, *Correspondance complète*, 36:196.
7. Marie-Élisabeth Duchez, "*Principe de la mélodie* et *Origine des langues*: Un brouillon inédit de Jean-Jacques Rousseau sur l'origine de la mélodie," *Revue de Musicologie* 60 (1974): 37.
8. Jacques Derrida, *Margins of Philosophy*, trans. Alan Bass (Chicago: University of Chicago Press, 1982), 151.
9. Lynn Festa, *Sentimental Figures of Empire in Eighteenth-Century Britain and France* (Baltimore: Johns Hopkins University Press, 2006), 3.
10. David J. Denby, *Sentimental Narrative and the Social Order in France, 1760–1820* (Cambridge: Cambridge University Press, 1994), 86; Stefano Castelvecchi, *Sentimental Opera: Questions of Genre in the Age of Bourgeois Drama* (Cambridge: Cambridge University Press, 2013), 129, 138–39, 167.
11. Denby, *Sentimental Narrative and the Social Order in France*, 47; Festa, *Sentimental Figures of Empire in Eighteenth-Century Britain and France*, 17; Castelvecchi, *Sentimental Opera*, 132.
12. See David Marshall, *The Surprising Effects of Sympathy: Marivaux, Diderot, Rousseau, and Mary Shelley* (Chicago: University of Chicago Press, 1988), 1–49; Anne C. Vila, *Enlightenment and Pathology: Sensibility in the Literature and Medicine of Eighteenth-Century France* (Baltimore: Johns Hopkins University Press, 1998), 119–27, 178–80; and Downing A. Thomas, *Aesthetics of Opera in the Ancien Régime, 1647–1785* (Cambridge: Cambridge University Press, 2008), 201–64.
13. Denby, *Sentimental Narrative and the Social Order in France*, 47.

14. Denby, *Sentimental Narrative and the Social Order in France*, 47; Festa, *Sentimental Figures of Empire in Eighteenth-Century Britain and France*, 39.
15. See Thomas, *Aesthetics of Opera in the Ancien Régime*, 179–200.
16. See Anne Vila's discussion of *morale sensitive* in Vila, *Enlightenment and Pathology*, 182–224.
17. François Hérissant, "Recherches sur les organes de la voix des quadrupèdes, et de celle des oiseaux," in *Histoire de l'Académie royale des sciences* (Paris: Imprimerie royale, 1753), 279–80.
18. Hérissant, "Recherches sur les organes de la voix," 282.
19. Hérissant, "Recherches sur les organes de la voix," 282–88.
20. Hérissant, "Recherches sur les organes de la voix," 290.
21. Hérissant, "Recherches sur les organes de la voix," 279.
22. Jean-Jacques Rousseau, *Essai sur l'origine des langues, Où il est parlé de la mélodie & de l'imitation musicale*, in *Collection complète des œuvres de J. J. Rousseau, citoyen de Geneve*, vol. 8 (Geneva: Du Peyrou, Pierre-Alexandre, 1782), 357.
23. Rousseau, *Essai sur l'origine des langues*, 8:363.
24. Rousseau, *Essai sur l'origine des langues*, 8:363.
25. Rousseau, *Essai sur l'origine des langues*, 8:417.
26. Rousseau, *Essai sur l'origine des langues*, 8:363.
27. Rousseau, *Essai sur l'origine des langues*, 8:363.
28. See Derrida, *De la grammatologie*; Michèle Duchet, *Anthropologie et histoire au siècle des Lumières: Buffon, Voltaire, Rousseau, Helvétius, Diderot* (Paris: Flammarion, 1971), 268; Jean Starobinski, *Jean-Jacques Rousseau: La transparence et l'obstacle* (Paris: Gallimard, 1971), 356–79; and Downing Thomas, *Music and the Origins of Language: Theories from the French Enlightenment* (Cambridge: Cambridge University Press, 1995), 82–142.
29. Étienne Bonnot de Condillac, *Essai sur l'origine des connoissances humaines*, vol. 2 (Amsterdam: Pierre Mortier, 1746), 97.
30. Condillac, *Essai sur l'origine des connoissances humaines*, 2:97.
31. See chapters 3 and 4 in Thomas, *Music and the Origins of Language*, 57–142.
32. Condillac, *Essai sur l'origine des connoissances humaines*, 2:9.
33. Condillac, *Essai sur l'origine des connoissances humaines*, 2:9.
34. Condillac, *Essai sur l'origine des connoissances humaines*, 2:10.
35. Condillac, *Essai sur l'origine des connoissances humaines*, 2:10.
36. Charles Pinot Duclos, "Mémoire sur l'art de partager l'action théâtrale," in *Œuvres complètes de Duclos*, vol. 9 (Paris: Colnet, 1806), 339.
37. Duclos, "Mémoire sur l'art de partager l'action théâtrale," 9:340.
38. Duclos, "Mémoire sur l'art de partager l'action théâtrale," 9:340.
39. Duclos, "Mémoire sur l'art de partager l'action théâtrale," 9:342.

40. Duclos, "Mémoire sur l'art de partager l'action théâtrale," 9:342.
41. Duclos, "Mémoire sur l'art de partager l'action théâtrale," 9:343.
42. Jean-Jacques Rousseau, *Dictionnaire de musique* (Paris: Duchesne la Venue, 1768), 542.
43. Rousseau, *Dictionnaire de musique*, 542.
44. Rousseau, *Dictionnaire de musique*, 67, 87, 387.
45. Rousseau, *Dictionnaire de musique*, 542.
46. Verba, *Music and the French Enlightenment*, 20n33.
47. Rousseau, *Dictionnaire de musique*, 1–2.
48. Rousseau, *Dictionnaire de musique*, 2–3.
49. Rousseau, *Dictionnaire de musique*, 3.
50. Jean-Jacques Rousseau, *Lettre sur la musique française*, 2nd ed. (Paris, 1753), 30.
51. Rousseau, *Lettre sur la musique française*, 30.
52. Rousseau, *Lettre sur la musique française*, 30.
53. Rousseau, *Lettre sur la musique française*, 30.
54. Verba, *Music and the French Enlightenment*, 43. See also Robert Wokler, "Rameau, Rousseau, and the *Essai sur l'origine des langues*," *Studies on Voltaire and the Eighteenth Century* 117 (1974): 179–238; and Marie-Élisabeth Duchez, "*Principe de la mélodie et Origine de langages*: Un brouillon inédit de Jean-Jacques Rousseau sur l'origine de la mélodie," *Revue de musicologie* 60, no. 1/2 (1974): 33–86.
55. Jean-Jacques Rousseau, "L'origine de la mélodie," in Duchez, "*Principe de la mélodie et Origine des langues*," 61.
56. Jean-Jacques Rousseau, *La Nouvelle Héloïse, ou Lettres de deux amans*, vol. 2 (Neuchâtel: Duchêne, 1764), 243.
57. Jean-Jacques Rousseau, *Émile, ou, De l'éducation*, vol. 1 (Amsterdam: J. Neaulme, 1762), 124.
58. Rousseau, *Essai sur l'origine des langues*, 8:375.
59. Rousseau, *Essai sur l'origine des langues*, 8:375.
60. Rousseau, *Essai sur l'origine des langues*, 8:370.
61. Rousseau, *Essai sur l'origine des langues*, 8:376.
62. Rousseau, *Essai sur l'origine des langues*, 8:405.
63. Étienne Bonnot de Condillac, "Du génie des langues," in *Essai sur l'origine des connaissances humaines*, vol. 2 (Amsterdam: Chez Pierre Mortier, 1746), 196–223.
64. Rousseau, *Essai sur l'origine des langues*, 8:403.
65. Rousseau, *Essai sur l'origine des langues*, 8:404.
66. Rousseau, *Essai sur l'origine des langues*, 8:405.

67. Rousseau, *Essai sur l'origine des langues*, 8:407.
68. Nina Sun Eidsheim, *Sensing Sound: Singing and Listening as Vibrational Practice* (Durham, NC: Duke University Press, 2015), 141, http://libcat.dartmouth.edu/record=b6280719~S1.
69. As I noted in the introduction, my research methodology includes a practical component because the works I study invite the reader to learn about the voice through speculative and performative experimentation. As a classically trained singer, I have experimented vocally with Rousseau's description of sonic passions. Combining my research with embodied practice, I imitated the harsh tones of the passion described in Rousseau's *Essai*. As I did so, I noticed how the mouth narrows and projects a shallow tone whose acoustic energy pools in the mouth.
70. Rousseau, *Essai sur l'origine des langues*, 8:429.
71. Rousseau, *Essai sur l'origine des langues*, 8:429.
72. Rousseau, *Essai sur l'origine des langues*, 8:429.
73. Denis Dodart, "MEMOIRE sur les Causes de la Voix de l'Homme, & de ses différens Tons," in *Histoire de l'Académie royale des sciences* (1700), 250.
74. Rousseau, *Essai sur l'origine des langues*, 8:407.
75. Rousseau, *Essai sur l'origine des langues*, 8:427.
76. Commas subdivide the semitone into minute intervals; as detailed in chapter 4, music theorists often reference the comma when discussing temperaments or the famous enharmonic ratio, or quarter tone (see Alexander Rehding, "Rousseau, Rameau, and Enharmonic Furies in the French Enlightenment," *Journal of Music Theory* 49, no. 1 [2005]: 141–80).
77. Rousseau, *Essai sur l'origine des langues*, 8:427.
78. Rousseau, "Chromatique," in *Dictionnaire de musique*, 98.
79. Rousseau, "Acteur," in *Dictionnaire de musique*, 26.
80. Rousseau, "Acteur," in *Dictionnaire de musique*, 26.
81. Victoria Malawey, *A Blaze of Light in Every Word: Analyzing the Popular Singing Voice* (Oxford: Oxford University Press, 2020), 7.
82. Malawey, *A Blaze of Light in Every Word*, 7.
83. Malawey, *A Blaze of Light in Every Word*, 7.
84. Malawey, *A Blaze of Light in Every Word*, 7.
85. Deirdre Loughridge, "Timbre before Timbre: Listening to the Effects of Organ Stops, Violin Mutes, and Piano Pedals ca. 1650–1800," in *The Oxford Handbook of Timbre*, ed. Emily I. Dolan and Alexander Rehding (Oxford: Oxford University Press, 2018), 10, https://www.oxfordhandbooks.com/view/10.1093/oxfordhb/9780190637224.001.0001/oxfordhb-9780190637224-e-16.

86. Loughridge, "Timbre before Timbre," 10.
87. Loughridge, "Timbre before Timbre," 10.
88. Rousseau, *Dictionnaire de musique*, 180.
89. Rousseau, *Dictionnaire de musique*, 321.
90. Rousseau, *Dictionnaire de musique*, 321.
91. Rousseau, *Dictionnaire de musique*, 498.
92. Rousseau, *Dictionnaire de musique*, 498.
93. Festa, *Sentimental Figures of Empire in Eighteenth-Century Britain and France*, 37.
94. Matthew Gelbart, "Rousseau and the Quest for Universals," in "Colloquy: Rousseau in 2013: Afterthoughts on a Tercentenary," ed. Jacqueline Waeber, *Journal of the American Musicological Society* 66, no. 1 (Spring 2013): 283.
95. This reflexive privileging of the male voice as the symbolic representative of the human race continued well after Rousseau, as evidenced in the work of the twentieth-century theorist Theodor Adorno, whose essay "The Curves of the Needle" posits that "male voices can be reproduced better [in vinyl recordings] than female voices. The female voice easily sounds shrill" (Adorno, "The Curves of the Needle," in *Essays on Music*, trans. Susan H. Gillespie [Berkeley: University of California Press, 2002], 274).
96. Rousseau, *Dictionnaire de musique*, 498.
97. Michael O'Dea, *Jean-Jacques Rousseau: Music, Illusion and Desire* (New York: St. Martin's, 1995), 83.
98. O'Dea, *Jean-Jacques Rousseau*, 100.
99. O'Dea, *Jean-Jacques Rousseau*, 101.
100. O'Dea, *Jean-Jacques Rousseau*, 101.
101. Rousseau, *Dictionnaire de musique*, 543.
102. Rousseau, *Dictionnaire de musique*, 543.
103. Rousseau, *Dictionnaire de musique*, 76.
104. Feldman, *The Castrato*, 184, 188.
105. Feldman, *The Castrato*, 185.
106. Rousseau, *Dictionnaire de musique*, 75.
107. Rousseau, *Dictionnaire de musique*, 75.
108. Rousseau, *Dictionnaire de musique*, 75–76.
109. Julia Simon offers a comparative analysis of Rousseau's musical and governmental theories (Simon, "Singing Democracy: Music and Politics," in *Rousseau among the Moderns: Music, Aesthetics, Politics* [University Park: Penn State University Press, 2013], 47–74).

110. Festa, *Sentimental Figures of Empire in Eighteenth-Century Britain and France*, 37.
111. Rousseau, *Dictionnaire de musique*, 453.
112. Emily Dolan, *The Orchestral Revolution: Haydn and the Technologies of Timbre* (Cambridge: Cambridge University Press, 2012), 56.
113. Dolan, *The Orchestral Revolution*, 55–56.
114. Rousseau, *Dictionnaire de musique*, 528.
115. Rousseau, *Dictionnaire de musique*, 528.
116. Rousseau, *Dictionnaire de musique*, 543.
117. Rousseau, *Dictionnaire de musique*, 26.
118. Rousseau, *Émile*, 4:62.
119. Rousseau, *Émile*, 4:62.
120. Rousseau, *Essai sur l'origine des langues*, 8:419.
121. Rousseau, *Émile*, 4:62.
122. Rousseau, *Émile*, 4:65.
123. Rousseau, *Dictionnaire de musique*, 236.
124. Rousseau, *Dictionnaire de musique*, 236.
125. Rousseau, *Dictionnaire de musique*, 236.
126. Rousseau, *Dictionnaire de musique*, 86–87.
127. Rousseau, *Essai sur l'origine des langues*, 8:421.
128. Rousseau, *Essai sur l'origine des langues*, 8:417.
129. David Kasunic, "Rousseau's Cat," in "Colloquy: Rousseau in 2013: Afterthoughts on a Tercentenary," ed. Jacqueline Waeber, *Journal of the American Musicological Society* 66, no. 1 (2013): 269.
130. Rousseau, *Lettre sur la musique française*, 30.
131. Rousseau, *Essai sur l'origine des langues*, 8:407.
132. Rousseau, *Émile*, 4:140.
133. Rousseau, *La Nouvelle Héloïse*, 1:141.
134. Rousseau, *Émile*, 1:134.
135. Rousseau, *Émile*, 1:134.
136. Rousseau, *Émile*, 1:413.
137. Rousseau, *Essai sur l'origine des langues*, 8:406.
138. Rousseau, *Essai sur l'origine des langues*, 8:406.
139. Rousseau, *Essai sur l'origine des langues*, 8:406.
140. Rousseau, *La Nouvelle Héloïse*, 2:286–87.

2. Fever Pitch

1. Denis Diderot, *Éloge de Richardson*, in *Œuvres Esthétiques*, ed. P. Verniere (Paris: Garnier, 1966), 35.
2. Diderot, *Éloge de Richardson*, 35.
3. Diderot, *Éloge de Richardson*, 30.
4. Samuel Johnson, *A Dictionary of the English Language, The fourth edition, revised by the author*, vol. 2 (Dublin: Thomas Ewing, 1775), 42.
5. Chevalier Louis de Jaucourt, "Style," in *Encyclopédie, ou dictionnaire raisonné des sciences, des arts et des métiers, etc.*, ed. Denis Diderot and Jean le Rond d'Alembert (Chicago: University of Chicago: ARTFL Encyclopédie Project [Autumn 2017 Edition], ed. Robert Morrissey and Glenn Roe), 15:553, http://encyclopedie.uchicago.edu.dartmouth.idm.oclc.org/.
6. Nina Sun Eidsheim, "Music's Material Dependency: What Underwater Opera Can Tell Us about Odysseus's Ears," in *Sensing Sound: Singing and Listening as Vibrational Practice* (Durham, NC: Duke University Press, 2015), 130, https://doi.org/10.1215/9780822374695.
7. Roland Barthes, *Image-Music-Text*, trans. Stephen Heath (New York: Hill and Wang, 1977), 182.
8. For a discussion on a multisensorial approach to music and the voice, see Eidsheim, "Music's Material Dependency."
9. See Tom Keymer's discussion of the *"audibility* of the narrating voice" in Fielding's novels (Keymer, *Richardson's "Clarissa" and the Eighteenth-Century Reader* [Cambridge: Cambridge University Press, 1992], xiii).
10. Ian P. Watt, *The Rise of the Novel: Studies in Defoe, Richardson, and Fielding* (Berkeley: University of California Press, 1957), 196, 201.
11. Keymer, *Richardson's "Clarissa" and the Eighteenth-Century Reader*, 51.
12. Mark Kinkead-Weekes, *Samuel Richardson, Dramatic Novelist* (Ithaca, NY: Cornell University Press, 1973), 396.
13. Kinkead-Weekes, *Samuel Richardson*, 407.
14. Cynthia Sundberg Wall, *The Prose of Things: Transformations of Description in the Eighteenth Century* (Chicago: University of Chicago Press, 2006), 145.
15. Diderot, *Éloge de Richardson*, 32.
16. For more on Richardson's epistolary writing, especially his letter writing to young women, see Louise Curran, "Trifling Scribes: Women's Letters and Patchwork Writing," in *Samuel Richardson and the Art of Letter-Writing* (Cambridge: Cambridge University Press, 2016), 89–123.
17. Samuel Richardson, "Samuel Richardson to Sophia Scudamore [née Westcomb]: 1746," in *Electronic Enlightenment Scholarly Edition of Correspondence*,

ed. Robert McNamee et al., vers. 3.0, University of Oxford, 2018, http://dx.doi.org.dartmouth.idm.oclc.org/10.13051/ee:doc/richsaOU0010064a1c.

18. Samuel Richardson, "Samuel Richardson to Lady Dorothy Bradshaigh [née Bellingham]: Wednesday, 6 November 1748," in *Electronic Enlightenment Scholarly Edition of Correspondence*, ed. Robert McNamee et al., vers. 3.0 University of Oxford, 2018, http://dx.doi.org.dartmouth.idm.oclc.org/10.13051/ee:doc/richsaOU0010089a1c.

19. Samuel Richardson, "Samuel Richardson to Edward Moore: 1748," in *Electronic Enlightenment Scholarly Edition of Correspondence*, ed. Robert McNamee et al., vers. 3.0, University of Oxford, 2018, http://dx.doi.org.dartmouth.idm.oclc.org/10.13051/ee:doc/richsaOU0010118a1c.

20. Naomi Tadmor, "'In the Even My Wife Read to Me': Women Reading and Household Life in the Eighteenth Century," in *The Practice and Representation of Reading in England*, ed. James Raven, Helen Small, and Tadmor (Cambridge: Cambridge University Press, 1996), 168–70; see also Roger Chartier, "Richardson, Diderot et La Lectrice Impatiente," *MLN* 114, no. 4 (1999): 647–66; and Abigail Williams, *The Social Life of Books: Reading Together in the Eighteenth-Century Home* (New Haven, CT: Yale University Press, 2017).

21. Janet M. Todd, *Sensibility: An Introduction* (London: Methuen, 1986), 77–81; Stefano Castelvecchi, *Sentimental Opera: Questions of Genre in the Age of Bourgeois Drama* (Cambridge: Cambridge University Press, 2013), 129, 138, 167.

22. See the following works with inserted musical scores: Madeleine de Scudéry, *Clélie, histoire romaine: Quatrième partie 1658* (Paris: Honoré Champion Éditeur, 2004), 387; Marie-Jeanne Lhéritier de Villandon, *La tour tenebreuse, et les jours lumineux: Contes Anglois, accompagnez d'Historiettes et tirez d'une ancienne Chronique composée par Richard, surnommé Coeur de Lion, Roy d'Angleterre* (Amsterdam: des Bordes, 1706), 1:96–97, 2:48–49; Charlotte Rose de Caumont de La Force, "La puissance de l'Amour," in *Les fées contes des contes* (Amerstdam, P. Mortier, 1711), 190–91; Mlle de Lubert, *La veillée galante, nouvelle* (La Haye, 1747); Godefroy Sellius, *La Double beauté, roman étranger* (Cantorbery, 1754), 34–35; Louis-Edme Billardon de Sauvigny, *Histoire amoureuse de Pierre Le Long, Et de sa très honorée Dame Blanche Bazu: Ecritte par iceluy [i.e., L. E. Billardon de Sauvigny] La Musique de Mr Philidor* (London: 1765), 121–38; François Thomas Marie de Baculard d'Arnaud, "Le Sire Créqui," in *Nouvelles historiques*, vol. 1 (Paris: chez Delalain, 1774), 487–89; Suzanne Bodin de Boismortier, *Histoire de Jacques Feru, et de valeureuse damoiselle Agathe Mignard*

(Hague: chez Cuissart, 1766), 61–66; Antoine d'Argenson Paulmy, *Histoire du Chevalier du Soleil, de son frère Rosiclair et de leurs descendants: Traduction libre et abrégée de l'Espagnol* (Amsterdam: Pissot, 1780), 1:365–67, 2:349–51; Etienne-François de Lantier, *Les Travaux de Monsieur l'abbé Mouche* (London, 1784), 169–72; Haudart, *Vie et amours d'un pauvre diable* (Geneva: J. Hilaire, 1788), 43–44, 134–35; Jean Claude Gorjy, *Blançay* vol. 1 (Paris: Guillot, 1789), 96, 161–63; William Toldervy, *The History of Two Orphans. In Four Volumes. By William Toldervy*, vol. 1 (London: William Owen, 1756), 100–101, 202–3.

23. I analyze Richardson's work as part of a broader narrative on French literature. I'm not concerned with the literary examples of musical scenes in British literature. This book is not a history of literary adaptations of musical scenes in British literature, and as such, I do not analyze musical scenes that appear in the novels of Henry Fielding, Eliza Haywood, Frances Burney, and Ann Radcliffe. It is about a specific type of musical scene in Richardson that Baculard d'Arnaud adapted into French literature.

24. Kinkead-Weekes, *Samuel Richardson*, 395. See also Samuel Richardson, "Samuel Richardson to Lady Dorothy Bradshaigh [née Bellingham]: Saturday, 9 October 1756," in *Electronic Enlightenment Scholarly Edition of Correspondence*, ed. Robert McNamee et al., vers. 3.0, University of Oxford, 2018, http://dx.doi.org.dartmouth.idm.oclc.org/10.13051/ee:doc/richsaOU0010329a1c.

25. Richardson, *Clarissa or, The History of a Young Lady* (London: S. Richardson, 1748), 1:286.

26. Richardson, *Clarissa* (1748), 1:286.
27. Richardson, *Clarissa* (1748), 1:286.
28. Richardson, *Clarissa* (1748), 1:293.
29. Richardson, *Clarissa* (1748), 2:205.
30. In addition to the voice, one can also read this scene in terms of drama's influence on Richardson (see Ira Konigsberg, *Samuel Richardson and the Dramatic Novel* [Lexington: University Press of Kentucky, 1968]).
31. Richardson, *Clarissa* (1748), 2:42.
32. Richardson, *Clarissa* (1748), 5:315.
33. Richardson, *Clarissa* (1748), 2:216.
34. Wall, *The Prose of Things*, 145.
35. Richardson, *Clarissa* (1748), 2:192.
36. Richardson, *Clarissa* (1748), 2:251.
37. Richardson, *Clarissa* (1748), 3:23.
38. Richardson, *Clarissa* (1748), 3:23.

39. Kathleen Lubey, "Sexual Remembrance in Clarissa," *Eighteenth-Century Fiction* 29, no. 2 (2016): 169–70.
40. My interest in an acousmatic regime is inspired by work that considers sound and unseen sound as a marker of communities as well as a form of control. Among many works that analyze sound through a historical anthropological or literary lens, I refer to the following works: Alain Corbin, "The Auditory Markers of the Village," in *Village Bells: Sound and Meaning in the Nineteenth-Century French Countryside*, trans. Martin Thom (New York: Columbia University Press, 1998), 95–158; Brian Kane, "The Baptism of the Acousmate," in *Sound Unseen: Acousmatic Sound in Theory and Practice* (Oxford: Oxford University Press, 2014), 73–94; Bruce R. Smith, *The Acoustic World of Early Modern England: Attending to the O-Factor* (Chicago: University of Chicago Press, 1999), 30–95; and Pierre Schaeffer, "Acousmatics," in *Treatise on Musical Objects: An Essay across Disciplines*, trans. Christine North and John Deck (Berkeley: University of California Press, 2017), 64–72.
41. Tita Chico, *Designing Women: The Dressing Room in Eighteenth-Century English Literature and Culture* (Lewisburg, PA: Bucknell University Press, 2005), 184.
42. Richardson, *Clarissa* (1748), 2:47.
43. Samuel Richardson, *Clarissa, or, the History of a Young Lady*, 3rd ed., vol. 8 (London: Samuel Richardson, 1750), 207.
44. Richardson, *Clarissa* (1750), 8:207.
45. Richardson, *Clarissa* (1750), 8:207.
46. Richardson, *Clarissa* (1750), 8:207–8.
47. Richardson, *Clarissa* (1748), 3:179.
48. Traditionally, domestic performance was an indispensable tool for women in the courtship process (see Regula Hohl Trillini, *The Gaze of the Listener: English Representations of Domestic Music-Making* [Amsterdam: Rodopi, 2008]).
49. For a discussion of *Clarissa*'s marginalia, see Florian Stuber, "Introduction: Text, Writer, Reader, World," in Samuel Richardson, *Clarissa, or, The History of a Young Lady*, vol. 1 (New York: AMS, 1990), 1–53.
50. For the first edition of *Clarissa*, Richardson only knew that a female author had penned "Ode to Wisdom." Elizabeth Carter subsequently wrote to Richardson and objected to her poem's uncredited appearance. Richardson then asked her permission to include her work in subsequent reprints.
51. "Original Letters of Miss E. Carter and Mr. Samuel Richardson," *Monthly Magazine, or, British Register*, July 1, 1812, 534.

52. Analyzing the sophistication of the musical setting, Thomas McGeary speculates about the composers who could have authored Clarissa's "Ode to Wisdom" (McGeary, "Clarissa Harlowe's 'Ode to Wisdom': Composition, Publishing History, and the Semiotics of Printed Music," *Eighteenth-Century Fiction* 24, no. 3 [March 29, 2012]: 436, https://doi.org/10.1353/ecf.2012.0007).
53. McGeary, "Clarissa Harlowe's 'Ode to Wisdom,'" 456.
54. Leslie Ritchie, *Women Writing Music in Late Eighteenth-Century England: Social Harmony in Literature and Performance* (Burlington, VT: Ashgate, 2008), 48–49.
55. Richardson, *Clarissa* (1748), 1:207.
56. Richardson, *Clarissa* (1748), 2:47–48.
57. Karen Lipsedge, Philippa Tristram, Simon Varey, and Cynthia Wall have analyzed Clarissa's domestic space in terms of privacy, confinement, family economy, and familial relationships. Karen Lipsedge discusses the configuration of architectural space in relation to family divisions (Lipsedge, *Domestic Space in Eighteenth-Century British Novels* [New York: Palgrave Macmillan, 2012], 59; see also Lipsedge, "Representations of the Domestic Parlour in Samuel Richardson's Clarissa, 1747–48," *Eighteenth-Century Fiction* 17, no. 3 [2005]: 391–423; Tristram, *Living Space: In Fact and Fiction* [New York: Routledge, 1989] 241, 244–45, 250, 256; Wall, "Gendering Rooms: Domestic Architecture and Literary Acts," *Eighteenth-Century Fiction* 5, no. 4 [1993]: 349–72; and Varey, *Space and the Eighteenth-Century Novel* [Cambridge: Cambridge University Press, 1990], 191).
58. Richardson, *Clarissa* (1748), 2:47–48.
59. Elizabeth Carter, *Poems on Several Occasions* (London: John, Francis and Charles Rivington, 1776), 85.
60. Richardson, *Clarissa* (1748), 2:48.
61. Here I evoke Shaftesbury's notion of the *Vocal looking glass*, in which a person's voice guides him toward a moment of self-awareness (Anthony Ashley Cooper, Earl of Shaftesbury, *Characteristicks of Men, Manners, Opinions, Times. In Three Volumes. By the Right Honourable Anthony, Earl of Shaftesbury*, vol. 1 [London, 1723], 171).
62. See Noelle Chao, "Musical Letters: Eighteenth-Century Writings on Music and the Fictions of Burney, Radcliffe, and Scott" (Ph.D. diss., University of California, Los Angeles, 2007), 55–68; and Penelope Gouk, "Music and the Nervous System in Eighteenth-Century British Medical Thought," in *Music and the Nerves, 1700–1900*, ed. James Kennaway (London: Palgrave Macmillan, 2014), 44–71.

63. Chao, "Musical Letters," 71. Chao offers a history of music writing that examines the influence of medical writings on literary and musicological approaches to music. Within British studies, literary scholars often consider music's influence on mid- to late eighteenth-century writers such as Frances Burney and Ann Radcliffe, and music historians acknowledge the influence of Charles Avison and Charles Burney on musicological writing. Unlike Chao's work, this chapter is not intended as a history of music's influence on British literature, musicology, or medicine. For the purpose of the current study, I analyze *Clarissa*'s musical scene due to its influence on French sentimental literature.
64. Richard Browne, *Medicina Musica: Or, A Mechanical Essay on the Effects of Singing, Musick, and Dancing, on Human Bodies. Revis'd and Corrected* (London: John Cooke, 1729), xiii–xiv.
65. George Cheyne to Samuel Richardson, September 30, 1738, in Cheyne, "Letters of Cheyne to Richardson," ed. Chales F. Mullet, *University of Missouri Studies 18 (1943)*: 42.
66. George Cheyne to Samuel Richardson, June 4, 1739, in Cheyne, "Letters of Cheyne to Richardson," 50.
67. George Cheyne to Samuel Richardson, July 1, 1739, and October 24, 1741, in Cheyne, "Letters of Cheyne to Richardson," 54, 71–72.
68. George Cheyne to Samuel Richardson, April 20, 1740, in Cheyne, "Letters of Cheyne to Richardson," 59.
69. Clive D. Edwards, *Eighteenth-Century Furniture* (Manchester: Manchester University Press, 1996), 117.
70. George Cheyne, *An Essay of Health and Long Life* (London: George Strahan [. . .] and J. Leake, 1725), 91.
71. See Hisao Ishizuka, "Elasticity of Animal Fiber: Motion, Tone, and Life of the Fiber Body," in *Fiber, Medicine, and Culture in the British Enlightenment* (New York: Palgrave Macmillan, 2016), 63–108.
72. Cheyne, *An Essay of Health and Long Life*, 94.
73. Cheyne, *An Essay of Health and Long Life*, 95.
74. Cheyne, *An Essay of Health and Long Life*, 144–45.
75. Cheyne, *An Essay of Health and Long Life*, 144–45.
76. Cheyne, *An Essay of Health and Long Life*, 159.
77. Cheyne, *An Essay of Health and Long Life*, 160.
78. Cheyne, *An Essay of Health and Long Life*, 160.
79. Cheyne, *An Essay of Health and Long Life*, 158.
80. See also Richardson's letter to Aaron Hill, which dramatizes the physiological effects of reading in a way that resembles Hill's acting theory

(Richardson, "Samuel Richardson to Aaron Hill: Wednesday, 9 November 1746," in *Electronic Enlightenment Scholarly Edition of Correspondence*, ed. Robert McNamee et al., vers. 3.0, University of Oxford, 2018, http://dx.doi.org/10.13051/ee:doc/richsaOU0010070a1c).

81. Richardson, *Clarissa* (1748), 2:47.
82. Richardson, *Clarissa* (1748), 2:48.
83. Richardson, *Clarissa* (1748), 2:51.
84. Richardson, *Clarissa* (1748), 2:50–51.
85. Richardson, *Clarissa* (1748), 2:50–51.
86. Richardson, *Clarissa* (1748), 2:50–51.
87. Samuel Richardson, "Samuel Richardson to Lady Dorothy Bradshaigh [née Bellingham]: Thursday, 26 December 1748," in *Electronic Enlightenment Scholarly Edition of Correspondence*, ed. Robert McNamee et al., vers. 3.0 University of Oxford, 2018, http://dx.doi.org/10.13051/ee:doc/richsaOU0010103a1c.
88. Richardson, "Samuel Richardson to Lady Dorothy Bradshaigh [née Bellingham]: Thursday, 26 December 1748."
89. I must qualify Clarissa's departure as brief because Carter's poem ends with "the sweet, engaging Ties / Of Still, Domestic Life" (Richardson, *Clarissa* [1748], 2:50).
90. See Janine Barchas, *Graphic Design, Print Culture, and the Eighteenth-Century Novel* (Cambridge: Cambridge University Press, 2003), 100; and Ritchie, *Women Writing Music in Late Eighteenth-Century England*, 49.
91. Pierre Dubois, in his work on eighteenth-century British depictions of music, even compares Clarissa's song to a sort of oratorio in which religious virtue and music combine (Dubois, *Music in the Georgian Novel* [Cambridge: Cambridge University Press, 2015], 35).
92. For a discussion of the instructional function of sentimental literature, see Todd, *Sensibility*, 70–77.
93. Clarissa's song is more sophisticated than a traditional English ballad. For more on Clarissa's song in relation to eighteenth-century English song genres, see McGeary, "Clarissa Harlowe's 'Ode to Wisdom,'" 436.
94. In the early eighteenth century, Marie-Jeanne Lhéritier de Villandon tried to purge the French *Air de cour* of its sexual connotations and even published a novel with antiquarian songs, translated from Provençal, titled *La Tour ténébreuse et les jours lumineux: Contes anglais* (1706) (see Marie-Jeanne Lhéritier de Villandon, "Marie-Jeanne Lhéritier de Villandon, *Diverse Works* [1696]," in *Fairy Tale Framed: Early Forewords, Afterwords, and Critical Words*, ed. Ruth B. Bottigheimer [Albany: State University of New York Press, 2012], 150–51).

95. Anne C. Vila, *Enlightenment and Pathology: Sensibility in the Literature and Medicine of Eighteenth-Century France* (Baltimore: Johns Hopkins University Press, 1998), 182–86.
96. Vila, *Enlightenment and Pathology*, 198–210.
97. Vila, *Enlightenment and Pathology*, 210–21.
98. Joseph-Louis Roger, *Traité des effets de la musique sur le corps humain* (Paris: Brunot, 1803), vii, xii–xvi.
99. Roger, *Traité des effets de la musique*, xxxii.
100. Roger, *Traité des effets de la musique*, xxxii.
101. Among many nuanced analyses on Rousseau and music, see Jacques Derrida, *De la grammatologie* (Paris: Minuit, 1967); Michael O'Dea, "Social Order and 'le pays des chimères,'" in *Jean-Jacques Rousseau: Music, Illusion and Desire* (New York: St. Martin's, 1995), 108–33; Julia Simon, *Rousseau among the Moderns: Music, Aesthetics, Politics* (University Park: Penn State University Press, 2013); Jean Starobinski, *Jean-Jacques Rousseau: La transparence et l'obstacle: Suivi de Sept essais sur Rousseau* (Paris: Gallimard, 1971); and Downing A. Thomas, *Music and the Origins of Language: Theories from the French Enlightenment* (Cambridge: Cambridge University Press, 1995).
102. Jean-Jacques Rousseau, "Lettre IV de Saint-Preux à Mylord Edouard," *La Nouvelle Héloïse*, vol. 4 (Paris and Neuchatel: Duchesne, 1764), 57.
103. Rousseau, *La Nouvelle Héloïse*, 4:57–58.
104. Rousseau, *La Nouvelle Héloïse*, 4:58.
105. Rousseau, *La Nouvelle Héloïse*, 4:58.
106. Rousseau, *La Nouvelle Héloïse*, 4:58.
107. Rousseau, *La Nouvelle Héloïse*, 4:58.
108. For more on the nostalgic effect of music, see Jean-Jacques Rousseau, *Dictionnaire de musique* (Paris: Duchesne la Veuve, 1768), 317.
109. Rousseau, *Dictionnaire de musique*, 317.
110. Previous scholarship has focused on Baculard d'Arnaud's imitation of Richardson with his *histoires anglaises*. I argue that Baculard d'Arnaud's use of musical scores also represents a point of contact between Richardson and Baculard d'Arnaud (see Lynn Festa, "Sentimental Bonds and Revolutionary Characters: Richardson's *Pamela* in England and France," in *The Literary Channel: The Inter-National Invention of the Novel*, ed. Margaret Cohen and Carolyn Dever [Princeton, NJ: Princeton University Press, 2009], 98n9).
111. Robert Dawson, *Baculard d'Arnaud: Life and Prose Fiction* ed. Theodore Bestermen (Oxford: Voltaire Foundation, 1976), 19.

112. Dawson, *Baculard d'Arnaud*, 19.
113. Dawson, *Baculard d'Arnaud*, 21.
114. François-Thomas-Marie de Baculard d'Arnaud, "Préface," in *Épreuves du sentiment* (Maastricht: Chez Jean Edme-Dufour and Philroux, 1784), xv.
115. François-Thomas-Marie de Baculard d'Arnaud, "The Character of Richardson," *Universal Magazine of Knowledge and Pleasure* 73 (December 1783): 327.
116. François-Thomas-Marie de Baculard d'Arnaud, "Préface," in *Nouvelles historiques*, vol. 1 (Paris: Delalain, 1774), xi.
117. For more on the physiological effects of reading, see Alexandre Wenger, *La Fibre littéraire: Le discours médical sur la lecture au XVIIIe siècle* (Geneva: Librairie Droz, 2007).
118. Roger, *Traité des effets de la musique*, xxxvii–xxxviii.
119. Roger, *Traité des effets de la musique*, ix.
120. François-Thomas-Marie de Baculard d'Arnaud, *Épreuves du sentiment*, vol. 3 (Paris: Delalain, 1775), 285.
121. Baculard d'Arnaud, *Épreuves du sentiment*, 3:285.
122. Jean-Jacques Rousseau, *La Nouvelle Héloïse, ou Lettre de deux amans, habitans d'une petite ville au pied des Alpes*, vol. 1 (Paris: Duchesne, 1764), 27.
123. Baculard d'Arnaud, *Épreuves du sentiment*, 3:270.
124. Baculard d'Arnaud, *Épreuves du sentiment*, 3:218.

3. Vitalist Voices in Diderot's Early Work

1. "Sur l'organe immédiat de la voix et de ses différens tons," *Histoire de l'Académie royale des sciences*, ed. J. Boudot (Paris: Imprimerie de Du Pont, 1741), 52.
2. "Sur l'organe immédiat de la voix et de ses différens tons," 54.
3. "Sur l'organe immédiat de la voix et de ses différens tons," 52.
4. The French anatomist François David Hérissant created a taxonomy of creaturely voices in his 1753 treatise *Recherches sur les organes de la voix des quadrupèdes et des oiseaux*.
5. "Sur l'organe immédiat de la voix et de ses différens tons," 54.
6. In chapter 3, I continue my discussion on the speciation of the voice as it took hold in the Académie royale des sciences in the 1750s.
7. Hans von Leden, "A Cultural History of the Larynx and Voice," in *Professional Voice: The Science and Art of Clinical Care*, ed. Robert Thayer Sataloff, 4th ed. (San Diego, CA: Plural, 2017), 79.

8. Steven Connor, *Dumbstruck: A Cultural History of Ventriloquism* (Oxford: Oxford University Press, 2000), 199–200.
9. See references to Denis Dodart and Claude Duclos in the articles on "Chant," "Résonnance," and "Voix," in Jean-Jacques Rousseau, *Dictionnaire de musique* (Paris: Duchesne la Veuve, 1768), 83, 414, 540–42. See also Denis Diderot, *Œuvres complètes: Éléments de physiologie*, ed. Jean Varloot et al., vol. 17 (Paris: Hermann, 1987), 396–97; and Albrecht von Haller, *Éléments de physiologie*, trans. Toussaint Bordenave, vol. 1 (Paris: Chez Guillyn, 1769), 193.
10. Denis Diderot, ed., "Voix [Physiologie]," in *Encyclopédie, ou dictionnaire raisonné des sciences, des arts et des métiers, etc.*, ed. Diderot and Jean le Rond d'Alembert (Chicago: University of Chicago: ARTFL Encyclopédie Project [Autumn 2017 Edition], ed. Robert Morrissey and Glenn Roe), http://encyclopedie.uchicago.edu.dartmouth.idm.oclc.org/, http://encyclopedie.uchicago.edu/.
11. Denis Diderot, *Œuvres complètes: Les Bijoux indiscrets*, ed. Jean Macary et al., vol. 3 (Paris: Hermann, 1978), 59–60.
12. Diderot, *Œuvres complètes: Les Bijoux indiscrets*, ed. Macary et al., 3:73.
13. Translations are mine except for quotations from *Bijoux*, which are taken from Denis Diderot, *Les Bijoux indiscrets: Or, The Indiscreet Toys* (Tobago: Freeman, 1749), 99.
14. Ann Thomson, *Bodies of Thought: Science, Religion, and the Soul in the Early Enlightenment* (Oxford: Oxford University Press, 2008), 194.
15. Georges-Louis Leclerc Buffon, *Histoire naturelle générale et particulière*, ed. Louis-Jean-Marie Daubenton, vol. 2 (The Hague: Pierre de Hondt, 1750), 9, https://gallica.bnf.fr/ark:/12148/bpt6k3188028.
16. Buffon, *Histoire naturelle générale et particulière*, 9.
17. Pierre-Louis Moreau de Maupertuis, *Vénus physique* (1745), 111–12, https://gallica.bnf.fr/ark:/12148/bpt6k15139332.
18. See also the writing of Julien Offray de La Mettrie. As one of the most rigid believers in matter's *vis viva*, he posited that an "innate force" resided in "every fibrous element, every vascular fiber" (La Mettrie, *Histoire naturelle de l'ame* [The Hague: Chez Jean Neaulme, libraire, 1745], 147).
19. Théophile de Bordeu, *Recherches anatomiques sur la position des glandes et sur leur action* (Paris: G. F. Quillau, pere, 1751), 452–53, 456, 515.
20. Bordeu, *Recherches anatomiques*, 452–53.
21. We find both a nod to the voice of sentience and the mechanical voice of inert matter in *Pensées philosophiques* (see Denis Diderot, *Pensées philosophiques* [The Hague: Aux dépens de la compagnie, 1746], 10–11, 34–36).

22. Thomson, *Bodies of Thought*, 195.
23. Denis Diderot, *Œuvres complètes: L'Interprétation de la nature (1753–1765)*, ed. Jean Varloot et al., vol. 9 (Paris: Hermann, 1981), 84; see also Ann Thomson's discussion of the divine consequences of vitalist molecules, as articulated by Diderot (Thomson, *Bodies of Thought*, 189–98).
24. Diderot, *Œuvres complètes: L'Interprétation de la nature (1753–1765)*, ed. Varloot et al., 9:84.
25. Denis Diderot, *Œuvres completes: Réfutations d'Helvétius*, ed. Jean Th. De Booy et al., vol. 24 (Paris: Hermann, 2004), 577.
26. Peter H. Reill, *Vitalizing Nature in the Enlightenment* (Berkeley: University of California Press, 2005), 31, 33–34, 162–63.
27. Reill, *Vitalizing Nature in the Enlightenment*, 39.
28. Reill, *Vitalizing Nature in the Enlightenment*, 38–40.
29. Hisao Ishizuka, "'Fibre Body': The Concept of Fibre in Eighteenth-Century Medicine, c. 1700–40," *Medical History* 56, no. 4 (October 2012): 563, https://doi.org/10.1017/mdh.2012.74.
30. Robert James, "Fibra, *fibre*," trans. Denis Diderot, Marc-Antoine Eidous, and François-Vincent Toussaint, *Dictionnaire universel de medicine*, vol. 3 (Paris: Briasson, David, Durand, 1747), 1500.
31. James, "Fibra, *fibre*," 1500.
32. James, "Fibra, *fibre*," 1517–18.
33. Anthony Ashley Cooper Shaftesbury (Earl of), *An Inquiry Concerning Virtue and Merit. The Moralists; A Philosophical Rhapsody* (printed by John Darby, 1732), 108.
34. For a discussion of interior listening and political harmony in Shaftesbury, see Maria Semi, *Music as a Science of Mankind in Eighteenth-Century Britain*, trans. Timothy Keates (Farnham, UK: Ashgate, 2012), 31–36.
35. Shaftesbury, *An Inquiry Concerning Virtue and Merit*, 94.
36. Shaftesbury, *An Inquiry Concerning Virtue and Merit*, 94.
37. Shaftesbury, *An Inquiry Concerning Virtue and Merit*, 95–96.
38. To hear differences in temperament, listen to this clip of Johann Sebastian Bach's "Prelude in C Major" from *The Well-Tempered Clavier*, book 1. The video includes renditions in Bach-Lehman well temperament, equal temperament, and Werckmeister well temperament (Arthur Bocaneanu, "Equal Temperament versus Bach-Lehman and Werckmeister—J.S. Bach: Prelude in C Major," https://www.youtube.com/watch?v=f8M-JzIwbog).
39. Thomas McGeary, "Shaftesbury on Opera, Spectacle and Liberty," *Music & Letters* 74, no. 4 (1993): 531.

40. In reconstructing Shaftesbury's and Diderot's period ears, we should acknowledge the historical and geographical contingencies of tuning systems. Equal temperament, first practiced in the late sixteenth century with fretted instruments such as lutes, increased in popularity around 1735. This is not to say that equal temperament was destined to be the most prevalent method of tuning. These systems coexisted for decades before equal temperament became more common. The difference between equal temperament and other tuning systems involves the capacity to modulate to distant keys. This system allows a musician to play seamlessly across different keys because it divides an octave into twelve equal semitones. Equal temperament also allows instruments from different families (woodwind, strings, and so on) to perform in harmony. To achieve this increased mobility and instrumental color, equal temperament must sacrifice the purer consonant thirds and more dissonant fifths of mean-tone temperament. In other words, the transition from mean-tone through well to equal temperament standardizes harmonic proportions across instrumental families.
41. Shaftesbury, *An Inquiry Concerning Virtue and Merit*, 94–95.
42. Mark Lindley, "Temperaments," *Grove Music Online*, http://www.oxfordmusiconline.com.dartmouth.idm.oclc.org/grovemusic/view/10.1093/gmo/9781561592630.001.0001/omo-9781561592630-e-0000027643. See Jean-Philippe Rameau, *Nouveau système de musique théorique, où l'on découvre le principe de toutes les règles nécessaires à la pratique: Pour servir d'introduction au Traité de l'harmonie* (De l'imprimerie de Jean-Baptiste-Christophe Ballard, 1726), 110.
43. Lindley, "Temperaments," *Grove Music Online*. See Rameau, *Nouveau système*, 110.
44. Anthony Ashley Cooper Shaftesbury (Earl of), *Principes de la philosophie morale*, trans. Denis Diderot (Amsterdam: Zacherie Chatelain, 1745), 165–66 (quotation from an unnumbered footnote by Diderot).
45. James, "Fibra, Fibre," 1520–21.
46. Ishizuka, "Fibre Body," 582.
47. Veit Erlmann, "String Theory: Denis Diderot's Philosophy of Sound and Everything," in *The Routledge Companion to Sounding Art*, ed. Marcel Cobussen, Vincent Meelberg, and Barry Truax (New York: Routledge, 2016), 146.
48. Denis Diderot, *Mémoires sur différens sujets de mathématiques* (Paris: Durand, 1748), 50.
49. According to a Buffonian-inflected reading of Diderot, his 1753 publication *Pensées sur l'interprétation de la nature* rejects the abstractions of

mathematics and instead embraces experimental physics. Indeed, scholars have often situated mathematics in opposition to the vitalist turn: its abstract and symbolic representations of natural forces represent an invented language, untethered from the infinite variations present in nature. Scholars have proposed many possible interpretations for the *Pensées sur l'interprétation de la nature*, including a movement toward biological science and the mechanical arts, a distrust of philosophical systems, an embrace of the descriptive science, and a rejection of conventional and arbitrary language (see Ernst Cassirer, *The Philosophy of the Enlightenment* trans. Fritz C. A. Koellin and James P. Pettegrove [Princeton, NJ: Princeton University Press, 1951], 74–75; and Suzanne Rodin Pucci, "Text as Document: Document as Text," *Diderot and a Poetics of Science* [New York: Peter Lang, 1986], 1–28).

50. See Kurt Ballstadt, "Mathematics," *Diderot: Natural Philosopher* (Oxford: Voltaire Foundation, 2008), 9–45.
51. Shaftesbury, *An Inquiry Concerning Virtue and Merit*, 124.
52. Shaftesbury, *Principes de la philosophie morale*, 213–14.
53. Diderot, *Œuvres complètes: Les Bijoux indiscrets*, ed. Macary et al., 3:169.
54. Denis Diderot, *Les Bijoux indiscrets: Or, The Indiscreet Toys*, vol. 2 (Tobago: reprinted for Pierrot Ragout, 1749), 75.
55. See Denis Diderot, "Chapitre XXV," in *Œuvres complètes: Les Bijoux indiscrets*, 3:112–18; Mary McAlpin, "Rape in Paradise: Naturalizing Sexual Violence in Diderot's Tahitian Reverie," *Eighteenth-Century Studies* 50, no. 3 (April 4, 2017): 300, https://doi.org/10.1353/ecs.2017.0012; for a discussion of rape depicted in Voltaire's fiction, see Georges Vigarello, *A History of Rape: Sexual Violence in France from the 16th to the 20th Century*, trans. Jean Birrell (Malden, MA: Polity, 2001), 64–65.
56. Michel Foucault, *Histoire de la sexualité: La volonté de savoir* (Paris: Gallimard, 1976), 101–5.
57. Diderot, *Œuvres complètes: Les Bijoux indiscrets*, ed. Macary et al., 3:99.
58. Diderot, *Les Bijoux indiscrets: Or, The Indiscreet Toys*, 1:169.
59. Jean-Jacques Rousseau, *Œuvres complètes de Jean-Jacques Rousseau*, ed. Bernard Gagnebin and Marcel Raymond, vol. 4 (Paris: Gallimard, 1959), 490, 715.
60. Nicolas Venette, *De la génération de l'homme, ou Tableau de l'amour conjugal* (Cologne: C. Joly, 1702), 107, 351 and 396, https://gallica.bnf.fr/ark:/12148/bpt6k9763528w.
61. Herman Boerhaave, *Institutions de médecine de Mr Herman Boerhaave*, vol. 7 (Paris: Huart, Briasson, Durand, 1743), 21, https://gallica.bnf.fr/ark:/12148/bpt6k97816003.

62. Charles Bonnet, *Considerations sur les corps organisés*, vol. 2 (Marc-Michel Rey, 1762), 233–34, https://gallica.bnf.fr/ark:/12148/bpt6k1040566r.
63. Joseph-Guichard Duverney, *Œuvres anatomiques de M. Duverney*, vol. 2 (Paris: Charles-Antoine Jombert, 1761), 338–39, https://gallica.bnf.fr/ark:/12148/bpt6k6227175g.
64. "Séance publique: De l'Académie royale des belles-lettres, sciences & arts de Bordeaux, Le Jour de Saint Louis, 24 Août 1749," *Mercure de France* 1 (January 1750): 3–33.
65. Duverney, *Œuvres anatomiques de M. Duverney*, 2:339.
66. Herman Boerhaave, *Institutions de médecine de Mr Herman Boerhaave*, 7:57; Albrecht von Haller, *Élémens de physiologie*, 2:253.
67. "Séance Publique," 12.
68. Charles Bonnet, *Considerations sur les corps organisés*, 2:233.
69. Bonnet, *Considerations sur les corps organisés*, 2:233.
70. Diderot, *Œuvres complètes: Éléments de physiologie*, ed. Varloot et al., 17:398.
71. Diderot, *Œuvres complètes: Éléments de physiologie*, ed. Varloot et al., 17:398.
72. Martha Feldman, *The Castrato: Reflections on Natures and Kinds* (Oakland: University of California Press, 2015), 96, 101.
73. Diderot, *Œuvres complètes: Éléments de physiologie*, ed. Varloot et al., 17:398.
74. Diderot, *Œuvres complètes: Éléments de physiologie*, ed. Varloot et al., 17:398.
75. Denis Diderot, *Œuvres complètes: La Religieuse*, ed. Georges May et al., vol. 11 (Paris: Hermann, 1975), 227.
76. Diderot, *Œuvres complètes: La Religieuse*, ed. May et al. 11:240–41.
77. Diderot, *Œuvres complètes: Les Bijoux indiscrets*, ed. Macary et al., 3:53.
78. Diderot, *Les Bijoux indiscrets: Or, The Indiscreet Toys*, 1:46.
79. Diderot, *Œuvres complètes: Les Bijoux indiscrets*, ed. Varloot, 3:53.
80. Diderot, *Les Bijoux Indiscrets: Or, The Indiscreet Toys* (1749), 46.
81. Diderot, *Œuvres complètes: Les Bijoux indiscrets*, ed. Varloot, 3:65.
82. Diderot, *Œuvres complètes: L'Interprétation de la nature* (1753–1765), 9:73.
83. Denis Diderot, "Affection," in *Encyclopédie, ou dictionnaire raisonné des sciences, des arts et des métiers, etc.*, ed. Diderot and Jean le Rond d'Alembert (Chicago: University of Chicago: ARTFL Encyclopédie Project [Autumn 2017 edition], ed. Robert Morrissey and Glenn Roe), http://encyclopedie.uchicago.edu/.

4. Sound and Sensibility

1. For more on the controversy, see Beverly Jerold, "Mystery in Paris, the German Connection and More: The Bérard–Blanchet Controversy Revisited," *Eighteenth-Century Music* 2, no. 1 (2005): 91–112.
2. Jean Blanchet, *L'art, ou les principes philosophiques du chant* (Paris: A. M. Lottin, 1756), xxii.
3. See Denis Diderot, *Lettre sur les aveugles, à l'usage de ceux qui voyent* (Londres [Paris?], 1749), 32.
4. Henri Coulet, introduction to Denis Diderot, *Œuvres complètes: Le Neveu de Rameau*, ed. Coulet et al., vol. 12 (Paris: Hermann, 1989), 33–35.
5. See Jacques Cazotte, *La nouvelle Raméide* (Amsterdam, 1766).
6. Auguste Jal, *Dictionnaire critique de biographie et d'histoire: Errata et supplement pour tous les dictionnaires historiques d'apres des documents authentiques inedits* (Paris: Plon, 1872), 1037–40.
7. Coulet, introduction to *Œuvres complètes: Le Neveu de Rameau*, ed. Coulet et al., 12:35.
8. Anne C. Vila, *Enlightenment and Pathology: Sensibility in the Literature and Medicine of Eighteenth-Century France* (Baltimore: Johns Hopkins University Press, 1998), 2–3.
9. David J. Denby, "Sensibility," in *Encyclopedia of the Enlightenment* (Oxford: Oxford University Press, 2002), http://www.oxfordreference.com/view/10.1093/acref/9780195104301.001.0001/acref-9780195104301-e-660.
10. Among the texts with which I frame my analysis of *sensibilité* in Diderot's corpus, I primarily focus on *Entretien entre Diderot et d'Alembert* and *Le Rêve de d'Alembert*.
11. Denis Diderot, *Lettre sur les sourds et muets: A l'usage de ceux qui entendent & qui parlent. Avec des additions* (Paris: Jean-Baptiste-Claude Bauche, 1751), 112; Denis Diderot, *Œuvres complètes: Le Rêve de d'Alembert*, ed. Jean Varloot et al., vol. 17 (Paris: Hermann, 1987), 148; Denis Diderot, *Œuvres complètes: La suite d'un entretien entre M. d'Alembert et M. Diderot*, ed. Jean Varloot et al., 17:102–3.
12. For more on the medical background of Diderot's use of the term *faisceau*, see François Duchesneau, "Diderot et la physiologie de la sensibilité," *Dix-Huitième Siècle* 31, no. 1 (1999): 195–216.
13. Denis Diderot, *Œuvres complètes: Le Neveu de Rameau*, ed. Coulet al., 12:125.
14. Diderot, *Œuvres complètes: Le Neveu de Rameau*, ed. Coulet et al., 12:168.
15. Blanchet, *L'art, ou les principes philosophiques du chant*, 26.

16. Coulet, introduction to Œuvres complètes: Le Neveu de Rameau, ed. Coulet et al., 12:35.
17. Denis Diderot, Œuvres complètes: Réfutations d'Helvétius, ed. Jean Th. De Booy et al., vol. 24 (Paris: Hermann, 2004), 578.
18. Diderot, Œuvres complètes: Réfutations d'Helvétius, ed. De Booy et al., 24:577.
19. Louis de La Caze, Idée de l'homme physique et moral, pour servir d'introduction à un traité de médecine (Paris: chez H. L. Guerin & L. F. Delatour, 1755), 294–95.
20. Mary McAlpin, Female Sexuality and Cultural Degradation in Enlightenment France: Medicine and Literature (Burlington, VT: Ashgate, 2012), 16.
21. McAlpin, Female Sexuality and Cultural Degradation in Enlightenment France, 16.
22. La Caze, Idée de l'homme physique et moral, 103, 112–19, 294–97, 381–82.
23. Denis Diderot, Œuvres complètes: Éléments de physiologie, ed. Jean Varloot et al., vol. 17 (Paris: Hermann, 1987)17:503.
24. Denis Diderot, Œuvres complètes: Paradoxe sur le comédien, ed. Jane Marsh Dieckmann et al., vol. 20 (Paris: Hermann, 1995), 57.
25. Diderot, Œuvres complètes: Paradoxe sur le comédien, ed. Dieckmann et al., 20:55.
26. Diderot, Œuvres complètes: Paradoxe sur le comédien, ed. Dieckmann et al., 20:49.
27. Diderot, Œuvres complètes: Paradoxe sur le comédien, ed. Dieckmann et al., 20:57.
28. Diderot, Œuvres complètes: Paradoxe sur le comédien, ed. Dieckmann et al., 20:58.
29. Diderot, Œuvres complètes: Paradoxe sur le comédien, ed. Dieckmann et al., 20:45, 57.
30. Diderot, Œuvres complètes: Paradoxe sur le comédien, ed. Dieckmann et al., 20:93.
31. Roland Desné introduction to Œuvres complètes: Réfutations d'Helvétius, ed. De Booy et al., 24:426.
32. Desné introduction to Œuvres complètes: Réfutations d'Helvétius, ed. De Booy et al., 24:426.
33. Desné introduction to Œuvres complètes: Réfutations d'Helvétius, ed. De Booy et al., 24:432.
34. Diderot, Œuvres complètes: Réfutations d'Helvétius, ed. De Booy et al., 24:577.

35. Diderot, Œuvres complètes: Réfutations d'Helvétius, ed. De Booy et al., 24:577.
36. Diderot, Œuvres complètes: Réfutations d'Helvétius, ed. De Booy et al., 24:577–78.
37. Diderot, Œuvres complètes: Réfutations d'Helvétius, ed. De Booy et al., 24:578.
38. Diderot, Œuvres complètes: Éléments de physiologie, ed. Varloot et al., 17:338.
39. Diderot, Œuvres complètes: Le Neveu de Rameau, ed. Coulet et al., 12:169.
40. See Dorothy S. Packer, "Horatian Moral Philosophy in French Song, 1649–1749," *Musical Quarterly* 61, no. 2 (1975): 240–71.
41. See Nicolas Clérambault, *Fables sur de petits airs et des Vaudevilles choisis avec une Basse en Musette* (Paris: G. Desprez et Jean Desessartz, 1730); Frédéric Desessartz, *Nouvelles poésies morales sur les plus airs de la musique française et italienne* (Paris: Lottin and Butard, 1732); *Trois cens fables en musique, dans le goût de M de la Fontaine notées sur des airs connus, vaudevilles, menuets, rondeaux & autres en six livres* (Liege: F. J. Desoer, n.d.); *Nouvelles étrennes utiles et agréables contenant un recueil de fables choisies dans le goût de La Fontaine sur des airs de vaudevilles notes, avec un calendrier* (Paris: Lottin, 1734); and *Nouvelles étrennes utiles et agréables, recueil de chansons morales et d'emblèmes sur de petits airs en vaudevilles connus* (Paris: Lottin, 1749).
42. Alain-René Lesage, "Préface des auteurs," in *Le theatre de la foire, ou L'opera comique* (Paris: chez Étienne Ganeau, 1721), vr.
43. *Nouvelles étrennes utiles et agréables, recueil de chansons morales et d'emblèmes sur de petits airs en vaudevilles connus*, iv.
44. Robert Darnton, *Poetry and the Police: Communication Networks in Eighteenth-Century Paris* (Cambridge, MA: Belknap Press of Harvard University Press, 2010), 80.
45. Derek Connon, "Music in the Parisian Fair Theatres: Medium or Message?," *Journal for Eighteenth-Century Studies* 31, no. 1 (2008): 122, https://doi.org/10.1111/j.1754-0208.2008.00007.x; Darnton, *Poetry and the Police*, 185.
46. Connon, "Music in the Parisian Fair Theatres," 122.
47. See Philip Robinson, "Les vaudevilles, un medium théâtral," *Dix-Huitième Siècle* 28, no. 1 (1996): 431–47, https://doi.org/10.3406/dhs.1996.2128; and Françoise Rubellin, "Lesage parodiste," in *Lesage, écrivain (1695–1735)*, ed. Jacques Wagner (Amsterdam: Rodopi, 1997), 95–123.
48. Connon, "Music in the Parisian Fair Theatres," 131.
49. Diderot, Œuvres complètes: Le Neveu de Rameau, ed. Coulet et al., 12:162.
50. In *Isle des fous* (1760), a governor oversees a penal colony in which the inhabitants can gain freedom only when the very unreasonable

inhabitants demonstrate reasonable behavior. In *Maréchal ferrant* (1761), a love intrigue develops when a marriage proposal almost separates the couples in love: the blacksmith's daughter Jeanette and her *soupirant* Colin, and Claudine and Jeanette's fiancé, la Bride.

51. Diderot, *Œuvres complètes: Le Neveu de Rameau*, ed. Coulet et al., 12:159. According to Henri Coulet's version of *Le Neveu*, the autograph version refers to the "vraies voyes d'un moribon," whereas the copyists' versions refer to the "vraies voix d'un moribond" (Diderot, *Œuvres complètes: Le Neveu de Rameau*, ed. Coulet et al., 12:159n257). My translation reflects Coulet's choice of "voies" as well as the copy editor's markings above "vraies," "voies," and "tour." The very literal meanings of these two terms, *path* and *tour*, seem to associate the line and movement of melody with the linear progression of human experience.

52. See James H. Johnson's chapter on musical imitation as well as the passage on Rousseau and Diderot (39–41) (Johnson, "Expression as Imitation," in *Listening in Paris: A Cultural History* [Berkeley: University of California Press, 1995], 35–50).

53. This aural style of reading resembles Wilda Anderson's description of reading *Le Rêve de d'Alembert*: "The text must induce in the reader the active-and-reactive state whose experience would be the most informative tactic Diderot could summon" (Anderson, *Diderot's Dream* [Baltimore: Johns Hopkins University Press, 1990], 62–63).

54. Daniel Heartz associates Lombard rhythms with a musical depiction of sobs (see Heartz, "Diderot et Le Théâtre Lyrique: 'Le Nouveau Stile' proposé par *Le Neveu de Rameau*," *Revue de Musicologie* 64, no. 2 (1978): 242, https://doi.org/10.2307/928237).

55. The music in *Le Neveu de Rameau* is also a commentary on the midcentury debate called the Querelle des Bouffons, which was a debate on the relative merits of French and Italian music.

56. Denis Diderot, *Œuvres completes: L'Interprétation de la nature (1753–1765)*, ed. Jean Varloot et al., vol. 9 (Paris: Hermann, 1981), 26.

57. Cristle Collins Judd, "Music in Dialogue: Conversational, Literary, and Didactic Discourse about Music in Renaissance," in "Essays in Honor of Sarah Fuller," special issue, *Journal of Music Theory*, 52, no. 1 (Spring 2008): 67.

58. Collins Judd, "Music in Dialogue," 64.

59. Collins Judd, "Music in Dialogue," 84.

60. See Denis Diderot and Bemetzrieder, *Leçons de clavecin et principes d'harmonie* in Diderot, *Œuvres complètes*, ed. Jean Mayer and Pierre

Citron, vol. 19 (Paris: Hermann, 1983), 59–391; Downing A. Thomas, "Sensible Sounds: Music and Theories of the Passions," in *Music and the Origins of Language: Theories from the French Enlightenment* (Cambridge: Cambridge University Press, 1995), 143–72.

61. See Béatrice Didier, *La musique des Lumières: Diderot—"L'Encyclopédie"—Rousseau* (Paris: PUF, 1985), 367–75; Daniel Heartz, "Diderot et Le Théâtre Lyrique: 'Le Nouveau Stile' proposé par *Le Neveu de Rameau*," 229–52; Daniel Heartz, "Locatelli and the Pantomime of the Violinist in *Le Neveu de Rameau*," *Diderot Studies* 27 (1998): 115–27; Marita P. McClymonds and Walter E. Rex, "'Ce beau récitatif obligé': *Le Neveu de Rameau* and Jommelli," *Diderot Studies* 22 (1986): 63–77; Jean-Christophe Rebejkow, "Nouvelles recherches sur la musique dans *Le Neveu de Rameau*," *Recherches sur Diderot et sur l'Encyclopédie* 20 (1996): 57–74; Jean-Christophe Rebejkow, "Diderot et la Pantomine: Vers un nouveau 'genre' musical," *Francofonia*, no. 19 (1990): 61–73; Cynthia Verba, "Music as Art and Science: Changing Conceptualizations by Diderot, 1748–1760," in *Music and the French Enlightenment: Reconstruction of a Dialogue 1750–1764* 2nd ed. (Oxford: Oxford University Press, 2016), 79–96; Tili Boon Cuillé, "Diderot and Musical Mimesis," in *Narrative Interludes: Musical Tableaux in Eighteenth-Century French Texts* (Toronto: University of Toronto Press, 2006), 25–55; and Mark Darlow, "Diderot's Voice(s): Music and Reform from the Querelle des Bouffons to *Le Neveu de Rameau*" in *New Essays on Diderot*, ed. James Fowler (Cambridge: Cambridge University Press, 2011), 203–19.

62. See Julia Kristeva, "La Musique parlée ou remarques sur la subjectivité dans la fiction à propos du *Neveu de Rameau*," in *Langue et langage de Leibniz à l'Encyclopédie*, ed. Michèle Duchet and Michèle Jalley (Paris: Union Général d'Éditions, 1977), 153–206; Jacques Chouillet, *La Formation des idées esthétiques de Diderot 1745–1763* (Paris: Colin, 1973), 520–52; Walter E. Rex, "Music and the Unity of *Le Neveu de Rameau*," *Diderot Studies* 29 (2003): 83–99; and John T. Hamilton, *Music, Madness, and the Unworking of Language* (New York: Columbia University Press, 2013), 67–70.

63. Marian Hobson, "Pantomime, spasme et parataxe: *Le Neveu de Rameau*," *Revue de Métaphysique et de Morale* 89, no. 2 (1984): 197–213.

64. This aural reading style is similar to but distinct from the one Anderson describes for *Le Rêve de d'Alembert* (see Anderson, *Diderot's Dream*, 62–63).

65. These passages are also relevant to the Querelle des Bouffons, the mid-century debate on French and Italian music (see Thomas Christensen,

Rameau and Musical Thought in the Enlightenment [Cambridge: Cambridge University Press, 1993], 249; Rameau, *Observations sur notre instinct pour la musique* [Paris: Prault fils, 1754], 63–68; and Verba, *Music and the French Enlightenment*, 41).

66. In an earlier passage, the nephew compares himself to the Greek herald Stentor (Diderot, *Œuvres complètes: Le Neveu de Rameau*, ed. Coulet et al., 12:125).
67. Diderot, *Œuvres complètes: Le Neveu de Rameau*, ed. Coulet et al., 12:167–68.
68. For an analysis of the chromaticism in "Tristes apprêts" and its affective meaning, see Christensen, *Rameau and Musical Thought in the Enlightenment*, 249; and Jean-Philippe Rameau, *Observations sur notre instinct pour la musique* (Paris: Prault fils, 1754), 63–68.
69. Diderot, *Œuvres complètes: Le Neveu de Rameau*, ed. Coulet et al., 12:158 and 169.
70. See Diderot, *Œuvres complètes: Paradoxe sur le comédien*, ed. Dieckmann et al., 20:55. For discussions of enharmonicism outside of Diderot, see Alexander Rehding, "Rousseau, Rameau, and Enharmonic Furies in the French Enlightenment," *Journal of Music Theory* 49, no. 1 (2005): 159, 167; Jean-Philippe Rameau, *Démonstration du principe de l'harmonie* (Paris: Durand, 1750), 99–100; and Jean-Philippe Rameau, "Remarques sur les pièces de ce livre, & sur les differens genres de musique," in *Nouvelles suites de pièces de clavecin* (Paris: Boivin, 1729).
71. Like Jean-Luc Filoche, I interpret the nephew's comments on enharmonicism as tinged with admiration for his uncle's musical experiments (see Filoche, "*Le Neveu de Rameau* et la Querelle des Bouffons: Un son de cloche inédit," *Diderot Studies* 21 [1983]: 103).
72. Rehding provides a lengthy musicological explanation of Rousseau's and Rameau's analysis of enharmonicism in eighteenth-century repertoire, namely Rameau's "Trio des Parques" from *Hippolyte et Aricie* and the furies in Christoph Willibald Gluck's *Orfeo ed Euridice* (see Rehding, "Rousseau, Rameau, and Enharmonic Furies," 141–80). As Rehding explains, the disagreement revolved around musical perspective. For Rousseau, singers should perform enharmonic tones with a microtonal variation because, depending on the system of tuning, they could be nonidentical pitches. Enharmonic notes are nonidentical pitches in just intonation (tuning from antiquity to the Middle Ages) and to a lesser degree in mean-tone temperament (tuning from the Renaissance to the nineteenth century), whereas enharmonic notes are identical pitches in equal temperament (mid-eighteenth century to the present).

73. See Downing Thomas's discussion of Rameau's "Trio des parques" and its association with horror in *Aesthetics of Opera in the Ancien Régime* (Cambridge: Cambridge University Press, 2002), 162–69.
74. Enharmonism in *Neveu* resembles Andrew Clark's interpretation of the figure of dissonance. Clark notes that the nephew uses poetic and musical dissonances to "force the reader and *Moi* to acknowledge the complexity and variety of positions and relations in each situation" (Clark, "The Figure of Dissonance," in *Diderot's Part* [Burlington, VT: Ashgate, 2008], 196).
75. Anderson, *Diderot's Dream*, 233–34.
76. Diderot, *Œuvres complètes: Le Neveu de Rameau*, ed. Coulet et al., 12:156.
77. Diderot, *Œuvres complètes: Le Neveu de Rameau*, ed. Coulet et al., 12:125. For a physiological description of coughing and laughter, see Denis Diderot, *Œuvres complètes: Le Rêve d'Alembert*, ed. Jean Varloot et al., vol. 17 (Paris: Hermann, 1987), 396.
78. Diderot, *Œuvres complètes: Le Neveu de Rameau*, ed. Coulet et al., 12:125.
79. Diderot, *Œuvres complètes: Le Neveu de Rameau*, ed. Coulet et al., 12:172.
80. Diderot, *Œuvres complètes: Le Neveu de Rameau*, ed. Coulet et al., 12:172.
81. Diderot, *Œuvres complètes: Le Neveu de Rameau*, ed. Coulet et al., 12:154, 164–68.
82. Diderot, *Œuvres complètes: Le Neveu de Rameau*, ed. Coulet et al., 12:156.
83. Diderot, *Lettre sur les sourds et muets*, 112.
84. Clark, *Diderot's Part*, 154.
85. Clark, *Diderot's Part*, 190.
86. Clark, *Diderot's Part*, 189.
87. Sophia Rosenfeld, *A Revolution in Language: The Problem of Signs in Late Eighteenth-Century France* (Stanford, CA: Stanford University Press, 2004), 46.
88. Diderot, *Œuvres complètes: Le Rêve de d'Alembert*, ed. Varloot et al., 17:101.
89. Diderot, *Œuvres complètes: Le Neveu de Rameau*, ed. Coulet et al., 12:169.
90. For alternate approaches to music and the *polype*, see Daniel Chua, *Absolute Music and the Construction of Meaning* (Cambridge: Cambridge University Press, 1999), 105–6; and Wye Jamison Allanbrook, "Comic Flux and Comic Precision," in *The Secular Commedia: Comic Mimesis in Late Eighteenth-Century Music*, ed. Mary Ann Smart and Richard Taruskin (Berkeley: University of California Press, 2014), 1–41.
91. Diderot, *Œuvres complètes: Le Neveu de Rameau*, ed. Coulet et al., 12:164–65.
92. David Charlton suggests that Pergolesi's *Tracollo* "most resembles a model" for the nephew's moment of madness (Charlton, *Opera in the Age*

of Rousseau: Music, Confrontation, Realism [Cambridge: Cambridge University Press, 2012], 263).
93. Diderot, *Œuvres complètes: Le Neveu de Rameau*, ed. Coulet et al., 12:164–65.
94. My reconstruction is an imperfect thought experiment in imagining the nephew's bizarre performance. Example 6, unfortunately, does not account for the many possible imagined scenarios. Melodies of varying tempi may intermingle, and thus my measured reconstruction would not accurately capture their overlap.
95. Diderot, *Œuvres complètes: Le Neveu de Rameau*, ed. Coulet et al., 12:166.
96. Diderot, *Œuvres complètes: Le Neveu de Rameau*, ed. Coulet et al., 12:165.
97. See Mary Cyr, "On Performing 18th-Century Haute-Contre Roles," *Musical Times* 118, no. 1610 (1977): 291–95.
98. This interpretation might also alter Didier's comparison of *Neveu*'s music to the Parisian social hierarchy (see Didier, *La musique des Lumières*, 372). Instead of Parisian society, I imagine the nephew's *opéra-comique* medley as a corollary to the beehive metaphor wherein individuals aggregate into a larger social organism.
99. This scene has a rich secondary literature, with many inspired critical interpretations of the role of madness; to name a few, it is interpreted as signifying consciousness freed from moral law (G. W. F. Hegel, *The Phenomenology of Mind*, trans. J. B. Baillie [New York: Harper Torchbooks, 1967], 543); LUI's demonstration of artistic conception (Cuillé, *Narrative Interludes*, 52); LUI's representation of the human subject as always contradictory and multiple (Hamilton, *Music, Madness and the Unworking of Language*, 74); and, finally, the incommensurability of two modes of thinking (Anderson, *Diderot's Dream*, 245). In highlighting the nephew's music, my interpretation compares Diderot's *clavecin* (the atomistic self of sensitive organs and vibrating nerve fibers) to musical figures.
100. Diderot, *Œuvres complètes: Le Rêve de d'Alembert*, ed. Varloot et al., 17:108–9.
101. Diderot, *Œuvres complètes: Le Neveu de Rameau*, ed. Coulet et al., 12:164–65.
102. Diderot, *Œuvres complètes: Le Neveu de Rameau*, ed. Coulet et al., 12:166.
103. Diderot, *Œuvres complètes: Le Neveu de Rameau*, ed. Coulet et al., 12:166.
104. David Charlton offers an interesting analysis of eighteenth-century metaphors comparing the orchestra with the singing voice (Charlton, "'Envoicing' the Orchestra: Enlightenment Metaphors in Theory and Practice," in *French Opera 1730–1830: Meaning and Media* [Aldershot, UK: Ashgate, 2000], 1–32).

214   NOTES TO PAGES 136–141

105. Rousseau, "Récitatif obligé," in *Dictionnaire de musique*, (Paris: Duchesne, 1768), 411–12. Rousseau asserts that the French do not use this recitative style, a notion that Charlton contests (Charlton, *Opera in the Age of Rousseau*, 47).
106. Denis Diderot, *Œuvres complètes: Entretiens sur le fils naturel*, ed. Jacques Chouillet and Anne-Marie Chouillet, vol. 10 (Paris: Hermann, 1980), 158.
107. This passage appears to be a "musical collage" of many sections of Jommelli's piece. Indeed, Walter Rex and Marita McClymonds note that the nephew could be quoting from any of several possible arias (see McClymonds and Rex, "'Ce beau récitatif obligé': *Le Neveu de Rameau* and Jommelli," *Diderot Studies* 22 [1986]: 63–77).
108. Diderot, *Œuvres complètes: Le Neveu de Rameau*, ed. Coulet et al., 12:166.
109. Jean-Baptiste Couvray, *Une année de la vie du Chevalier Faublas* in *Romanciers du XVIIIe siècle*, vol. 2, ed. Etiemble (Paris: Gallimard, 1960), 556.
110. Denis Diderot, *Œuvres complètes: Le Neveu de Rameau*, ed. Coulet et al., 12:196.

5. The Haunted Listener

1. Trevor Burnard and John Garrigus, *The Plantation Machine: Atlantic Capitalism in French Saint-Domingue and British Jamaica* (Philadelphia: University of Pennsylvania Press, 2016), 67.
2. The 1772 and 1776 editions present two versions of the supernatural. In the 1776 edition, we encounter an Orientalist version, akin to the *Arabian Nights*. Literary scholars have often associated *le merveilleux* in *Diable* with that of *Aladin et sa lampe merveilleuse* (see Claudine Hunting, "Les Mille et une sources du *Diable amoureux* de Cazotte," *Studies on Voltaire and the Eighteenth Century* 230 [1985]: 247–71). This reading is apt for the 1776 edition because it includes a passage with Egyptian fortune-tellers. In the first edition, however, the supernatural emerges as a representational strategy that ironically critiques Enlightenment ideals, and specifically the search for knowledge both natural and humanistic. As part of this representational strategy, the narrator describes uncanny voices with two distinct inflections: the accents of Italian lyricism and of English sentimentality. *Diable*'s first edition represents voices whose cultural presence in France eroded the prestige of French opera (*Tragédie en musique*) and significantly influenced French literary production. Within my critical narrative, the uncanny voices in *Diable* represent

an attack on the vitalist voices of chapters 3 and 4 and the sentimental voices in chapters 1 and 2.
3. Most scholarship on *Diable* ignores the first edition's denouement, which confirms Béelzébuth's supernatural origin, and instead focuses on Cazotte's definitive version, which leaves open the question of Béelzébuth's origin. In the definitive version, the reader and protagonist never know whether the spirit is imaginary, supernatural, or demonic. An analysis of the voice in the first edition contributes to scholarship on the definitive edition, from Tzvetan Todorov's definition of the Fantastic as a moment of doubt (a hesitation between rational explanations and supernatural beliefs) to Georges Décote's interpretation of *Diable* as a critique of the Enlightenment and its praise of human emotion (*passions*) because the supernatural voice generates doubt in the protagonist's mind (see Todorov, *Introduction à la littérature fantastique* [Éditions du Seuil: Paris, 1970], 37–38; and Décote, *L'Itinéraire de Jacques Cazotte (1719–1792): De la fiction littéraire au mysticisme politique* [Geneva: Droz, 1984], 295).
4. My version of the uncanny does not consider whether the erosion of class and geographic boundaries contributed to what Francesca Brittan describes as the "characteristic wavering between supernatural and rational, exotic and domestic domains" in the literary and musical depictions of the fantastic (Brittan, *Music and Fantasy in the Age of Berlioz* [Cambridge: Cambridge University Press, 2017], 32).
5. Rosemary Jackson, *Fantasy: The Literature of Subversion* (London: Routledge, 1981, 2003), 66; José B. Monleón, *A Specter Is Haunting Europe: A Sociohistorical Approach to the Fantastic* (Princeton, NJ: Princeton University Press, 1990), 12–13.
6. See Terry Castle, *The Female Thermometer: Eighteenth-Century Culture and the Invention of the Uncanny* (New York: Oxford University Press, 1995), 3–20.
7. Gary Tomlinson, *Metaphysical Song: An Essay on Opera* (Princeton, NJ: Princeton University Press, 1999), 73.
8. Tomlinson, *Metaphysical Song*, 83–84.
9. Jacques Cazotte, "Lettre 53," in *Correspondence de Jacques Cazotte*, ed. Georges Décote (Paris: Klincksieck, 1982), 134.
10. Christopher McIntosh, *Eliphas Lévi and the French Occult Revival* (Albany: State University of New York Press, 1972, 2011), 34. See also Décote, *L'Itinéraire de Jacques Cazotte*, 315–37.
11. Georges Décote finds evidence to suggest that Cazotte entered a Martinist order in 1777 (Décote, *L'Itinéraire de Jacques Cazotte*, 319).
12. Jacques Cazotte, "Lettre 53," in *Correspondance de Jacques Cazotte*, 134.

13. Jacques Cazotte wrote three successive versions of *Le Diable amoureux* (1772, 1774, and 1776), the second of which he never published but read aloud to friends. Tili Boon Cuillé, *Narrative Interludes: Musical Tableaux in Eighteenth-Century French Texts* (Toronto: Toronto University Press, 2006), 112, 231n77.

14. Jacques Cazotte, *Œuvres badines et morales*, vol. 4 (London, 1788), 277.

15. Cazotte, "Lettre 53," in *Correspondance de Jacques Cazotte*, 135.

16. Cazotte, "Lettre 53," in *Correspondance de Jacques Cazotte*, 136.

17. In the following paragraph, Cazotte even questions a pillar of eighteenth-century scientific discoveries, the polyp. This small organism helped inspire theories of the materialist soul (Cazotte, "Lettre 53," in *Correspondance de Jacques Cazotte*, 136; see also Aram Vartanian, "Trembley's Polyp, La Mettrie, and Eighteenth-Century French Materialism," *Journal of the History of Ideas* 11, no. 3 [1950]: 259–86).

18. Cazotte, "Lettre 53," in *Correspondance de Jacques Cazotte*, 136. For more on the supernatural and the Enlightenment, see Dan Edelstein, "Introduction to the Super-Enlightenment," in *The Super-Enlightenment: Daring to Know Too Much*, ed. Edelstein (Oxford: Voltaire Foundation, 2010), 1–33.

19. Fabienne Moore, "The Poetry of the Super-Enlightenment: The Theories and Practices of Cazotte, Chassaignon, Mercier, Saint-Martin and Bonneville," in *The Super-Enlightenment: Daring to Know Too Much*, ed. Dan Edelstein (Oxford: Voltaire Foundation, 2010), 137.

20. Moore, "The Poetry of the Super-Enlightenment," 153, 154.

21. Baculard d'Arnaud, *Euphémie ou le triomphe de la religion* (Paris: Le Jay, 1768), ix.

22. Cazotte's correspondence contains a passage in which he explicitly imitates Baculard d'Arnaud's exuberant use of exclamation points (Cazotte, "Lettre 62," in *Correspondance de Jacques Cazotte*, 161–62). Other eighteenth-century figures attempted to transcribe the voice in print. As Noelle Chao notes, Joshua Steele's 1775 *Essay towards Establishing the Melody and Measure of Speech* "was a complex system for recording the voice in print . . . [and] making sound into something a person could hold in his hands" (Chao, "Listening to the Voice on the Page: Joshua Steele and Technologies of Recording," *The Eighteenth Century: Theory and Interpretation* 54, no. 2 [Summer 2013]: 245). Discussions also took place in the eighteenth century on the connection between orality and print culture (see Denis Diderot, in *Œuvres complètes: Entretiens sur le fils naturel*, ed. Jacques Chouillet and Anne-Marie Chouillet, vol. 10 [Paris: Hermann, 1980], 84;

Roger Chartier, *The Cultural Use of Print in Early Modern France* trans. Lydia G. Cochrane [Princeton, NJ: Princeton University Press, 1987]; and Robert Darnton, *Poetry and the Police* [Cambridge, MA: Belknap Press of Harvard University Press, 2010]).

23. Brian Kane, "The Voice: A Diagnosis," in "Music and the Modes of Production," ed. Lidia Klein and Karim Wissa, special issue, *Polygraph: An International Journal of Culture & Politics* 25 (2016): 106, https://www.academia.edu/31894038/The_Voice_a_Diagnosis.

24. Cazotte, "Lettre 60" in *Correspondance de Jacques Cazotte*, 156. Although in this letter Cazotte specifically describes the French Revolution as "the work of the Devil," he imagined a causal link between the ideas of the *philosophes* and the outbreak of the Revolution (see Georges Décote's annotation in Cazotte, *Correspondance de Jacques Cazotte*, 146n24, 150n13, 156n17, 160n8).

25. I do not include in the vitalist voice the one described in the *Paradoxe sur le comédien*. See chapter 4 on the distinction between a vitalist voice that is embodied, and the voice of an acting genius that is dispassionate and untethered from the audible sentience of human physiology.

26. Anonymous, "Extrait d'une lettre écrite de Bourgogne à M. D. L. R. Le 4 fevrier 1731, contenant quelques reflexions sur l'Akousmate d'Ansacq, dont il est parlé dans le second volume du mercure de decembre dernier," *Mercure de France*, February 1731, 334–35.

27. Anonymous, "Extrait d'une lettre écrite de Bourgogne," 336.
28. Anonymous, "Extrait d'une lettre écrite de Bourgogne," 336.
29. Anonymous, "Extrait d'une lettre écrite de Bourgogne," 336.
30. Anonymous, "Extrait d'une lettre écrite de Bourgogne," 336.
31. René Descartes, "René Descartes to Henry More: Thursday, 15 April 1649," in *Electronic Enlightenment Scholarly Edition of Correspondence*, ed. Robert Mcnamee et al., vers. 3.0, University of Oxford, 2018, http://dx.doi.org.dartmouth.idm.oclc.org/10.13051/ee:doc/descreCU0030371a1c.

32. Augustin Calmet, *Dictionnaire historique, critique, chronologique, géographique et litteral de la Bible*, vol. 1 (Paris: Emery, Saugrain and Pierre Martin, 1730), 89.

33. Claude-François Nonnotte, *Dictionnaire philosophique de la religion: Où l'on établit tous les points de la religion, attaqués par les incrédules, et où l'on répond à toutes leurs objections* (Brussels: J. Van den Berghen, 1773), 398.

34. Nonnotte, *Dictionnaire philosophique de la religion*, 399.

35. Calmet, *Dissertations sur les apparitions des anges, des démons [et] des esprits* (Paris: Bure l'aïné: ambridge, 1746), 230–31, 472.

36. See Lalouat de Soalaines, "Seconde lettre de M. Lalouat de Soalaines, sur les Akousmates," *Mercure de France,* July 1731, 1637.
37. Calmet, *Dissertations sur les apparitions des anges, des démons [et] des esprits,* 472.
38. This ritual allegedly allowed Martinists to reintegrate with God through commerce with benevolent spirits (see Robert Darnton, *Mesmerism and the End of the Enlightenment* [Cambridge, MA: Harvard University Press, 1968], 69).
39. Calmet, *Dictionnaire historique, critique, chronologique, géographique et litteral de la Bible,* 1:531.
40. Sébastien Michaelis, "Actes recueillis et dressez par le Père Michaelis," in *Histoire admirable de la possession et conversion d'une pénitente, séduite par un magicien, la faisant sorcière et princesse des sorciers au païs de Prouence, conduite à la Ste.-Baume pour y estre exorcizée: Ensemble La Pneumalogie, ou discours des esprits,* 2nd ed. (Paris: Charles Chastellain, 1613), 26.
41. Jehan Boulaese, *Le manuel de l'admirable victoire du corps de Dieu sur l'esprit maling Beelzebub: prins pour l'extrait & souverain sommaire de toute l'histoire notoire, par les hérétiques impugnée & publiquement avérée par la veue de plus de 150 000 personnes* [. . .] (Liège Henry Houius, 1598), 88–89.
42. Boulaese, *Le manuel de l'admirable victoire du corps de Dieu,* 204.
43. Boulaese, *Le manuel de l'admirable victoire du corps de Dieu,* 204.
44. Bloechl describes vocal signs of demonic possession as "uncanny vocality." In this chapter, I extend Bloechl's uncanny vocality beyond possession to include the voice's ability to disguise a being's material or spiritual substance, and a supernatural voice, which exhibits a supernatural power over the material world (see Bloechl, *Native American Song at the Frontiers of Early Modern Music* [Cambridge: Cambridge University Press, 2008], 68–69).
45. Jacques Cazotte, *Le Diable amoureux: Nouvelle espagnole* (Naples [i.e., Paris]: Le Jay, 1772), v.
46. Cazotte, *Le Diable amoureux,* 14.
47. Cazotte, *Le Diable amoureux,* 14.
48. Cazotte, *Le Diable amoureux,* 15.
49. Boulaese, *Le manuel de l'admirable victoire du corps de Dieu,* 209.
50. Cazotte, *Le Diable amoureux,* 14–5.
51. Cazotte, *Le Diable amoureux,* 15.
52. Michaelis, *Histoire admirable de la possession et conversion d'une pénitente,* 88.

53. Bloechl, *Native American Song at the Frontiers of Early Modern Music*, 86. Whereas Bloechl specifically discusses the "ecstatic voice of prophecy," I interpret both demonic and conjuring voices as possessing a noncorporeal force.
54. Cazotte, *Le Diable amoureux*, 14.
55. Edme-François Mallet, "Conjuration," in *Encyclopédie, ou dictionnaire raisonné des sciences, des arts et des métiers, etc.*, ed. Denis Diderot and Jean le Rond d'Alembert (University of Chicago: ARTFL Encyclopédie Project [Autumn 2017 edition], ed. Robert Morrissey and Glenn Roe), 3:885, http://encyclopedie.uchicago.edu.dartmouth.idm.oclc.org/.
56. The third use of italicization occurs when Biondetta dictates the terms of her servitude to Alvare. Alvare binds Biondetta to him with borrowed words. With this incantation, he becomes the ventriloquizing subject of a supernatural spirit (Cazotte, *Le Diable*, 48–49).
57. Jacques Matter, *Saint-Martin, le Philosophe Inconnu: Sa vie et ses écrits, son maître Martinez et leurs groupes d'après des documents inédits* (Paris: Didier et comapgnie, 1862), 59.
58. Matter, *Saint-Martin*, 388–91.
59. Matter, *Saint-Martin*, 390.
60. See Downing Thomas, *Aesthetics of Opera in the Ancien Régime, 1647–1785* (Cambridge: Cambridge University Press, 2002), 190–92. See also Joseph-Louis Roger, *Traité des effets de la musique sur le corps humain* (Paris: Brunot, 1803).
61. Darnton, *Mesmerism and the End of the Enlightenment in France*, 133.
62. Cazotte, *Le Diable amoureux*, vii.
63. Cazotte, *Le Diable amoureux*, 9.
64. Cazotte, *Le Diable amoureux*, 8.
65. *Diable* blurs the lines between the gender roles associated with demonic possession. While men often exercised or conjured spirits, women more frequently fell victim to possession. Alvare's voice strangely modifies the historical accounts and gender roles associated with demonic possession and Martinist rituals. Alvare combines these two roles to create a new gender category, which, as Dorothea von Mücke suggests, is the role of bachelorhood (von Mücke, *The Seduction of the Occult and the Rise of the Fantastic Tale* [Stanford, CA: Stanford University Press, 2003], 20, 49).
66. Cazotte, *Le Diable amoureux*, 39, 82.
67. "Obsession du démon," in *Encyclopédie*, 11:325.

68. Bloechl, *Native American Song at the Frontiers of Early Modern Music*, 59.
69. Jean-Jacques Rousseau, "Improviser," in *Dictionnaire de musique* (Paris: Veuve Duchesne, 1768), 255.
70. In addition to evoking uncanniness, the unnaturalness of Italian music offers a counterargument to a pro-Italian, especially Rousseauan, critique of French music (harmony) as the unnatural creation of artificial conventions (see Cynthia Verba, *Music and the French Enlightenment: Reconstruction of a Dialogue, 1750–1764*, 2nd ed. [Oxford: Oxford University Press, 2016], 46).
71. Denis Diderot, *Œuvres complètes: Paradoxe sur le comédien*, ed. Jane Marsh Dieckmann et al., vol. 20 (Paris: Hermann, 1995), 123.
72. Diderot, *Œuvres complètes: Paradoxe sur le comédien*, ed. Dieckmann et al., 20:123–24.
73. Denis Diderot, *Œuvres complètes: La Religieuse*, ed. Georges May et al. (Paris: Hermann, 1975), 240–41.
74. Johann Caspar Lavater, *Essai sur la physiognomonie, destiné à faire connoître l'homme et à le faire aimer*, trans. Antoine-Bernard Caillard et al., vol. 1 (The Hague, 1781), 22, https://gallica.bnf.fr/ark:/12148/bpt6k56987922.
75. Johann Caspar Lavater, *Essai sur la physiognomonie, destiné à faire connoître l'homme et à le faire aimer*, trans. Antoine-Bernard Caillard et al., vol. 3 (The Hague, 1781), 212, https://gallica.bnf.fr/ark:/12148/bpt6k5606379q.
76. Lavater, *Essai sur la physiognomonie*, 3:212.
77. Since my study is on the voice, I have focused on passages from Lavater that examine the voice's physiological temperament. This is not to say that Lavater privileges the voice over other physiological signs. The voice is one of many organs through which a person expresses their moral temperament.
78. Cazotte, *Le Diable amoureux*, 83.
79. Elisabeth Le Guin's description of sonic *sensibilité* involves an embodied and sonic expression of inwardness and softness. Although her argument applies to Boccherini, her connection between sensibility and the qualities of softness and inwardness are easily applied to *Diable* (see Le Guin, "Virtuosity, Virtuality, Virtue," in *Boccherini's Body: An Essay on Carnal Musicology* [Berkeley: University of California Press, 2006], 105–59).
80. James H. Johnson, *Listening in Paris: A Cultural History* (Berkeley: University of California Press, 1995), 61.
81. Johnson, *Listening in Paris*, 65.
82. Cazotte, *Le Diable amoureux*, 82.

83. Fanny de Beauharnais, *Les Illuminés* in *Le Somnambule: Œuvres posthumes en prose et en vers, où l'on trouve l'histoire générale d'une isle très singulière aux grandes Indes en 1784* (Paris: Didot, 1786), 200.
84. Jacques Cazotte, *Le Lord Impromptu, nouvelle Romanesque, traduite de l'Anglois* (Amsterdam: Arkstée and Merkus, 1767), 34, 37, 40, and 61.
85. This is a recurring theme in Cazotte's work. In addition to his pamphlet letter and two novels, *Le Diable amoureux* and *Le Lord impromptu*, Cazotte wrote an epic poem called *Ollivier*, which includes a short story about music as a language of emotion (see Cuillé, *Narrative Interludes*, 62–71).
86. Jacques Cazotte and Louis de Cahusac, *La Guerre de l'opéra, lettre écrite à une dame en province*, (1753), 18.
87. Cazotte, *Le Diable amoureux*, 83.
88. *Dictionnaire de l'Académie française*, 4th ed. (Paris, 1762), s.v. "connoitre."
89. Nina Sun Eidsheim, *Sensing Sound: Singing and Listening as Vibrational Practice* (Durham, NC: Duke University Press, 2015), 68, http://libcat.dartmouth.edu/record=b6280719~S1.
90. Nicolas Beauzée, "Métaphore," in *Encyclopédie*, 10:437.
91. Samuel Richardson, *Clarissa, or, the History of a Young Lady*, vol. 3 (London: Samuel Richardson, 1748), 333.
92. Castle, *The Female Thermometer*, 59.
93. Samuel Richardson, *Clarissa, or, the History of a Young Lady*, vol. 5 (London: John Osborn, 1751), 111.
94. Martha Feldman, *The Castrato: Reflections on Natures and Kinds* (Oakland: University of California Press, 2015), 188.
95. Feldman, *The Castrato*, 177–78, 211.
96. Cazotte, *Le Diable amoureux*, 23.
97. Cazotte, *Le Diable amoureux*, 25.
98. Cazotte, *Le Diable amoureux*, 26.
99. Cazotte, *Le Diable amoureux*, 26.
100. Cazotte, *Le Diable Amoureux*, 26.
101. Cazotte, *Le Diable amoureux*, 26.
102. Alvare constantly struggles with this process of unveiling. After this scene, Alvare gazes at Biondetta and imagines that a transparent film covers her beautiful complexion (Cazotte, *Le Diable amoureux*, 50). Alvare's recognition resembles what Jean Starobinski calls the *théorie de dévoilement*. Starobinski posits that in Rousseau's work, there is a process of unveiling. First, one recognizes the illusion of the veil. One then discovers and describes what is hidden (Starobinski, *Jean-Jacques Rousseau: La transparence et l'obstacle* [Paris: Gallimard, 1971], 94).

Epilogue

1. Thomas L. Hankins and Robert J. Silverman, *Instruments and the Imagination* (Princeton, NJ: Princeton University Press, 1995), 186.
2. See Hankins and Silverman, *Instruments and the Imagination*, 186; and Louis-Gabriel Michaud, *Biographie universelle, ancienne et moderne* vol. 28 (Paris: Delagrave, 1843), 186–87.
3. "Mécanique," *Journal de Paris*, no. 122 (May 1, 1784): 533.
4. Mathon de La Cour, *Journal de Lyon: ou Annonces et variétés littéraires*, no. 10 (Lyon: Chez Aimé de la Roche, 1784), 156.
5. La Cour, *Journal de Lyon: ou Annonces et variétés littéraires*, 156.
6. "Mécanique," *Journal de Paris*, no. 102 (April 11, 1784): 449.
7. "Mécanique," *Journal de Paris*, no. 143 (May 22, 1784): 624.
8. "Mécanique," *Journal de Paris*, no. 143 (May 22, 1784): 624; Jacques Mallet du Pan, "Variétés: Lettre au rédacteur du Mercure," *Mercure de France*, July 1784, 182–83.
9. "Mécanique," *Journal de Paris*, no. 143 (May 22, 1784): 624.
10. "Mécanique," *Journal de Paris*, no. 143 (May 22, 1784): 624.
11. "Mécanique," *Journal de Paris*, no. 143 (May 22, 1784): 624.
12. "Mécanique," *Journal de Paris*, no. 102 (April 11, 1784): 449.
13. "Mécanique," *Journal de Paris*, no. 143 (May 22, 1784): 624.
14. Antoine de Rivarol, *De l'universalité de la langue française* (Berlin: Prault and Bailley, 1785), 142.
15. Rivarol, *De l'universalité de la langue française*, 142.
16. Antoine de Rivarol, *Lettre à Monsieur le président de ***: Sur le globe airostatique, sur les têtes parlantes, & sur l'état présent de l'opinion publique à Paris* in *Œuvres completes de Rivarol* (Paris: Léopold Collin, 1808), 236.
17. Rivarol, *De l'universalité de la langue française*, 95–99.
18. Rivarol, *De l'universalité de la langue française*, 95.
19. Rivarol, *De l'universalité de la langue française*, 146.
20. "Mécanique," *Journal de Paris*, no. 143 (May 22, 1784), 624.
21. Mallet du Pan, "Variétés: Lettre au rédacteur du Mercure," 179.
22. Mallet du Pan, "Variétés: Lettre au rédacteur du Mercure," 179.
23. Jean-Antoine-Nicolas de Caritat Condorcet, *Œuvres de Condorcet*, vol. 12 (Paris: Didot frères, 1847), 239.
24. Mallet du Pan, "Variétés: Lettre au rédacteur du Mercure," 183.
25. Mallet du Pan, "Variétés: Lettre au rédacteur du Mercure," 182.
26. Mallet du Pan, "Variétés: Lettre au rédacteur du Mercure," 177.
27. Mallet du Pan, "Variétés. Lettre au rédacteur du Mercure," 182.

28. The critique of Mical's voices could also be directed at the object of their praise, the monarchy (Mallet du Pan, "Variétés: Lettre au rédacteur du Mercure," 182).
29. Mallet du Pan, "Variétés: Lettre au rédacteur du Mercure," 184–85.
30. Jonathan Sterne, "Machines to Hear for Them," in *The Audible Past: Cultural Origins of Sound Reproduction* (Durham, NH: Duke University Press, 2003), 31–85.

INDEX

Page numbers in italics refer to illustrations.

Académie royale des sciences, 9, 20–21
accent, 27–28; emotional, 54, 72; female, 61–62; male, 62; musical, 24, 26; physiology of, 15–51; sentimental, 53; vocal, 22–23, 146; and writing, 31. *See also* timbre; voice
acoustics: laws of, 7; mechanical understanding of, 176; of the vibrating string, 11, 92, 99–101. *See also* sound
Adorno, Theodor, 190n95
aesthetics: mathematical logic and, 92; musical, 38, 121–22. *See also* art; music
affection: definition of, 108; external signs of natural, 95; mathematical and moral theory of, 108; social, 76. *See also* emotion
allegory, 103, 106
analogy, 87; history and, 92, 99
Anderson, Wilda, 125, 209n53
Ansacq, 4–8, 19, 146, 176; scientific explanations for the event at, 148–49
Antoinette, Marie, 77
Appelbaum, David, 2
Arabian Nights, 140, 214n2
Aristotle, 117–18
art: as a form of emotional therapy, 73; of imitation, 44; physics of, 43. *See also* aesthetics; music
Avison, Charles, 68, 197n63

Bach, J. S., *The Well-Tempered Clavier*, 95, 202n38
Baculard d'Arnaud, François, 2, 9–10, 58, 144, 194n23, 199n110; "Anecdote sicilienne," 54, 73–74, 77–85, *82*, *83*; *Épreuves du sentiment*, 78; *Euphémie* (preface), 144; *Nouvelles historiques* (preface), 78
Balzac, Honoré de, *Sarrasine*, 12, 179
Barthes, Roland, 53
Behaurnais, Fanny de, *Les Illuminés*, 162
Bérard, Jean-Antoine, 109
Bertin, Joseph-Exupère, 88
Blanchet, Jean, 109, 112
Bloechl, Olivia, 152–53
body: aerial, 150; fiber theory of, 69, 86–87, 91–107, 111, 117, 122, 127–28, 133–35; limited form of sentience expressed through sound by, 11; materiality of, 53; mechanical, 10, 90; mind and, 70, 130; and musical instruments, 69, 86–87, 129; pneumatic theory of, 69; reproductive organs of, 11, 87, 102–6; of singer, 54, 84; unspoken desire of, 13; vitalist, 10, 89–91, 102–8, 115, 122, 139, 159, 180. *See also* medicine; vitalism
Boerhaave, Herman, 93, 103–4, 111
Boissier de Sauvages, François, 90
Bonnet, Charles, 103–4
Bordeu, Théophile de, 90–91
Boulaese, Jean, 153
Bradshaigh, Dorothy, 56
Brittan, Francesca, 215n4
Brocklesby, Richard, 68
Browne, Richard, *Medicina Musica: A Mechanical Essay on Singing, Musick and Dancing*, 68
Burney, Charles, 197n63
Burney, Frances, 197n63

Cahusac, Louis de, 1
Calmet, Antoine Augustin: *Dictionnaire historique, critique, chronologique, géographique et littéral de la Bible*, 148, 151; *Dissertations sur les apparitions des anges, des demons et des esprits*, 147–50
Carter, Elizabeth, "Ode to Wisdom," 65, 66, 67, 71–73, 195n50, 198n89
Castle, Terry, 142, 165
Castor et Pollux (Rameau), 123–24, 124
castrati, 39–40, 105, 185n33; Italian, 158–59, 166. *See also* singing
Catholicism, 145, 147. *See also* religion
Cazotte, Jacques, 2, 12, 110, 216n17, 221n85; correspondence of, 216n22, 217n24; *Le Diable amoureux*, 8, 12, 139–70, 151, 161, 164, 179, 214–15nn2–3, 216n13, 219n65; *Lettre à une dame*, 163; *Le Lord Impromptu*, 163; Martinism of, 215n11; *Ollivier*, 221n85; pamphlet on opera, 163
Chanvlon, Jean-Baptiste Thibault de, 103–4
Chao, Noelle, 68, 197n63
Charlton, David, 212n92, 213n104
Cheyne, George, 68–69, 74, 92–93; *An Essay of Health and Long Life*, 69–70
Chopin, Frédéric, *Funeral March*, 119
Clark, Andrew, 129, 212n74
clavecin, 112, 128, 134, 213n99
Condillac, Étienne Bonnot de, 22–23; *Essai sur les connaissances humaines*, 30–32
Condorcet, Nicolas de, "Lettre d'un jeune mécanicien," 176
consciousness: of a character, 55; momentary form of, 91, 134; moral, 74; tensions beneath human, 175. *See also* mind
Cooper, Anthony Ashley (third Earl of Shaftesbury), 11, 69–70, 196n61, 202n34; *An Inquiry on Virtue or Merit*, 87, 91–97, 100

Correte, Michel, *Le parfait maître à chanter*, 134
Coulet, Henri, 113, 209n51
Couvray, Jean-Baptiste Louvey de, 137
Cuillé, Tili Boon, 3

Décote, Georges, 215n3, 215n11
deism, 91
demons, 7, 123, 150–55; angels and, 147–50; possession by, 152–53, 158; voice of, 140–41, 152–53, 157, 179, 219n53. *See also* exorcism
Derrida, Jacques, 15; *De la grammatologie*, 3; *Marges . . . de la philosophie*, 17
Desaugiers, Marc-Antoine, "Quatrième romance," 82, 83
Descartes, René, 142, 147–48
desire: aversion and, 11, 91, 106, 170, 180; deleterious effects of, 9; and fertility, 105; impulses of physical, 9, 11, 13; insalubrious, 74–75; masculine, 10, 58, 73–74, 83, 180; monstrous, 12–13; moral, 116; pure music as physical language of, 163; of reproductive organs, 103; revulsion and, 12; sexual, 157, 166; unsanctioned, 76; vocal expression of, 84. *See also* emotion; love; sexuality
Desné, Roland, 115
diaphragm, 11, 112–17, 128; mobile, 127; sensibility of, 120–23, 126–27, 134. *See also* voice
didactic dialogues, 121–22
Diderot, Denis, 2, 9, 11–13, 55, 69–70, 176–78; *Les Bijoux indiscrets*, 11, 87–89, 101–2, 104, 106–9, 113; *Correspondance littéraire*, 111; *Dictionnaire universel de médecine* (translation), 94; early works, 86–108; *Éléments de physiologie*, 88, 104–5, 111, 114, 128–29, 135; *Éloge de Richardson*, 52; *Encyclopédie* (articles), 88, 93, 108; *Entretien entre d'Alembert et Diderot*, 110, 129, 134; *Entretiens sur*

le fils naturel, 136; *Essai sur le mérite et la vertu* (translation), 87, 91–97, 100, 108; figurative model of simultaneous resonance of, 130–31; *Interprétation de la nature*, 121; *Leçons de clavecin*, 122; *Lettre sur les aveugles*, 109–10, 112; *Lettre sur les sourds et muets*, 110, 112, 129, 136; mathematical work of, 42, 87, 98–102; *Le Neveu de Rameau*, 11, 109–38, 209n51, 209n55, 212n74, 213n98; *Paradoxe sur le comédien*, 114–15, 159, 217n25; *Pensées sur l'interprétation de la nature*, 91, 203n49; physiological theory of, 106–7, 206n12; *Principes généraux d'acoustique*, 42, 87, 98–99, 109; *Réfutations d'Helvétius*, 111, 113–17; *La Religieuse*, 105–6, 139, 159–60; *Le Rêve de d'Alembert*, 110–12; scientific method of, 107; vocal theory of, 85–109
Didier, Béatrice, 213n98
Dodart, Denis, 1, 18, 20–21, 24–25, 34, 88, 176–78
Dolan, Emily, 42
Dolar, Mladen, 185n33
Dubois, Pierre, 198n91
Duclos, Charles Pinot, 88; "Déclamation des anciens," 23–24; *Mémoire sur l'art de partager l'action théâtrale*, 23–25
Duverney, Joseph-Guichard, 103–4

education: cultural, 43–44; moral, 58, 77; musical, 79
Eidsheim, Nina Sun, 4, 33, 53, 164–65
emotion: aural memory of, 133; calming of, 71–72; communication of, 50–51, 57; dysregulated, 63, 75; expression of, 95; harmony of, 81; involuntary vocalizations of, 57; language and, 31–32; melody and, 120; natural, 83–84; of singing, 11, 36, 57–58, 71–72, 127; socially beneficial, 86; vocal physiology and, 35. See also affection; desire; love; sentimentality; suffering
Encyclopédie, ou dictionnaire raisonné des sciences, des arts et des métiers (Diderot and le Rond d'Alembert), 1, 9, 23, 52, 88, 93, 154, 157–58, 165, 174
enharmonicism, 125, 189n76, 211nn70–72, 212n74. See also music
Enlightenment, 2, 111, 142, 177, 215n3; as form of diabolic power, 155; ideals of, 214n2; philosophy of, 170; science of, 142, 145; supernatural and, 216n18. See also *philosophes*
Erlmann, Veit, 98
exorcism, 152–53, 158. See also demons

fairy tales: literary devices of, 7; musical scores inserted into, 57. See also literature
Fel, Marie, 28
Feldman, Martha, 3, 40, 105, 166
Ferrein, Antoine, 1, 18, 20–22, 87–89, 176–78
Festa, Lynn, 18, 38
Filoche, Jean-Luc, 211n71
Foucault, Michel, *Histoire de la sexualité*, 102
Frederick the Great, 77
Freemasonry, 140, 143–44
French anatomists, 1, 17, 28, 50, 109, 200n4
French Revolution, 217n24

Galen, 104
Garrick, David, 15
Gelbart, Matthew, 38
gender: distinction of, 47–48, 50; dynamic of, 180; identity of, 13; roles of, 106, 219n65; timbres as acoustic mark of, 10. See also sexuality
glottis, 1, 20, 35, 113; flexibility of, 46. See also vocal anatomy

INDEX

Gluck, Christoph Willibald, *Orfeo ed Euridice*, 211n72

harmony, 17; abstract notion of, 95; transhuman, 142. *See also* music
Heartz, Daniel, 209n54
Hérissant, François David, 1, 18, 20, 176; *Recherches sur les organes de la voix des quadrupèdes et celles des oiseaux*, 20–22, 200n4
history: and analogy, 99; cultural, 4; intellectual, 4; of language, 23, 31; of melodic dexterity, 36; of music writing, 197n63; occult, 143; of vocal anatomy, 87
hoax, 7
Hoeveler, Diane Long, 12
Horace, 117–18
horror, 125–27
Hume, David, 15

identity: cultural, 33, 53; demonic, 164; female, 146, 168, 179; gender, 13, 40, 53, 166; human, 3, 9, 116; moral, 117, 127; sentimental, 169; transcendental, 180; uncanny, 167; vocal, 72
imagination: acoustical, 53; libertine, 156; role of, 12; of suffering, 145
Ishizuka, Hisao, 93, 98
Islam, 49. *See also* religion
Isle des fous (Duni and Goldoni), 119, 131–33, 132, 208n50

James, Robert, 11, 93, 111; *A Medicinal Dictionary*, 92–95, 97–98
Jaucourt, Chevalier, 52
Jélyotte, Pierre de, 28
Johnson, James, 120, 162, 209n52
Johnson, Samuel, 52
Jommelli, Niccolò, *Lamentatione prima*, 128, 135–37, 214n107
Journal de Paris, 171–73

Journal du Physique et d'Histoire naturelle, 142
Judd, Cristle Collins, 121

Kane, Brian, 7, 144
Keymer, Tom, 55
Kinkead-Weekes, Mark, 55
Kusinic, David, 45

La Bruyère, Jean de, 117–18; *Nouvelles étrennes utiles et agréables, recueil de chansons morales et d'emblèmes sur de petits airs en vaudevilles connus*, 118
La Caze, Louis, 90; *Idée de l'homme physique et moral*, 113–14
La Mettrie, Julien Offray de, 201n18
language: acquisition of, 30; affective limits of, 122; conventional, 22; and emotion, 31–32; French, 173–74; invention of, 22–23; melodic features of, 23, 26–27, 30; and music, 3, 10, 22–23, 26, 34; mythical origins of, 43; of nature, 91–92; physiological point of view in explanation of, 17; sentimental, 162; songlike, 35; speech and, 21; supernatural properties of, 155; theory of origins of, 27; vocal organs and, 23; and vocal physiology, 27, 30–34. *See also* metaphor; music; speech
La Rochefoucauld, François de, *Maximes*, 117–18
Lavater, Johann Caspar, 160, 220n77
Le Cat, Claude-Nicolas, 156
Leclerc, Georges-Louis (Comte de Buffon), *Histoire naturelle*, 90
Le Guin, Elisabeth, 162, 220n79
Lesage, Alain-René, 119
Lhéritier de Villandon, Marie-Jeanne, 198n94
Lipsedge, Karen, 196n57
literary simulation, 8–9. *See also* literature; rhetoric

literary studies, 54–55, 197n63. *See also* literature
literature: eighteenth-century medical, 113; epistolary, 52, 55–56, 58–59; imaginative power of, 89; musical scenes in, 194n23; sentimental, 50, 52–85, 197n63, 198n92; uncanny, 12, 142. *See also* fairy tales; literary simulation; literary studies; mythology; novel; poetry; rhetoric; satire; sentimentality
Locke, John, 2
Loughridge, Deirdre, 37
Louis XVI, King, 171
love: expression of, 19; marital, 10, 82; moral feeling of communitarian, 41; passion of, 82, 119; sickness of, 76, 81–82. *See also* desire; emotion; sexuality

Malawey, Victoria, 36–37, 45; "comprehensive model" for voice analysis of, 36–37, 37
Mallet, Edme-François, 154
Mallet du Pan, Jacques, 174–79
Maréchal ferrant, Le (Philidor and Quétant), 119–20, 120, 209n50
Martinism, 140, 143–44, 155–56, 215n11, 218n38; ritual incantations of, 144, 150, 157; rituals of, 219n65
mathematics, 42, 87, 92, 98–102, 107; abstractions of, 203n49; music and, 101
Matter, Jacques, 155–56
Maupertuis, Pierre Louis Moreau de, 90–91
McGeary, Thomas, 196n52
medicine, 10–11, 92–93; eighteenth-century exercise, 69–70; science of magnetism of, 144; of singing, 68; theories of, 70, 74, 79. *See also* body; therapy
melody, 10, 17, 31, 35–36, 67, 124, 213n94; basic contour of, 23; memory of, 120–21; musical parameters of, 26, 120;

strophic, 82; sustained, 72; sympathetic vibrations of, 71; transformation of, 81. *See also* music
memory: affective, 76; aural, 120–21, 133; emotional, 76–77; of languages, 34; musical, 79; reconstruction from, 56; sensations of, 111; social, 77. *See also* mind
Mercure de France, 4, 6, 173–74
Mesmerism, 156, 162
metaphor, 87, 93, 95–96, 103, 107; of desire, 156; musical, 116, 126, 129, 213n104. *See also* language
Mical, Abbé, 171–78, 223n28
Michaelis, Sébastien, 151
mind: abstract conversation in reader's, 56; and body, 70, 130; mechanical body and spiritual, 10. *See also* consciousness; memory; self; soul
Montagnat, Henri Joseph Bernard, 88
Montesquieu, *L'Esprit des lois*, 174
Montpellier medical school, 74–75, 79, 90, 113
Moore, Edward, 56
Moore, Fabienne, 144
morale sensitive, 74, 79
morality: materialist conception of, 116; musical form of, 58, 66, 71–73, 75; perspective of, 11; sensationalist, 160; sentiment in, 9, 18; of women in marriage, 44
More, Henry, 147
music: diabolical, 149; expression in, 57; French, 220n70; Italian, 220n70; language and, 3, 10, 22–23, 26, 34; and laws of nature, 79; and mathematics, 101; medical notions about making of, 10, 70–71, 156; and morality, 66; painting and, 43; and social obligations, 64, 66; as spiritually dangerous activity, 163; sublime, 137; traditional purpose of making, 71; tuning systems of, 95, 203n40. *See also* aesthetics; art;

music (*continued*)
    enharmonicism; harmony; language; melody; musical instruments; music theory; opera; singing; therapy
musical instruments: animal constitutions and, 95; human physiology and, 69, 116; human sentience and, 129; Pythagorean tuning of ancient lyre, 96; sounds of, 5; subversion of, 64; timbre of, 37, 42; vocal cords of dissected animals as, 1, 87–88. *See also* music
music theory: didactic dialogues with musical examples in, 121–22; enharmonic ratio in, 189n76; of Rousseau, 3, 22, 29, 34, 37–38, 58, 79, 125, 190n109, 199n101, 211n72. *See also* music
mythology, 112, 179. *See also* literature

nature: contemplation of, 73; divine author of, 21; humanity and, 77, 92; language of, 91–92; mathematical representation of, 92; as moral guide, 83; music and laws of, 79; universal accent of, 27
Nonnotte, Claude-François, *Dictionnaire philosophique de la religion*, 147–49
novel: canonical, 54; epistolary, 78, 81; libertine, 87; music inserted into fictional depictions in, 54, 57, 65, 145; representation of emotion in, 18; sentimental, 10, 18–19, 50, 52–85. *See also* literature; *roman noir*

O'Dea, Michael, 15, 39
opera: French, 140, 214, 214n2; Italian, 140, 158; listening to, 162; medley of airs, 128; of Rousseau, 125; sentimental, 18–19, 50; singers of, 36. *See also* music; *opéra comique*; theater; *Tragédie en musique*
opéra comique, 119, 123, 130, 213n98. *See also* opera
Ovid, 117–18

Paris, 20
Pascal, Blaise, *Pensées*, 117–18
Perrault, Claude, 1, 21
philosophes, 142–43, 145; fictional, 148; and the French Revolution, 217n24. *See also* Enlightenment
philosophical dialogue, 11
philosophy: moral, 11, 92, 94; natural, 11–12, 103, 144, 148–49, 176; vocal physiology in, 12. *See also* science
phonographs, 181
physics, 11; experimental, 107; phenomenon of, 146
pleasure: and aversion, 105, 108; and pain, 107, 114, 116–17, 127; sensual, 43; sexual, 106; of sharing contentment and delight with others, 94
Pliny, 117–18
poetry: rational, 144; and song, 65; spiritual, 144. *See also* literature
Poizat, Michel, 185n33
polype, 130, 133, 137, 212n90
psychology, 12

Querelle des Bouffons, 28–29, 140, 163, 209n55, 210n65

Radcliffe, Ann, 68, 197n63
Rameau, Jean-François, 110
Rameau, Jean-Philippe, 96–97, 110, 123–26, 124, 125, 126; *Hippolyte et Aricie* (opera), 125–26, 211n72
Raynal, Abbé, *Histoire des deux Indes*, 174
reading: of letters in novels, 81; of novels by women, 56; and performance practices, 8–9; physiological effects of, 197n80, 200n117; and singing, 117–19; as style of vocalization, 63; by virtual form of listening, 56. *See also* writing
Rehding, Alexander, 125, 211n72
Reill, Peter, 91–92

religion: contradictory presences of, 2; Enlightenment science and, 142; false, 100. *See also* Catholicism; Islam

representation: false sense of unmediated, 58; fictional, 12; literary, 178, 181

rhetoric: strategies of, 7–8, 91–92; as style of voice, 157. *See also* literary simulation; literature

Richardson, Samuel, 52, 192n16, 194n23, 197n80; *Clarissa*, 8, 10, 54–74, 60, 66, 77–78, 195n50

Ritchie, Leslie, 65

Rivarol, Antoine, 173–74

Roger, Joseph-Louis: musical hygiene of, 79, 156; *Tentamen de vi soni et musices in corpus humanum*, 75, 77

romance: as intrasubjective reflection, 79; as naturalized sounding board for thoughts and passions, 80–81, 84–85; songs of genre, 73–77

roman noir, 77. *See also* novel

Rosenfeld, Sophia, 129

Rousseau, Jean-Jacques, 2–3, 9–51, 78, 178; aesthetic theory of, 38; *Confessions*, 19; *Du contrat social*, 41; *Le Devin du village* (musical *intermède*), 19; *Dictionnaire de musique*, 9, 17, 24–27, 30, 34, 39, 43–44, 76, 134, 136, 158, 214n105; *Émile, ou De l'éducation*, 17, 30, 41, 43–44, 47–50; emotion theory of, 58; *Encyclopédie* (articles), 17, 39, 42–43; *Essai de l'origine de l'inégalité parmi les hommes*, 19; *Essai sur l'origine des langues*, 9–10, 17, 21–22, 29–34, 41, 44, 47–49; *Examens des deux principes avancés par M. Rameau dans sa brochure intitulée Erreurs sur la musique dans l'Encyclopédie*, 29; *Julie, ou La Nouvelle Héloïse*, 10, 17, 19, 29, 41, 47, 49, 54, 74–76, 81; *Lettre à d'Alembert sur les spectacles*, 17, 39–41; *Lettre sur la musique française*, 17, 28–29, 45; *Le Matérialisme du sage*, 74; music theory of, 3, 22, 29, 34, 37–38, 58, 79, 125, 190n109, 199n101, 211n72; *organe musical* of, 17, 22, 30–34; *Origine de la mélodie*, 29; *Pygmalion* (musical *intermède*), 19; social theory of, 41; speculative anthropology of, 19; vocal theory of, 10, 17, 28–30, 33, 36–51, 88, 103, 189n69

Rozier, François, 142

Saint-Martin, Louis-Claude de, 155

satire, 57, 89, 101. *See also* literature

Schmidt, Leigh Eric, 2

science: acoustical, 149; Enlightenment, 142, 145; French, 89–90, 101; medical, 7; partial understanding of voice in, 9; popular, 145; and spirituality, 146; vitalist, 91–92. *See also* philosophy

Scudamore, Sophia, 55–56, 67

self: atomistic, 137–38, 213n99; Husserlian voices of interior, 16; intellect and wisdom directed to, 71; knowledge of, 81. *See also* mind

Seneca, 117–18

sensation: acoustical, 8; aural, 161; external and internal, 133; moral, 43–45, 80

sensation, physical, 41, 43, 56, 129; and cognition, 72; and emotional response, 120–21; of suffering, 18

sensibility, 109–38; chaotic matrix of, 134; cult of, 162; diaphragmatic, 120–23, 126–27, 134; materialist, 135; monstrous, 159; physical, 120–22, 127; secular belief in human, 143. *See also* sentimentality; vitalism

sentimentalism, 105; vitalism and, 142, 160. *See also* sentimentality

sentimentality, 18–19, 162; English, 78, 165–66, 214n2; French, 38; moral, 181; sound of, 80; vitalism and, 142; of voice, 9–20, 31, 41, 50–51, 57–58, 72–73, 77, 80, 85–86, 139, 145–46, 157, 160, 165–66. *See also* emotion; literature; sensibility; sentimentalism

Serva padrona, La (Pergolesi), 131–33, 132
sexuality: discourse of, 102; female, 105–6; monstrous forms of, 104; and voice, 11, 102–6, 157. *See also* desire; gender; love
singing: and composition exercises, 121; diaphragmatic control in, 112–13; emotion of, 11, 36, 57–58, 71–72, 127; fashionable, 44; Italian, 45; monstrous, 127; moral, 63–64, 77, 146; as multisensory physical activity, 53–54, 192n8; opera, 36; sentimental, 77, 165; sound-based notion of, 33; and speech, 24–26, 28; vocal physiology of, 86. *See also* castrati; music; vocal performance; voice
social inequality, 18–19
soul: body and, 69; inner turmoil of, 66; materialist, 75, 111–12, 130, 216n17. *See also* mind
sound: acousmatic, 7, 62, 184n24, 195n40; events of, 4–8, 149, 176; instrumental, 25; invisibility of, 149; mathematical notion of, 42; musical, 71; physical sensations of nonhuman, 45; and sensibility, 109–38; of sentiment, 80; spiritual, 150; uncanny, 12, 45, 178; vocal, 4, 11, 22–23, 27–28, 54, 89–90; vocal, uniqueness of, 42–43. *See also* acoustics; voice
space, 147
speech: abstract notion of, 22; imagination and, 1; intellectual faculty of, 1; and language, 21; singing and, 24–26, 28; vocal physiology's role in, 12. *See also* language; vocal physiology
Starobinski, Jean, 221n102
subjectivity: gendered, 33; modern theories of, 12
suffering, 18–19; imagination of, 145; lyrical expression of, 145; sentimental voices as signs of, 57; sonic imitation of, 137; virtuous, 78. *See also* emotion

supernatural, the: Caribbean, 140; and Enlightenment, 216n18; orientalist, 140, 214n2; Pygmalion as, 179; superstitious beliefs of, 144; voices of, 1–3, 140–70, 215n3, 218n44. *See also* uncanny, the
Swedenborg, Emanuel, 144
syphilis, 105

Tadmor, Naomi, 56
Temple de la gloire (Rameau), 123–25, 125
Têtes parlantes (vocal machine), 12, 171–76, 172
theater: eighteenth-century, 120; French lyric, 119. *See also* opera
theism, 147–49
therapy: moral, 10, 83; music, 10, 73–74, 77, 80, 83–84; vocal, 54, 72–73. *See also* medicine; music
Thomas, Downing, 3, 15
Thomson, Ann, 91, 113, 202n23
timbre: definition of, 41; gendered, 15–51; of musical instruments, 37, 42; physical and moral attributes of, 41; Rousseauan, 46; sentimental, 40; vocal, 28, 34–36, 50, 89. *See also* accent; voice
Todorov, Tzvetan, 170, 215n3
Tomlinson, Gary, 142
Tragédie en musique, 140, 214n2. *See also* opera

uncanny, the: Freudian notion of, 141; literature of, 12, 142; sound of, 12, 45; vitalism and, 179; voice of, 3, 9, 11–13, 139–70, 178–81, 214n2, 218n44. *See also* supernatural, the

vaudeville, 119–20, 124, 130
Verba, Cynthia, 15, 27
Verne, Jules, *Le Château des Carpathes*, 179
Vicq d'Azyr, Félix, 171
Vila, Anne, 74–75

Villiers de l'Isle-Adam, Auguste, *L'Ève future*, 179
vitalism, 10, 12, 90–91, 102–8, 122, 146, 170, 176, 179; binary aspects of, 105–6; and enharmonicism, 125; and sentimentalism, 142, 160; and uncanny, 179. *See also* body; sensibility; voice
vocal anatomy, 7–8, 20, 180; comparative, 9, 20–22; textual construction of, 17. *See also* glottis; vocal physiology; voice
vocal performance, 8–11, 16, 33, 46, 63, 71, 83, 167; emotionally vibrant melodies in, 10; and human physiology, 127; and reading experience, 9; variety of discrete meanings of, 137. *See also* singing; voice
vocal physiology, 1–4, 16–22, 28–30, 34–35, 50–54, 57, 105, 169, 181; as avenue of philosophical inquiry, 12; and emotion, 35; experimental, 88; and human experience, 13; language and, 27, 30–34; mechanics of, 176; and moral and physiological composition of speaker, 12; of singing, 9, 11, 19, 86; of vitalist voice, 128. *See also* sound; speech; vocal anatomy; voice
voice: acousmatic, 8, 176; analysis of, 36–37, 37, 53–56; anatomical, 8, 18, 178; animal, 1, 15, 20–22, 88, 91, 94–97, 200n4; avian, 20–21, 200n4; biomechanical conceptions of, 9, 24; of castrati, 39–40, 105, 185n33; demonic, 140–41, 152–53, 157, 179, 219n53; diaphragmatic, 127–28, 135; diseased, 105; embodied, 73, 107, 142; epistolary, 52, 56; feline, 45; female, 39–41, 47–48, 157–58, 179, 185n33, 190n95; glottal, 88; human, 1, 5, 21; imagined, 73; imitation of, 3, 8; literary descriptions of, 8–9, 36, 178; male, 38–40, 47–49, 103–5, 190n95; materiality of, 2–4, 8–9, 11, 16, 34, 53; mechanical, 12, 171–73, 175–79, 201n21; metaphorical, 16; multidisciplinary approach to, 11; multimodal, 53, 84; musical representation of reactive, 11; operatic, 36, 142, 185n33; of possession, 139–70; postlapsarian, 48; reproductions of, 144, 180–81; and reproductive organs, 11, 102–7; sentimental, 9–20, 31, 41, 50–51, 57–58, 72–73, 77, 80, 85–86, 139, 145–46, 157, 160, 165–69, 178–81; sexuality and, 11, 102–6, 157; supernatural, 1–3, 140–70, 215n3, 218n44; tenor, 38–39; terrorizing, 68; textual representations of, 4, 8, 53; theorization of, 3, 8–10, 85; uncanny, 3, 9, 11–13, 139–70, 178–81, 214n2, 218n44; uniqueness of, 42–43; virtual, 59–62, 67, 73; vitalist, 9–13, 70, 85–108, 117, 127–28, 139–46, 159–60, 165, 169, 175–81, 217n25; and vocal organs, 3, 15–21, 24, 29–38, 48, 53–54, 59, 84–86, 89, 103; vocal range of, 134. *See also* accent; diaphragm; singing; sound; timbre; vitalism; vocal anatomy; vocal performance; vocal physiology
Voltaire, 77, 204n55; *La Henriade* (epic poem), 174
von Haller, Albrecht, 88, 98, 103, 111, 160
von Leden, Hans, 88
von Mücke, Dorothea, 219n65

Wall, Cynthia, 55–56, 61
Watt, Ian, 55
women: domestic performance of, 195n48, 196n57; independence of, 71–72, 83; musical performance of, 167–68; Platonic ideal of beauty of, 179; reading aloud of novels by, 56; taxonomy of temperament of, 102–3; traditional wisdom of, 71–73; voices of, 39–41, 47–48, 157–58, 179, 185n33, 190n95
writing: accent and, 31; epistolary, 192n16; of harpsichord pieces, 110. *See also* reading

WINNERS OF THE
Walker Cowen Memorial Prize

*The Usufructuary Ethos: Power, Politics, and
Environment in the Long Eighteenth Century*
Erin Drew

*Staging Civilization: A Transnational History of French
Theater in Eighteenth-Century Europe*
Rahul Markovits, translated by Jane Marie Todd

The Shortest Way with Defoe: "Robinson Crusoe," Deism, and the Novel
Michael B. Prince

Public Vows: Fictions of Marriage in the English Enlightenment
Melissa J. Ganz

*Citizens of Convenience: The Imperial Origins of American
Nationhood on the U.S.-Canadian Border*
Lawrence B. A. Hatter

*Empiricist Devotions: Science, Religion, and Poetry
in Early Eighteenth-Century England*
Courtney Weiss Smith

*Nationalizing France's Army: Foreign, Black, and Jewish
Troops in the French Military, 1715–1831*
Christopher J. Tozzi

Prose Immortality, 1711–1819
Jacob Sider Jost

*The Evil Necessity: British Naval Impressment in
the Eighteenth-Century Atlantic World*
Denver Brunsman

*Be It Ever So Humble: Poverty, Fiction, and the
Invention of the Middle-Class Home*
Scott R. MacKenzie

Backstage in the Novel: Frances Burney and the Theater Arts
Francesca Saggini, translated by Laura Kopp

*The Nation's Nature: How Continental Presumptions
Gave Rise to the United States of America*
James D. Drake

Our Coquettes: Capacious Desire in the Eighteenth Century
Theresa Braunschneider

*Virginians Reborn: Anglican Monopoly, Evangelical Dissent, and
the Rise of the Baptists in the Late Eighteenth Century*
Jewel L. Spangler

*Ending the French Revolution: Violence, Justice, and
Repression from the Terror to Napoleon*
Howard G. Brown

Wild Enlightenment: The Borders of Human Identity in the Eighteenth Century
Richard Nash

*Poems of Nation, Anthems of Empire: English
Verse in the Long Eighteenth Century*
Suvir Kaul

If the King Only Knew: Seditious Speech in the Reign of Louis XV
Lisa Jane Graham

No Tomorrow: The Ethics of Pleasure in the French Enlightenment
Catherine Cusset

The Unfinished Manner: Essays on the Fragment in the Later Eighteenth Century
Elizabeth Wanning Harries

www.ingramcontent.com/pod-product-compliance
Lightning Source LLC
Chambersburg PA
CBHW030619230426
43661CB00053B/2064